# MONEY AND EMPLOYMENT

# MONEY AND EMPLOYMENT

**R. J. Ball**
*Principal, London Business School*

*First published 1982 by*
THE MACMILLAN PRESS LTD
*London and Basingstoke*
*Companies and representatives*
*throughout the world*

ISBN 0 333 28795 9 (hardcover)
ISBN 0 333 28796 7 (paperback)

*Printed in Hong Kong*

For Lindsay, for patience

# Contents

# List of Figures and Tables

# Preface

This book originates from a series of lectures on the macroeconomy delivered to executive participants and post
graduate students at the London Business School. I hope that
it will be of use to their successors and to others who seek
to clarify the economic issues of the day.

It is based empirically on research conducted at the London Business School Centre for Economic Forecasting into the
working of the economy. This has been supported for a number
of years by the Social Science Research Council, to whom the
Centre is highly indebted. I am grateful to the Leverhulme
Trust for a personal research grant which has made this book
possible by funding research assistance from Heather Morley
and Patrick Willcocks.

Kind friends and colleagues have given time to reading the
book in draft form, and I am particularly indebted to Michael
Beesley, Samuel Brittan, Alan Budd, Ruth Leavitt and Harold
Rose for helpful comments directed toward the elimination of
errors and failures of presentation. I am grateful to Jeremy
Morse for comments on Chapter 6. My thanks are also due to
my secretary, Judith O'Connor, who coped with the organisation of the typescript in the midst of many other responsibilities.

My thinking on the matters set forth has been shaped by
discussion with my former colleague, Terry Burns, and with
Alan Budd, Michael Beenstock and Bill Robinson of the London
Business School. Needless to say, they bear no responsibility for the conclusions that I draw or for any deficiencies
that remain.

*February 1981*                                    R.J. Ball

# 1 Introduction

The aim of this book is to clarify some of the issues that
have featured in public and professional discussions about
economic management in recent years. The last decade has
seen a greater polarisation of views about how the economy
functions and the economic policies that can and should be
pursued. Debates have taken place in the press, in bank
reviews and periodicals and in the professional economic
journals. What follows is a bringing together of what has
been discussed, and the suggestion of some conclusions.

The text is chiefly concerned with macroeconomic policies,
although the distinction between macro- and microeconomic
policies is blurred at the margin. Some attention is given
to the role of industrial policies in affecting the supply
side of the economy, but the principal focus is on monetary
and fiscal policies, the role of exchange rates and incomes
policies, and the implications of protection for economic
management.

In analysing the behaviour of the economy, and the conduct
of economic policy, three themes recur throughout. The first
is the nature of the interaction between the supply potential of the economy and the level and rate of growth of
nominal or monetary demand. This affects the determination
of employment, the analysis of inflation, the significance
of the behaviour of the balance of payments, and the consequences of exchange rate changes and protection. It also
throws light on the role of aggregate supply and aggregate
demand in the process of economic growth, and on the analysis of the consequences of North Sea oil.

Secondly, the analysis carries implications for the conduct of economic policy. The behaviour of the economy imposes limitations on what governments can achieve in the
framework of a free society. The nature and extent of these
limits are much disputed. Accordingly attention is focussed
throughout on the consequences of government action, and on
the role that government can legitimately be expected to

1

play.

Thirdly, there is the international dimension. The economic problems of the United Kingdom are not unique. The economy functions in an international world to which it is tied
by trade and capital flows. Through them, economic events in
the world outside have an impact on inflation, employment
and growth. The international environment sets limits on the
extent to which domestic economic policies can be pursued
unilaterally. While from time to time it is helpful for ex-
positive purposes to ignore international complications, in
the last analysis an international approach is essential.
An understanding of the international economic environment
is critical.


## EFFECTIVE DEMAND AND EFFECTIVE SUPPLY

Assuming that average prices are not falling, an increase in
production or output sold implies an increase in the level
of nominal spending. An increase in nominal spending that
calls forth an increase in domestic output represents an increase in domestic *effective demand*. This reflects a demand
or a desire to obtain certain goods and services. It is effective demand to the extent that such goods and services
are obtained.

However, an increase in nominal spending may not result in
any ultimate increase in the level of effective demand for
domestic output. If goods and services are not made available, the excess nominal demand for them will eventually result in a rise in prices, so eliminating any real effect on
domestic output. In an open economy, i.e. an economy with
foreign trade, the increase in nominal spending may simply
lead to a rise in imports. Prices may not increase, but
neither will domestic output.

In simple Keynesian economics, the international complications were largely neglected and prices held constant. At the
time that Keynes presented *The General Theory of Employment,
Interest and Money*, prices had been falling for nearly a decade so the latter assumption did not seem as implausible as
it does today. Given these assumptions, it was argued that
government should pursue policies to raise nominal expenditure and so effective demand, increasing output to the
point where the physical limitations of either labour or
capital or both prevented increased production. At this
point, the economy would be supply-constrained in a physical
sense. Further increases in the rate of nominal spending
would be inflationary. Full employment would have been reached.
However it is clear that Keynes himself - although not his

later followers - took a much more modest view of how much
unemployment could be eliminated by increases in the general
level of monetary demand. As recalled by Lord Kahn, in 1937
when unemployment as measured at the time was at 10 per cent
of the labour force Keynes, in an article in *The Times*, recorded that:

> It is natural to interject that it is premature to abate
> our efforts to increase employment so long as the figures
> of unemployment remain so high. . . . I believe that we
> are approaching or have approached the point where there
> is not much advantage in applying a further general stimu-
> lus at the centre. . . . The economic structure is unfor-
> tunately rigid. . . . The later stages of recovery require
> a different technique. To remedy the condition of the dis-
> tressed areas, *ad hoc* measures are necessary. (*The Times*,
> 11 March 1937)

There is a further problem. The existence of excess capacity either in terms of labour or of equipment does not
necessarily imply that it can be profitably utilised in the
face of a general increase in the level of monetary demand.
By analogy with the concept of effective demand, we may also
define the concept of *effective supply*, which is the profitable level of output that can be sustained at any given level
of monetary demand. Amongst other things, this will depend
on the costs of production and, in an open economy, on the
degree of competition. It is not obvious that a high rate of
unemployment in the long run is due to a lack of effective
demand rather than a lack of effective supply.

As we have seen, however aggregate supply is determined,
an expansion in nominal demand may be dissipated in inflation or imports. This has led to demand for incomes policies
to control inflation and for protection to control imports
in order that the level of effective demand can be increased.
If, however, there are limits imposed by effective supply,
it will be impossible permanently to increase effective demand by simply expanding the monetary level of expenditure.
The behaviour of aggregate supply is therefore critical in
much of the analysis of this book.

## THE ROLE OF GOVERNMENT

Since the Second World War, it has been widely believed in
the United Kingdom that government can and should accept responsibility for the overall rate of employment. Keynesian
thinking provided the basis on which intervention was to be

undertaken to promote output and employment in the short
run.

It is argued in this book that, both internationally and
domestically, the high levels of employment experienced in
the first twenty-five years after the war had little to do
with some new-found expertise on the part of governments.
The exceptional growth rate of the OECD countries was due to
particular influences that have been reversed. In the United
Kingdom, the scope for independent monetary and fiscal policies was limited by the commitment to maintain the parity of
sterling with the dollar. Increased flexibility resulting
from the abandonment of this commitment, and the floating of
sterling in 1972, has been associated with more rapidly
rising unemployment and high and variable rates of inflation. This has not been due solely to the behaviour of monetary and fiscal policies, although this accounts for much of
the poor performance of the United Kingdom *vis-à-vis* the
rest of the world. The shift in the terms of trade of the
manufacturing countries resulting from the rise in the real
price of energy has been an important factor, requiring an
adjustment in real wage levels. Attempts to avoid this adjustment have weighed heavily on the rate of return on manufacturing capital, with consequent effects on both output
and jobs.

The capacity of government to determine employment in a
market economy has been challenged by two arguments. The
first is that, under floating exchange rates, increases in
nominal spending resulting from government action will be
largely dissipated in inflation. In the medium term, monetary and fiscal expansion will be neutral in their effects
on output and employment. Secondly, even if there are short-
run effects on output, these will be limited, since expectations will speed up the inflationary adjustment. Government
may set targets and pursue objectives in monetary terms,
i.e. by aiming at a given rate of increase in nominal spending, but the precise implications for real output and employment will be determined by market forces that are beyond
government control.

As seen in Figure 1.1, the trend in unemployment in Britain has been upward since 1963, irrespective of the government in power, the policies pursued and the exchange rate
regime in force. The ingredients of this sad tale are repeated bouts of monetary and fiscal expansion resulting from
tax cuts and increases in public spending, followed by rising inflation. In the process of bringing the inflation under control, unemployment rises above its long-term trend.
The inflation itself, and the adjustment that follows it,
destroys output and jobs. Each time, the capacity of indus-

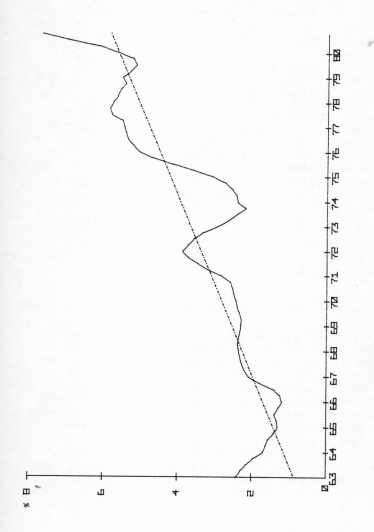

FIGURE 1.1   Percentage of the labour force unemployed in Great Britain
             (seasonally adjusted, excluding school-leavers)

             SOURCE   *Department of Employment Gazette.*

try to meet the challenge of inflation is weakened, together
with its capacity to create new business to absorb the
rising core of unemployment. As unemployment rises there is
pressure for yet another round of monetary and fiscal expansion, with the best of intentions, but with disastrous results.

Simple Keynesianism relies on the pull of increases in
monetary demand to induce an increase in supply in the long
run. But this has failed. Simple monetarism suggests that
inflation interacts with the behaviour of output when the
economy is in disequilibrium. When it is in balance, the
growth of output and the behaviour of employment are determined by real factors that underly competitiveness, such as
technology and productivity. Monetary and fiscal policy can
be used in an attempt to control the flow of nominal spending and hence inflation. Bringing inflation under control
eliminates the cyclical component of inflation. This is
necessary to enable the growth potential of the economy to
be realised. If inflation is out of control nothing goes
right. But a stable financial framework is only a necessary
and not a sufficient condition for a desired rate of economic growth and a reduction in the core rate of unemployment.
Monetarism, and especially simple monetarism, is 'not
enough'.

The heart of the problem lies in the supply side of the
economy. On this there may be more agreement than is commonly supposed. Supply side economics holds the key to unemployment. It emphasises the important connection between
real wages, profitability and employment. It throws into
relief the importance of new business development, the role
of incentives, the need for skills, the flexibility of labour and housing markets, and the need for enterprise.

In tackling these problems, there are important divergences of opinion with regard to the role of the state and
the contribution of private business, which are taken up
later in this book. However, we stop short of any detailed
assessment of particular policies. The principal intention
is to establish the nature of the problem and to make clear
that there are important choices to be made. The central
conclusion is that these problems have no facile solution
deriving from monetary control, the management of demand,
incomes policies or protectionism. They are firmly rooted in
the current structure of our industrial society.

THE INTERNATIONAL DIMENSION

An economy which is as open as the United Kingdom's is subject to external shocks from changes in world output and

prices. The stability of the external economic world is a matter of direct concern. The behaviour of the world economy is important, as we shall see, in understanding the economic history of the United Kingdom. The recession of the thirties was not due simply to inappropriate domestic economic policies pursued by the government of the time. The 30 per cent fall in exports in 1931 and 1932 was not the result of an overvalued exchange rate alone, but also of the massive fall in world demand that followed in the wake of the collapse of the United States. The rise in real energy and commodity prices in the seventies had an impact on the economy. The collapse of the international monetary system established at Bretton Woods had a major effect on world inflation, before the rise in the real price of energy, with knock-on effects for the rate of inflation in Britain.

International monetary and trading relationships impose limitations on the economic freedom of national governments. The pegging of the exchange rate after the war imposed limits on the freedom of the United Kingdom authorities to determine the rate of growth of monetary demand independently. Unfortunately this lack of freedom was interpreted to mean that the growth of the economy was 'constrained' by the behaviour of the balance of payments, an issue that recurs in this book. This viewpoint failed to appreciate that so-called balance of payments problems arose from a lack of effective supply and competitiveness. The behaviour of balance of payments was a symptom and not a constraint in any fundamental sense. This misconception led to the belief that the 'constraint' could be eliminated either by altering the nominal exchange rate or by protection.

When sterling was floated in 1972, it was widely believed that this would enable the authorities to regain control over the level of real demand. The balance of payments would no longer act as a constraint. In practice, the collapse of the Bretton Woods system imposed greater responsibilities on individual countries to manage their fiscal and monetary policies in the interests of restraining inflation. The failure to understand this, when combined with the impact of world inflation and the rise in energy prices, led to near disaster. For some at least, including the present writer, this episode led to an agonising reappraisal of the economic views that had dominated both official and academic thinking for a quarter of a century.

It is important to understand not only the nature of international economic linkages and their effects on domestic economic policy, but also the way in which the international monetary and trading system works as a whole. Throughout the sixties and the early seventies, there was much discussion

of the reform of the system. Since 1973 there has been an
increase in protectionism in manufactures and a move towards
flexible exchange rates. More recently there has in some
quarters been a call for 'managed trade'. While no major re-
forms in the international monetary system have taken place,
some members of the EEC have taken matters into their own
hands by the establishment of a European Monetary System.
These issues are all of major concern with regard to the
future of the international economy, in the face of widespread inflation and unemployment and the problems arising
from increased energy costs, and are accordingly discussed
in some detail.


ECONOMICS AND POLITICS

This book is primarily concerned with the technical issues
that underlie the desirability and feasibility of particular economic policies. In a democratic society, the policies
that are pursued are evidently those that are regarded as
politically feasible. Their success or failure is determined by their acceptability.

Economists no less than politicians reflect different
value judgements about the consequences of particular
economic policies. That is why the study of economics was
in the past described as the study of political economy. In
a modern context, those who believe that the power of government to determine the level of employment and economic
growth is limited are saddled with the accusation either
that they do not care about unemployment or that they place
a high value on other economic objectives such as the rate
of inflation. The moral high-ground is seized, not on technical grounds, but in the name of the majority whose concerns are pressing and immediate: the unemployed, declining
businesses and those who are least able to protect themselves against the damaging consequences of both inflation
and recession.

A central thesis of this book is that there is no medium-
term choice between inflation on the one hand and growth
and employment on the other. Inflation is both a cause and
a consequence of the incompatibility of individual and collective aspirations. The economic problems that we face
constitute a challenge to the very basis of the mixed economy to which, in some measure, both major political parties
have in the past subscribed. Keynesian economics provided
the intellectual basis for the middle ground of British
politics, but it has failed to stand the test of the seventies, once the umbrella of a stable international financial

system, largely provided by the United States, was swept away. The polarisation of economic views reflects the reality of choice that the community faces, albeit less starkly than presented by the political parties and the media.

The reconstruction of simple Keynesianism, supplemented by incomes policies or protection, will prove to be a failure. The problem is how to reconcile the virtues of the welfare state and a constructive role for government in industrial affairs with sound money and a stable financial environment. The alternative is the dismantling of any pretence at a social market economy and its replacement by state intervention and bureaucratic control. The choice is a real one which, under the pressure of current economic events, might well be ignored. In that event, the future of what is left of the private enterprise system is at risk. In the interests of short-term economic and political expediency, it could be washed away with the tide.

## THE STRUCTURE OF THE BOOK

Chapter 2 sets the scene by reviewing the economic history of the United Kingdom and the world economy over the last hundred years. In the course of this review, the familiar problems of growth and unemployment, inflation and trade, emerge from the course of events.

While this is not a book written by an economist for economists, but for a wider audience, Chapters 3 and 4 set out in some detail the principal ideas and theories which underlie many of the policy conclusions that emerge at a later stage. The discussion is primarily theoretical and unrelated to the flow of events. One would not wish to discourage people from reading these chapters, but it is possible to pass directly to Chapter 5, which discusses the problem of economic growth, without too much of a loss of continuity.

Chapter 6 examines the international monetary and trading system in two parts. The first reverts to the style of Chapter 2 and focusses in some detail on international economic problems in the historical setting of the period after the Second World War. The second part contains some analysis of the problems of balance of payments adjustment between countries, and looks at the arguments for 'managed' trade and protection on an international basis.

Chapters 7 and 8 set out, with the help of what has gone before, to discuss economic policy. In Chapter 7 attention is focussed on the scope for, and limits to, what governments may achieve by the pursuit of discretionary monetary and fiscal policy, by the use of incomes policies, and by the use of protection, when seen from a national viewpoint. Chapter 8 follows on to consider public spending in a wider context than that of macroeconomic policy, the role of industrial policy and the issues that result from the existence of North Sea oil.

No attempt has been made to document the sources from which most of the material comes. They will be familiar to professional economists. Neither is there any systematic attempt to set forth empirical evidence for the statements made and the conclusions drawn. There are no footnotes. Such source material as is referred to in the text is to be found in the short reference section under the name of the author. In addition, other references have been given to enable the reader to probe further should he or she desire.

# 2 The Historical Background

At the outset of *The Economic Consequences of Democracy*
Samuel Brittan wrote:

> The besetting sin of much discussion of current issues is
> to concentrate on the immediate present. Although there
> are no easy lessons from history, the past is an invalua-
> ble storehouse for enriching understanding. One way of
> bringing perspective to today's events is to look back
> with the wisdom of hindsight.

Current ideas are often not as novel as may appear either
to those who propound them or to those who listen to them.
Their antecedents are often as significant as their content.
Attention to the development of ideas is not simply an academic exercise. It helps to gain perspective and acts as a
guard against reinventing the wheel. Obviously not only
ideas themselves are significant but also the events that
stimulate them. Economic thinking takes place against a
background of events producing an ebb and flow as ideas are
challenged. In economics, it is sometimes said, the questions remain stubbornly the same, it is only the answers
that change.

History never precisely repeats itself. Nevertheless the
discovery of recurrent patterns tests the generality of
thought. Moreover the course of historical events generates
recurrent themes which lie at the heart of contemporary discussion. Balance of payments problems in the United Kingdom
date back to the First World War. For the major industrial
countries the thirties was a period of massive unemployment.
Today those same countries are concerned at rates of unemployment which are exceptional compared with the average
over much of the post-1945 period. As in the thirties the
international monetary system is in disorder.

An examination of these issues in an historical context
is important not only from the point of view of the search

for general explanations, but also in assessing possible
'solutions'. Many currently see the problem of 'de-
industrialisation' (see Chapter 5) at the heart of British
economic difficulties, representing a situation in which our
exports of manufactures have not risen fast enough to pay
for the imports generated at full employment. But in a recent essay Sir Alec Cairncross wrote:

> Is the situation any different from what it must have
> looked like in the 1870s, when rising imports of food-
> stuffs threatened the balance of payments and it was
> doubtful whether exports in the face of increasing com-
> petition from industrial countries could pay the bill?

This suggests that contemporary problems may not be easy to
explain and points to a high degree of humility toward the
possibility of generating facile 'solutions'. The phenomenon
of modest economic growth in Britain goes back to the nineteenth century when the tax system was different, trades
unions were less powerful and when, paraphrasing Browning,
God was in his heaven and all was right with the world.

A second besetting sin that has characterised much of the
debate about Britain's economic problems since the Second
World War is to regard those problems as unique. It is not
the history of the United Kingdom economy alone that is relevant to the discussion of contemporary affairs. It is true
that at different times the incidence of particular problems
in the United Kingdom has been different from elsewhere in
the industrial world. Industrial employment in Britain has
fallen faster than in most industrial countries. In the middle seventies she became an exceptionally high-inflation
economy. The balance of payments problem has been seen to be
one of preventing deficit rather than surplus. But in a
world of highly interconnected trade and payments, of capital
flows between countries, and of competitive interreaction,
the relationship between the British economy and the outside
world becomes a fundamental part of the economic story.

Over much of the post-1945 period there has been a tendency to see British economic problems as confined by the
Straits of Dover. In part no doubt this arose as a manifes-
tation of insularity born of political predominance and Empire which has militated against a global view of economic
affairs. In part it also stemmed from an intellectual tradition, which suggested that the economy, both internally
and externally, could be balanced unilaterally by appropriate mixes of fiscal and monetary policies, supplemented
with administrative *ad hoc*ery as exemplified by the variety
of incomes policies pursued by governments of both left and

right.

In this Chapter we review the economic history of the last hundred years or so both from the British standpoint and from that of the industrial economic world. The starting point must be arbitrary but it is useful to begin with some observations on the world before 1914, and then the inter-war period divided by the Great Crash in the United States in 1929. The Second World War divides the years of depression of the thirties from the years of prosperity, through the comparative turbulence of the 1970s – to the intellectual and practical challenge of today's economic world.


THE WORLD BEFORE 1914

In 1871 the Franco-Prussian War ended and the German Empire emerged. The American Civil War ended in 1865 and by the early 1870s the period of reconstruction could be said to be complete. For Britain the early 1870s marked the climacteric of her industrial pre-eminence. From then on, if it was not exactly downhill all the way, it was certainly true that international competition  from Germany and the United States began to erode Britain's dominant position.

Not that Britain's economic progress, following the industrial revolution and into the mid-nineteenth century, had been as spectacular as many suppose. Fluctuations in trade apart, the growth of national output insofar as we can measure it had been modest, certainly by the standards of many of the industrial countries after the Second World War. There had been little international competition. Moreover, despite the nostalgia about Britain as the erstwhile workshop of the world, Napoleon had much of the truth when he described the British as a nation of shopkeepers. The Empire was not created by manufacturers but by traders, by seamen, and those who sold services as well as goods on international markets. Typically the British ran a deficit on visible trade, offset by services supplied and by a growing income from investments overseas. As the nineteenth century progressed the visible trade balance deteriorated and, by the early twentieth century, international competition in manufactures had reached a level that stimulated demands for industrial protection personified by Joseph Chamberlain, a theme that was to recur in the early 1930s and which is the subject of debate today.

For much of the nineteenth century, however, the current account of the United Kingdom balance of payments was strong. Such dominance might have led to considerable difficulties

for the world at large since it meant that, on current account, Britain was potentially withdrawing funds from the
rest of the world. In recent years we have become accustomed
to the difficulties posed by the large current account surpluses earned by the oil-producing countries, which require
'recycling' if they are not to lead to deflationary consequences for others. In the case of nineteenth-century Britain, no such problem arose because the surplus on current
account was roughly matched by an outflow on capital account. So overseas investment, the Empire, and a supply of
cheap food and raw materials  grew on the back of the current account surplus. Income from overseas capital con-
cealed, if barely in its later stages, the problems of an
increasingly uncompetitive and deteriorating position on
visible trade. By the twentieth century the stock of overseas capital was the North Sea oil of its time.

   The situation that developed had marked consequences both
for the pound sterling and for the growth of Britain's
financial system. In over-simplified terms, the rest of the
world owed Britain money. The currency was widely used as a
medium of exchange in international trade. It was an international store of financial wealth in which private individuals and governments could hold their reserves. It became
what was later called a key currency; it spanned the trading
world and, supported by the strength of the current account
of the balance of payments, it was 'as good as gold'. It was
the basis on which the City of London became the world's
leading financial centre, providing the financial machinery
to deal with capital flows and the role of sterling as the
reserve currency, central to the international monetary system.

   An efficient international monetary system should facilitate the resolution of payments imbalances between countries
at something like full employment and provide the desired
increase in international money both to finance trade and
the level of reserves that countries wish to hold. Resolving
payments imbalances does not mean that all countries should
balance their books on current account. But if a country or
group of countries cannot achieve the desired balance without having to resort to excessive unemployment, lower growth
than its potential and a general under-utilisation of resources, this situation is not only unsatisfactory from the
point of view of those individual countries but also for the
world as a whole. In current times the persistence of large
trade surpluses in Germany and Japan has created problems
for the rest of the world. As we shall see later this implies that the international monetary system in the world
today is not working efficiently.

An efficient monetary system needs to deal with two central problems. The first is the problem of adjustment, or
the elimination of undesirable trade imbalances. The second
is the problem of liquidity, i.e. of providing adequate international working capital and reserves, the nature of the
problem depending on exchange rate policies. In the period
before 1914, the main adjustment problem occurred between
the United Kingdom and the rest of the world, which the market effectively solved through the export of capital. *Ex
post* there was no major recycling problem because of the
dominance of the United Kingdom.

Neither was there a problem of international liquidity. Up
to 1914 the world by and large operated on what was known as
the Gold Standard. That is to say the value of currencies
was fixed in terms of gold and currencies were freely ex-
changeable into gold. The world before 1914 experienced relative monetary stability. Many supposed, and some still do,
that this was attributable to the existence of the Gold
Standard which imposed monetary discipline on individual
countries. Although there is something in the idea that stable exchange rates are associated with international monetary stability, the monetary system before the First World
War reflected not only dependence on gold as a reserve asset, but also dependence on sterling. Sterling itself constituted an essential part of international liquidity. It
was the growth of sterling rather than the increase in the
stocks of gold available that kept the wheels of international trade turning smoothly.

There was no very clear idea that the economy, in a macroeconomic sense, might not function very well. The economics
of the time supposed that markets functioned efficiently,
and public debates on problems as we see them today were
noticeably absent. True, there had been extensive debates
about protectionism, but hardly in the context in which such
debates are carried out today. Economics was seen to be concerned with economic efficiency in the allocation of resources on the one hand and with equity on the other. There
was no place for extensive discussions about the economy as
a whole, of the kind that had characterised Marx and some of
the earlier so-called classical economists. It was recognised that government intervention on efficiency grounds
would be justified where social costs and benefits of economic activities diverge from private ones. On the other hand
the growing concern with the consequences of *laissez-faire*
for the distribution of income and wealth was a more potent
force leading to concern with poverty and minimum living
standards. These stimulated the budgets introduced by Lloyd
George, often seen as the beginnings of the welfare state.

But economists, politicians and the public at large were far
from the concepts of modern economic policy-making which
dominate, indeed excessively dominate, public debate today

## THE WORLD OF THE TWENTIES

The First World War had far-reaching social and economic effects. It shifted the balance of economic power between the
Old World and the New. It marked the emergence of the United
States as the world's major economic power, the consequences
of which were not fully integrated into the international
economic order for over a quarter of a century. For the British, the war forced upon them the economic realities that
had been growing before the war itself. The cost of the war
had been heavy, and in order to finance it it had been
necessary to draw on the overseas stock of capital which had
shored up the visible trade account. Not only was there a
loss of investment income, but also a loss of trade and
shipping particularly in the New World. The modern problem
of balance of payments adjustment, which has been a sustained feature of the British economy for so long, began in
the 1920s.
  The situation in continental Europe was if anything worse.
The mainland had borne the brunt of the physical destruction
of the war. Germany had been brought to its knees, and was
saddled with a ridiculous burden of reparations which was
impossible to discharge and which *a fortiori* was inconsistent with a healthy economic recovery. Further east the
break-up of the old Austro-Hungarian Empire left economic
destruction and anomalies which added to the European burden.
On the continent political disorder and instability went
hand-in-hand with economic depression.
  In the United Kingdom unemployment began to rise in 1920
reaching 11.3 per cent of the work-force in 1921. It never
fell below 6.8 per cent in the inter-war years, with a peak
of 15.6 per cent in 1932, after the slump in the United
States. The most popular explanation of this situation turns
on the decision made in 1925 to adopt something called the
Gold Exchange Standard and in particular to set the pound
sterling at a fixed parity with the dollar at the pre-war
rate of $4.86 to the £.
  The Gold Standard had been formally suspended as far as
the United Kingdom was concerned in 1914. However, as already pointed out, many believed that the apparent monetary
stability of the pre-war period had been associated with the
Gold Standard system and that a return to a stable international order meant returning to it. Accordingly in 1925,

with Winston Churchill as Chancellor of the Exchequer, a modified version of the Gold Standard, the Gold Exchange Standard, was adopted, the modification being that while overseas holders of sterling could convert into gold, domestic residents could not.

The fly in the ointment was the parity set against the dollar which many, at the time and later, believed was excessively high. So, despite the fall in British wages and prices, British industry was uncompetitive in international markets. The result, it is said, was high unemployment, particularly in the heavy export industries which had provided much of Britain's industrial advance in the nineteenth century.

Despite the high exchange rate the balance of payments overall appeared to remain, broadly speaking, satisfactory. Overseas investment continued to be undertaken and the stock of overseas assets again began to climb. But this soundness was in part illusory since, in the later twenties particularly, it rested on short-term borrowings from abroad stimulated by exceptionally high real interest rates. However, the main consequence of the high parity was said to be not on the balance of payments, but on the volume of exports and thence on total output and employment. The problem is echoed by those who today fear the consequences on output and employment in Britain from the existence of North Sea oil, a strong currency and, in relative terms, a declining non-oil competitive position.

It is clear that up to the First World War British industry had become structurally ill-equipped to deal with changing technologies and with changing patterns of world demand. Part of the problem arose because the old commodity industries were no longer in such demand, and it was inevitably in the traditional industries such as iron and steel, textiles, and shipbuilding, that the severest unemployment occurred. Newer developments in electrical and other lighter forms of engineering were relatively absent. In these areas the United Kingdom had been outstripped even before the First World War by Germany and the United States. In a very general sense there is little doubt that the United Kingdom had become uncompetitive in a non-price sense.

To believe that a lower parity would have had such a marked effect on British output and employment is, as we shall see in Chapter 4, to ask the exchange rate to have achieved more than might reasonably have been expected. The fragility of the British balance of payments, culminating in the suspension of the Gold Exchange Standard, and the devaluation of the pound against the dollar in 1931, did not originate solely from an excessively high parity in the 1920s, but

also from the dangerous and unsound financial practice of
borrowing short and lending long, without adequate protection. It was the strain imposed on the balance of payments
by excessive overseas investment propped up by short-term
loans that played a major role in the subsequent collapse,
in addition to the costs imposed by the desire to return to
gold.

Part of the explanation of stagnation in the 1920s is attributable to too high an exchange rate. But the rest of the
world outside the United States remained depressed, partly
for some of the reasons already described. However the major
problem that affected everyone lay in the imbalance between
the United States and the rest of the world. This transcends
any simple British explanation of its own unemployment.
Trade outside the United States remained continually depressed and it is the explanation of this that is of central
importance.

The major problem for the world outside the United States
was an inability to balance the books with the United States
at higher rates of economic growth and employment. The outflow of private capital from Britain in the nineteenth century had offset the surplus on current account. The United
States after the First World War went into isolation, refus-
ing even to ratify the Treaty of Versailles. In isolationist
America there was neither the custom nor the will to follow
Britain particularly as British investment overseas to build
an empire was regarded as imperialism. Such American overseas investment as there was went largely to support ailing
governments in repaying money that was already owed to the
Americans. The self-sufficiency of the United States enabled
it to embark on the greatest boom in its history without
fear or favour. The depression of trade output and employment in the 1920s for the rest of the world outside the
United States was the direct consequence of the collapse of
any semblance of an efficient international monetary system
which permitted the efficient use of all the world's major
industrial resources. It was inevitable that Britain should
have experienced its share of this depressed state of the
rest of the world, accentuated by problems of industrial
structure, even apart from the question of whether the parity set in 1925 was too high.


AFTER THE SLUMP

In splendid isolation self-sufficient America, pulling itself
up by its own bootstraps, had embarked on a path of economic
expansion that lasted a decade. The Great Crash of 1929 that

followed was both spectacular and disastrous, not only for
the United States itself but also for the rest of a world
which had just limped its way through the twenties.

A detailed analysis of the causes and subsequent development of the recession in the United States, and its consequences for the rest of the world, is beyond the scope of
this book, but some examination of it is necessary. As in
the analysis of recession in 1975 and the persistent unemployment in the industrial world that has followed it, it is
important to separate the underlying behaviour of the real
economy from financial and monetary behaviour of both the
private financial system and of governments. In addition account must be taken of subsequent legislation relating to
trade, with its concomitant effects on trading relationships
and exchange rate behaviour.

The American recession had its immediate origins in the
real cyclical behaviour of the economy. The boom of the
twenties was based on major investment, both in housing and
in industry. Towards the end of the period the rate of investment accelerated, and between 1927 and 1929 the output
of capital goods rose by nearly a quarter. All the conditions appeared to be present for an overshoot in investment,
an excessive rate of capital accumulation, to be followed by
an inevitable contraction of the type predicted by a wide
class of economic theories concerning the trade cycle. The
evidence suggests that, by 1929, the downturn was under way.

The trade or business cycle is a discernible phenomenon of
the nineteenth century. The central question that arose was
not so much why such a boom should come to an end - a matter
on which there might be a large measure of agreement - but
why in this case the slump and the subsequent recession
should be so great. By any standards the real boom was substantial and one might suppose that, the greater the boom,
the greater the subsequent adjustment would be expected to
be. But even on this assumption it is doubtful whether the
severity of the subsequent recession can be adequately explained in terms of a trade cycle theory, which focusses on
real as opposed to monetary phenomena, and which also excludes the subsequent reaction of the policy-making authorities to rising unemployment.

To begin with, the boom in the United States had created
a state of euphoria that was unhealthy. The steady rise in
profits throughout the period, the length of the boom, and
the sharp acceleration toward the end of the period  encouraged both real and financial investment alike. In Wall
Street financial investors fought to obtain a share in the
growing prosperity. Stock market fever gripped the private
investor, and the felony was compounded by the pernicious

practice of buying shares on margin, i.e., borrowing money
in order to purchase shares. The net effect was that by the
time the real decline in the economy began to be understood,
a massive speculative position had been taken by private investors. The Wall Street Crash that followed had a profound
effect on the inflated values of private wealth holdings,
which rebounded to an abnormal extent on the investment of
private businesses and the spending of consumers. At the
outset the real downturn in the cycle was strongly reinforced by the pervasive financial failure of individual
persons causing a major disruption in the capital market. A
new South Sea Bubble had burst, with calamitous effects for
an economy that was already on the way down.

The real downturn in the economy and the collapse on Wall
Street were followed by a sharp contraction in the supply
of money and credit. Reduced credit-worthiness, brought
about both by the real downturn and by financial failure,
brought reduced credit and further monetary contraction,
each round tightening the screws on falling output and rising unemployment. The industrial decline, accompanied by
falling capital and consumer spending, brought major second-
round effects on farm prices and farmers' incomes, in a
country in which agriculture and the farming community still
played a major role.

The international consequence of the American collapse
manifested itself in several ways. Despite the small significance of foreign trade to the United States, its absolute
size and influence was such that the fall in demand had direct and damaging effects on world trade and other trading
nations. Exports and imports began to move sharply downward.
The fall in trade and the collapse of commodity and farm
prices in the United States strongly influenced world prices
of food and raw materials, so spreading the recession to
farming communities and commodity producers in the world at
large.

Concurrently, the sharp monetary contraction that followed
the real downturn made itself felt in international capital
markets. As already recorded, at a government level American
money had been used to assist Germany to deal with the problem of reparations payments, some of which had been redistributed among the other Allies, notably the United Kingdom and France. While American investment abroad had been
inadequate to sustain a real recovery in economic growth, in
Europe it was significant enough to cause serious problems,
most immediately for Germany, when it began to dry up. The
growing shortage of money and credit in the United States
prompted the repatriation of funds and the calling in of international loans. The reduction in the flow of international

lending triggered off a general calling in of loans and the repatriation of funds. The consequences for Britain were direct, substantial and unfortunate.

Towards the end of the twenties, Britain had been supporting its capital outflow with short-term borrowings from abroad, which required exceptionally high real rates of interest and led to a major exposure to capital flight. The problem of capital flight was compounded by the earlier decision to adopt the Gold Exchange Standard which meant that the repatriation of short-term debts constituted a direct charge on the gold reserves. With general pressure on international capital markets the rot started and gold began to flow out.

At the same time unemployment was rising sharply, and the direct costs of the unemployed began to weigh heavily on the National Insurance Fund, out of which unemployment benefit was paid. This resulted in two perceived problems. First it was believed that financial probity required the government to balance its books on current account - that is to say that government expenditure should be roughly offset by the income it collected in taxes. The rights and wrongs of this are discussed subsequently in this book. The point to note here is simply that this belief was widely held and had a distinct influence on behaviour.

Of course governments in general do not finance their expenditure out of taxation and the British Government during the twenties was no exception to the rule. In order to make ends meet it had to borrow as well as collect taxes. However, the persistent drain on government funds caused by the exceptional rise in unemployment resulted in fear being felt by the Treasury and others, which was ultimately accepted by Ministers, that a continuation of the rising pressure on the government's financial deficit would result in a loss of confidence in the British financial system.

Notice that this had two elements. The first suggested the need to balance the government's budget, in order to stimulate domestic confidence and so output and employment. The second was the fear of a decline in overseas confidence, with pressure both directly on the gold reserves through the repatriation of capital, and on the exchange rate. Even the Labour government of the day was persuaded that steps would have to be taken to preserve some semblance of budgetary equilibrium. None of this discussion took place within the context of any coherent view of how a budget deficit interacted with either output or the exchange rate. It was something of an act of faith.

But the fat was in the fire. The pressure on the gold reserves increased as money flowed out while, paradoxically, decisions to cut unemployment benefit and public sector

wages caused as much alarm as they did good to the deficit.
By this stage external expectations were too strong, and in
September 1931 it became necessary to suspend the Gold
Exchange Standard. The convertibility of sterling into gold
ceased, and with it went a fixed sterling exchange rate *vis-
à-vis* the dollar. Effective immediately, the pound was devalued from $4.86 to the £ to $4 to the £ and allowed to
float, and by mid-1932 had lost virtually another 50¢. The
devaluation of the pound marked a gear change in the international system in much the same way as the devaluation of
sterling in 1967. The thirties, like the seventies, became
a period of flexible exchange rates or 'dirty floating'.
For those who had bemoaned the parity in 1925, it must have
seemed like a casting-off of chains, as indeed the devaluation of 1967 seemed to many others at the time. In both
cases they turned out to be wrong, although in the case of
1931 there were unfortunately more insidious forces at
work, to undermine whatever good a depreciation of sterling
might have achieved.

As trade cascaded downwards and unemployment rose throughout the world, individual countries grasped at straws to
save themselves. Perhaps, like economists, common sense in
economics is not always to be trusted. In the early thirties, what could seem more commonsensical than the view that
a solution of the internal problem of unemployment was to
ensure that expenditures made by domestic residents should
be diverted to domestic products, so raising domestic output and creating jobs at home? Unfortunately the general
move to protection, to the imposition of tariffs and import
quotas, and to the imposition of exchange control, served
only to intensify the downward spiral of trade and employment. Everyone's imports are someone else's exports, so that
the attempt to raise domestic employment by restricting imports was simply a device to shift one's domestic unemployment on to someone else. Protection led to falling imports
which led to falling exports, and by 1933 the combination of
the fall in world demand, the competitive depreciation of
currencies, and the extension of tariff barriers and quantitative controls, resulted in the volume of manufactured
goods traded falling to about 50 per cent of its 1929 level.
It was an ominous year in which National Socialism in
Germany came to power. Not for the first time was it
demonstrated that economics and politics are interdependent.

From 1933 onwards there was moderate improvement. In Britain, Keynes and others called for more public works and increased government spending. Indeed, the advocacy of public
works had been included on Keynes' influence in the Liberal

Party Manifesto in 1929. It was generally agreed that interest rates in the late twenties had been too high· and,
from a level of 6 per cent in 1929, Bank Rate was brought
down to 2 per cent in 1932, where it stayed with the exception of a few weeks in 1939 until 1951. Lower interest
rates combined with government subsidies produced something
of a housing boom – the 1930s houses and buildings con-
spicuously remain to testify to the period. Unemployment as
a percentage of the labour force fell from 22 per cent at
the peak to an average of 12 per cent in 1939.

In the United States, Roosevelt as President inauguarated
the New Deal, a new set of public works and spending policies designed to do for the United States what others
wanted for the United Kingdom. There did appear to be an
upturn in America in 1937 but, although the situation had
improved, it began to peter out in the following year. Re-
grettably the buoyant component of demand that put some life
into the world economy was the growth of rearmament as the
spectre of the Second World War began to rear its ugly head.

What should one conclude from this disastrous episode? At
one time there was broad agreement that the commercial
policies pursued by individual countries in response to the
recession were totally inappropriate. Import controls,
tariffs and competitive depreciation were to be eschewed.
This profoundly affected those who at a later date attempt-
ed to provide a better economic framework for the post-1945
era. But agreement may now be less certain when we observe
the advocacy of some of these policies today, in a period of
unemployment well above the average for the twenty-five
years after 1945.

While many agree that across countries commercial policies
were inhibiting to trade and economic recovery, the popular
predilection in Britain has been to suggest that matters
would have been radically better in the United Kingdom if
only two things had been more clearly understood. The first,
which has already been discussed, is the parity set for the
pound in 1925. The second is the role of fiscal policy in
determining the rate of unemployment, and in particular the
need to adjust the public sector financial deficit to generate the desired rate of employment, rather than being sub-
servient to outmoded criteria for budget balance that had
no roots in any comprehensive theory of how the economy actually functioned.

There would seem to be little doubt that domestic action
with regard to the public sector deficit was indeed inappropriate for the circumstances, since its general effect
was to reduce the growth of the money supply below what,
other things being equal, might have seemed desirable.

Nevertheless, it is an open question as to whether domestic fiscal and monetary policy could in large measure have off-set the major shock administered by the enormous monetary contraction in the United States following the Wall Street Crash.

It has already been argued that the world of the twenties was dominated by the imbalance between the United States and the rest of the world, in the absence of any mechanism to bring about adjustment without relatively slow growth in the world outside. The situation of the thirties after the slump, and the subsequent behaviour of exchange rates, dramatically underlined the absence of any effective international monetary system and the lack of any mechanisms for coordinating monetary and fiscal policies between countries. The combination of repressive commercial policies in the world at large, and monetary instability after the slump of 1929, presented problems that affected all countries and from which no one was immune. That is the important lesson to be learned from the experience of the thirties and it has direct relevance to the problem of growth and exchange rate behaviour in the world today.


AFTER THE SECOND WORLD WAR : THE EARLY YEARS

The events of the thirties were indelibly stamped on the minds of the policy-makers who gathered together toward the end of the Second World War to prepare an economic world fit for heroes to come home to. Unemployment and the disruption of international trade that had followed the slump of 1929, and the subsequent recession, dominated their agendas. There had to be a world in which unemployment was banished, and stable patterns of trade restored.

It was recognised that, in an efficient international monetary system, the two problems of adjustment and liquidity had to be dealt with. In the event the bulk of the attention was focussed on the latter rather than the former, partly it seems in the belief that the trade and balance of payments problems that tended to emerge were of an essentially cyclical nature, and it was these cyclical problems that became central. It was agreed that cyclical fluctuations would be materially amplified, if balance of payments problems experienced during the cycle had to be met by contractionary fiscal and monetary policies, exacerbating the downward movement of output and employment. There was a perceived need for international credit facilities which would enable individual countries to weather such storms without recourse to deflation, and the supply of credit for this purpose was

institutionalised in the creation of the International
Monetary Fund.

Each individual country was to contribute to the Fund according to its quota which was established on the basis of
size and importance. The IMF became a potential supplier of
short-term loans, which would provide a breathing space for
individual countries in difficulties, with an implicit assumption that over the course of the cycle there would be
some balancing out. It is true that the Charter of the Fund
did give some clues as to what might have to be done in the
cases of individual countries whose balance of payments
were ruled to be in fundamental, rather than cyclical, disequilibrium. Import quotas and controls were permitted only
under special circumstances. Similarly, while the intention
was to stabilise exchange rates and avoid the competitive
depreciations of the thirties, it was recognised that the
existing structure of exchange rates was not immutable, and
that there could be circumstances which would require parity
changes. Accordingly changes of parity exceeding 10 per cent
required that the Fund should be consulted. Despite this,
the emphasis tended to be on the need for international
liquidity and reserves rather than on the mechanisms through
which persistent imbalances between countries might be removed.

The liquidity problem suggested that gold production,
which was to some extent arbitrary, and the operations of
domestic monetary systems would not result in adequate
liquidity, either in terms of its total or its distribution
between individual countries. In consequence Keynes proposed
a much more ambitious plan for the setting up of a world
central bank, which would create a new international money
called bancor in which the individual countries would hold
deposits. This new international money could then be used
to settle inter-country debts, and the total amount of it
available adjusted to the needs of world trade and employment, offsetting the vagaries of gold production and the
supplies of domestic currencies. Roughly speaking, the
amount of bancor was to be increased in line with the growth
in world trade. Opposition to the plan largely turned on
issues of monetary sovereignty, i.e. domestic control over
monetary matters affecting one's individual economy, and
more generally on the question as to how the world money
was to be controlled and by whom.

Parallel with concern for the international monetary system was concern about the commercial policies that had been
pursued during the recession. It was widely accepted that
the tariffs and import controls of the thirties were inimical to trade and that there was a need to return to some-

thing approaching free trade. While the inimical effects of
the restrictions on trade were indeed widely recognised, it
was the United States above all which espoused the cause of
free trade with the greatest enthusiasm, while others were
less certain. Exchange control, and restrictions on imports
largely through licences, had been a feature of the economic apparatus constructed by Britain as part of her wartime
economic programme, and there were considerable doubts as
to the wisdom of dismantling such restrictions too rapidly
in the face of expected post-war problems. In the event, it
was not until 1954 that the last vestiges of trade restriction in this form were swept away, although exchange control remained in some form for a considerable period of
time. While exchange controls relating to the current account were abolished in the late fifties with the convertibility of the major industrial currencies, controls in the
capital account were only abolished in the United Kingdom
in 1979. The General Agreement on Tariffs and Trade (GATT)
reflected the attempts of the policy-makers to transform
their intentions with regard to freer trade into actuality.

Finally there was concern about the developing countries,
with their high dependence on commodity trade and their low
standards of living and economic advancement, which had suffered the enormous slump in commodity prices associated with
the inter-war recession. At the outset, this reflected itself in the creation of the International Bank for Reconstruction and Development (the World Bank) to serve as a
financial intermediary between the richer and poorer countries. Thus the three main objectives of the founding
fathers of the post-war international economy - balance of
payments equilibrium without unemployment, freer trade, and
greater help for the developing nations - had their institutional counterparts in the IMF, GATT and the World Bank.

It all sounded fine on paper, but reality is a hard task-
master. The United States was anxious to return almost immediately to a free trading world with full convertibility
of currencies. But it was not to be. The details of what
followed, particularly with regard to the United Kingdom,
made it clear that this was to prove very difficult. The
central problem that in the event dominated economic
affairs, as indeed it had after the First World War, was the
overwhelming economic power of the United States *vis-à-vis*
the rest of the world. This was a problem that had been
recognised by many in the United Kingdom, but she was in no
position to impose her views. The Allies in continental Europe had suffered destruction and disorganisation. Germany
was once again on its knees together with Japan. The imbalance between the United States and the rest of the world was,

if anything, greater than it had been after the First World
War. Such an imbalance could not have been cured by the rest
of the world depreciating against the dollar, since it
would have been unable to supply the goods necessary to re-
move this imbalance. The problem of adjustment between
America and the outside world stood in the way of European
reconstruction, again creating a potential recycling problem if recovery in Europe were to be completed and full
employment restored.

As we have seen, in the nineteenth century British overseas investment offset the persistent surplus on its current
account of the balance of payments. The United States solved
the problem initially not through overseas investment, but
by the simple expedient of giving resources away. As far as
Europe was concerned, this was achieved through the Marshall
Plan, which gave aid for European reconstruction, and other
forms of aid continued to flow out from the United States
through the 1950s. It was this that provided the basis for
recovery in the world outside America.

The giving of aid and the financial arrangements made at
the end of the war between the United States and its Allies,
including in the British case the writing off of Lend Lease,
meant that the early post-war recovery was financed by
America, without creating a lasting burden of deadweight
debt in the world outside. The economic dominance of America,
however, meant that a shortage of dollars became the key
factor in the progress made by those countries. For the
world at large, just as sterling had been the key reserve
currency in the nineteenth century, so the dollar became the
key reserve currency in the 1950s and 1960s. It was not the
only reserve currency since sterling continued to play an
important role. After the devaluation of sterling in 1931
the world had divided into a number of trading currency
areas of which the sterling area was one, encompassing more
or less what became the Commonwealth, with the exception of
Canada which tied itself to the dollar, and including the
Republic of Ireland and others who continued to use sterling.
But in Britain itself the position was summed up in the ex-
pression 'the gold and dollar reserves', which emphasised
the primacy of the dollar in world economic affairs. The
world at large was effectively on a dollar standard, the
dollar being supported - as we shall see in Chapter 6 - by
the commitment of the United States to convert dollar holdings into gold.

## THE YEARS OF PROSPERITY

Dates are arbitrary and the slicing up of time artificial.
To say that the period from 1950 to 1970 constitutes the
years of prosperity is not to say that either date marks a
point of identifiable change. Indeed, from 1959, which
some regard as symbolising the completion of post-war economic recovery with the establishment of currency convertibility, there was discernible change in the economic world
on a number of fronts. Nevertheless, the period as a whole
reflected a remarkable growth in world trade, relative
price stability as compared with the seventies and exceptional growth in many industrial countries, notably in Germany and Japan. True, such rapid rates of growth were not
shared either by Britain or by the United States. But in
all countries there had been relatively full employment by
any historical standards and, certainly by the standards of
the inter-war period, world growth in the industrial countries must be regarded as remarkable.

Unfortunately the same could not be said of the developing countries, about whom concern had been expressed by the
founding fathers of the post-war economic world. It has become more difficult to talk about the developing countries
with much generality. There are those with oil. There are
those whose growth in industrial potential has become a
source of increasing competition for the old industrial
countries themselves. But there are also those whose problems seemed to remain intractable, still highly dependent
on the vagaries of commodity markets rather than on industrial products or oil. For them, the gap between rich and
poor widened. By and large efficiency increases in the industrial countries were initially directly absorbed by increased money incomes, while increased efficiency in the
production of commodities went directly to the industrial
consumer in the form of lower prices. The terms of trade
were much in favour of the industrial nations.

The factors explaining the years of relative prosperity
are a matter of some dispute. With slower growth during the
seventies and rising levels of unemployment, what has gone
wrong? It is convenient to consider the question in terms
of the effects of government policies, the character of the
international monetary system and secular forces underlying
the rate of growth of world output.

Keynes' *General Theory of Employment, Interest and Money*,
published in 1936, is often taken to be the most important
work published in the social sciences since Marx's *Das Kapi-
tal*. Its importance stems from its theoretical contribution
to economic thinking, its practical contribution to the

making of economic policy and, not least, its political significance. The first and third of these are taken up in subsequent chapters. Here we are concerned only with the second,
namely the extent to which the practical policies advocated
by Keynes, and refined by those who came after him, exercised
a major influence in creating the years of prosperity that
followed the Second World War.

The almost total acceptance of Keynesian prescriptions by
economists, public servants, and politicians of both left
and right in the United Kingdom has tended to exaggerate the
practical influence of Keynesianism on affairs. Much British
writing extrapolates this influence to the world at large
outside but the evidence is at best patchy. In terms of the
development of professional economic thinking, the United
States and the Scandinavian countries were probably most affected, and in practical terms there is little doubt that
economic policies in the latter were set in an essentially
Keynesian framework. The central objective of policy was to
relate the state of the budget deficit to the general level
of demand required to give something like full employment.
From time to time, the side effects of inflation and balance
of payments difficulties deflected the aim from its proper
target, but there was little or no theoretical disagreement
about the target or the predominance of fiscal policy (government spending and tax policy) in achieving it. In this
world monetary policy as such was for the most part purely
accommodating. That is to say, the supply of money simply
responded to the demand for it.

But, while it is fair to say that in academic economic
circles in the United States Keynesianism was supported by
the majority, its impact on the actual conduct of economic
policy is far less clear. Indeed, for much of the recovery
period after the war through to the 1960s, economic policy
in the United States was clearly conducted according to
quite different principles. In 1952 President Eisenhower
came to power with the avowed aims of ending the Korean
War, which he did, and balancing the budget, which he didn't.
However, the Eisenhower attitude profoundly affected the
policies pursued until the Kennedy era when, with the tax
cut of 1964, the practical impact of Keynesianism on American domestic policy can be said to have reached its peak.

A balanced assessment of Keynesian influence on American
economic policy-making during the years of prosperity is
that it was at best spotty. It must be emphasised that the
issue at this stage is not whether the policies followed
were right or wrong. Those pursued by the Eisenhower Administration, for example, were heavily criticised in many
quarters. The issue is simply whether delicate control and
fine-tuning based on Keynesian principles could be said to

have exercised a consistent influence on American domestic
economic affairs, and to account for the major difference
in the performance of the economy with regard to employment
and output when compared to the pre-war period. On this
issue the answer must be no.

The separation of economic powers in the United States
must also be recognised. In America, monetary policy is the
concern of the Federal Reserve Board, while fiscal policy
is the concern of Congress. In Germany too there is a wider
separation between monetary and fiscal powers, given the
Federal nature of the Republic. Unlike the situation in Britain, in both the United States and Germany monetary policy
exercises a more independent and significant role. There is
little evidence in either Germany or Japan that budgetary
policy carried out on Keynesian lines can provide a major
part of the explanation of the rapid rates of economic
growth that were prevalent, and the persistence of what
would now be regarded as full employment. In Germany the
fear of inflation focussed the attention of the authorities
on monetary rather than fiscal control, and Keynesian principles contributed little to the German economic miracle.

However, in Britain, at least on the surface there would
appear to be no doubt of the influence of Keynesian thinking on the practical conduct of economic affairs. For most
of the period fiscal policy was at the heart of economic
decision-making, and monetary policy appeared to play only
an accommodating role. What have come to be referred to as
demand management policies were framed and discussed in
Keynesian terms and in Keynesian language. Budgets were
classified as reflationary, neutral or deflationary, i.e.
they were assessed in terms of the likely effects of fiscal
changes on output and employment. There were from time to
time debates as to whether government fiscal intervention
was actually stabilising or de-stabilising. But there is
little doubt that governments of both left and right were
trying to be Keynesian. Criticism of policy was directed at
errors in implementing an agreed set of principles, rather
than directly challenging the principles themselves. For the
most part, criticisms of budgetary policy were based on domestic considerations, on such issues as whether the timing
of measures was correct or incorrect, or whether the implied
value judgements in policy-making, e.g. between less unemployment and more inflation, were to be regarded as acceptable.

But, in assessing the influence of Keynesian principles
during this period little attention has been paid to the
international circumstances of the time, and in particular
to the way in which the international monetary system func-

tioned. As has already been described, the world after the
Second World War went on to a dollar/gold exchange standard, and parity with the dollar in what was a pegged exchange rate system became central to the policies pursued
by many countries including the United Kingdom. After the
war itself the United Kingdom did not make what was to many
the fundamental error of the 1920s, which was to maintain
the pre-war parity with the dollar. Instead Britain massive-
ly devalued the pound sterling by some 30 per cent in 1949,
and maintained the new parity of $2.80 to the £ for a period
of eighteen years until the devaluation of 1967. The
implications of this require some anticipation of the discussion of the implications of a fixed exchange rate regime
which will be seen in Chapter 4.

There are three important points to make. The first is
that, subject to a number of qualifying factors discussed in
Chapter 4, nominal exchange rate parities are not determined
in any simple way only by flows of trade, but also by relative rates of monetary growth. Exchange rates are determined in capital markets as well as by trade flows. Consequently constraints are imposed on the relative monetary
rates of growth of the countries in the system. For a given
country there is something that we may describe as a 'warranted' rate of monetary growth, which will keep the currency in line with the others that are pegged in the system.
If a country pursues a monetary policy that is tighter than
the warranted rate, then its currency will tend to appreciate, and vice versa.

Secondly, in a pegged exchange rate system, there will be
a tendency for inflation rates to be drawn together by the
process of competition in international markets, although
this process will be modified by the different balances in
different economies between traded and non-traded goods. For
example, in the case of Japan, while the prices of traded
goods remained highly competitive, the Japanese domestic
inflation rate was considerably above that of other countries due to low productivity in non-traded goods. Nevertheless under pegged exchange rates there is some limit on how
far inflation rates can diverge, subject to this qualifica-
tion, and still remain consistent with a pegged exchange
rate system. Finally, under a pegged exchange rate system,
the major effect of an excessive monetary expansion shows
up directly not so much in an increase in the domestic inflation rate, but in a deterioration in the current account
of the balance of payments as imports are sucked in from
abroad.

The consequences of this for Britain during the years of
prosperity are manifest. The emergence of unemployment, even

on a modest scale as in the early fifties, the late fifties, and the early sixties, was followed by reflation. The economy was expanded through tax cuts and increases in public spending which promoted monetary expansion. In these episodes some direct effects of price inflation were observed, but the major consequence in each case was a deterioration in the balance of payments which, if left to carry on, would have threatened the existing parity with the dollar. The result was a retreat from the previous expansion, although in the aftermath of the 1963/4 expansion, too late as it turned out to save the pound from devaluation.

Thus, during the years between the devaluations, the United Kingdom engaged in what became familiarly known as 'stop/go'. Given the objectives of maintaining parity with the dollar, at the end of the day the scope for independent demand management and fine-tuning based on Keynesian principles turned out to be remarkably limited. In a sense the United Kingdom tried to be Keynesian and failed. As we shall see later, the attempt to do so after 1973 - when the exchange rate was floating - was near disastrous.

But the dollar/gold exchange standard was obviously of wider significance for the world as a whole. Insofar as the world pegged itself to the dollar, it was directly influenced both by American monetary policy and by its rate of inflation. Even so exchange rates did not remain completely fixed after 1949 and there was devaluation in France and revaluation in Germany at a later stage. During the 1960s the system showed signs of creaking and in the end collapsed. But for a period of some twenty years the dollar/gold exchange standard brought a cohesion into the international monetary system that had been lacking since before the First World War. Temporary as it was, it provided international monetary stability that had been lacking in the twenties and thirties. It was the gradual breakdown in this system that paved the way for the years of relative turbulence that were to follow.

However international monetary stability must be seen only as a necessary and not as a sufficient condition for growing prosperity. If, as has been suggested, it is doubtful whether Keynesian thinking was ever as widely effective in determining policies in individual countries as the British commonly suppose, a major role must be assigned to other real factors in the world economy in explaining the high levels of employment. Typically in the past wars have been followed by both booms and inflation. The notable exception to this is of course the First World War, after which the boom was short-lived, but specific reasons have already been given as to why the international monetary system of the day

prevented it being sustained. Following the management of
European reconstruction and in a relatively settled international monetary environment, it was possible to exploit
the new technologies and investment opportunities that the
war itself stimulated. In particular, as we shall see in
Chapter 5, great opportunity was provided for a catching up
process between the United States at the frontier of technology and the rest of the industrial world. Conditions
were favourable for a long-drawn-out and sustained boom. The
war itself not only led to the need for capital replenish-
ment but also, through growing technology, to new demands
for capital goods coupled with a long-term expansion in the
demand for consumer durable goods and housing. Many countries, unlike the United Kingdom, were in a particularly
favourable position to divert labour from other occupations
into industrial employment in order to supply the growing
demand for industrial goods. The reduction of barriers to
trade enlarged the world market for tradeable goods. At the
same time, with the exception of the Korean War period, the
industrial countries were blessed with relatively stable
commodity prices, with cheap sources of raw material and
energy, all of which facilitated rapid industrial growth.
The monetary stability of the period, coupled with these
particularly favourable circumstances, provides a more plausible explanation of the economic growth of the industrial
countries at large, than that it was due to a fundamental
shift in the abilities of governments to manipulate and
fine-tune their economies according to Keynesian principles.


THE YEARS OF TURBULENCE

There is no sudden transition from what has been described
as the years of prosperity to the problems of the 1970s for
the industrial world. From the peak of post-war recovery in
the late fifties there were signs of change. Paradoxically
it was the growing strength of the rest of the world *vis-à-
vis* the United States that was partially responsible for
some of the difficulties that were to come. The combination
of this growing strength, with the particular policies pursued by the United States, was sufficient to end the long
period of relative international monetary stability on
which the progress of the post-war period had rested.
    As we have explained, the dollar/gold exchange standard
depended on the willingness of the other industrial countries to regard dollars as being as good as gold. This status of the dollar depended crucially on the economic
strength of the United States as manifest in its balance of

payments and in its willingness to redeem dollar liabilities in terms of gold. But as the period wore on there were
signs in the early sixties and after that central banks
were no longer so keen to hold such a large proportion of
their reserves in dollars, a development that would have
been almost inevitable given the change in the economic balance of power following the full post-war recovery. Other
currencies became strong too, and the privileged position of
the dollar was, with hindsight, bound to weaken.

But the growing economic strength of the rest of the
world, particularly in continental Europe, also led to the
raising of principles. The pragmatic approach to dollar supremacy associated with the earlier post-war years gave way
to questioning. In simple terms, insofar as the dollar was
regarded as being as good as gold, and the United States
controlled the supply of dollars, it had the unique privilege of being able to print gold – as long, that is, as the
central banks were prepared to absorb dollars without limit
at the ruling exchange rate. However the balance of the
American dollar outflow had begun to change. There was a
shift towards more overseas private investment as a part of
the outflow, compared to operations on official account.
Thus it seemed that the dollar standard gave the United
States a privileged position in being able to create international money for investment overseas. This began to be
seen by countries such as France as insupportable both in
practice, insofar as it meant some absorption by American of
European industry, and in principle, since it came to be
thought that such concentration of international monetary
power was inherently undesirable.

This shift in attitude was compounded by the fact that the
overall position of the American balance of payments began
to get weaker, which was at a later stage reinforced by the
financing of the Vietnam War. The dollar shortage of the
fifties began to turn into a dollar glut, the consequences
of which were for a time largely offset by the continuing
practice of absorbing excess dollars into reserves. It was
argued that the United States, and Britain, were aided by
the reserve nature of their currencies and were shielded
from the necessity of maintaining strict discipline over
their payments. The wider consequence of these issues are
discussed in Chapter 6. The result was the ending of the
*de facto* commitment of many countries to accepting the American inflation rate as the world standard, and to accepting
American leadership with regard to world monetary policies.

The United States was accused of exporting inflation to
the rest of the world by the excessive creation of dollars,
and the French in particular sought to take action to break

the power of the dollar by switching from dollar holdings
into gold. In Germany, upward pressure on the mark was created by the refusal of the monetary authorities to expand
the money supply fast enough to maintain parity with the
dollar. There was sustained pressure on the United States
during the late sixties to devalue the dollar which occurred
with a general realignment of currencies after the Smithsonian agreement of 1971. The pound sterling had already been
devalued in 1967, which in many respects marks the end of an
era. By 1971, the currency realignments that took place
marked the end of the dollar/gold exchange standard which
had been declining over the previous decade. The stability
of the international monetary system as it had operated for
most of the post-war period, based on the strength of the
dollar and conservative American monetary policies, was
over. The ship had dragged its anchor and was left to drift
without direction into the subsequent problems of the seventies.

While the Smithsonian agreement of 1971 was intended to
effect a once-and-for-all realignment of exchange rates, in
practice the result was an uncomfortable halfway house between a system of fixed exchange rates on the one hand and
fully floating rates on the other. The dollar continued to
be important as a reserve currency, although without the *de
facto* guarantees from central bank behaviour that had ruled
during much of the post-war period. In principle one of the
supposed advantages of floating rates is that a country is
free to determine its monetary policy, in terms of monetary
growth, without reference to the monetary policies being
pursued by others. There is no pegged exchange rate system
to maintain. In practice, however, old habits die hard and
the rest of the world was unwilling to abandon some of the
advantages of the dollar standard. So for some time it was
prepared to go on absorbing the dollar outflow from the
United States.

This continued outflow put pressure on the outside world,
which resulted in upward pressure on other exchange rates
*vis-à-vis* the dollar or, in the absence of effective action
to offset it, in an expansionary effect on the money supplies of other countries. Combined with domestic attempts at
expansion and a reduction in unemployment, as for example
under the Heath administration in the United Kingdom,this
resulted in a sharp and synchronised world boom. Growth accelerated, unemployment fell and inflation rose as commodity
prices took off in a manner not seen since the political
scare brought about by the Korean war. As the boom reached
its peak, conflict broke out in the Middle East, and the
dramatic uplift in the price of oil added a major supply

shock to a system that was already excessively inflationary.
Within two years, the industrial world was suffering the
sharpest downturn in output and employment since the Second
World War.

The downturn itself was a combination of three things. The
first was the sharp rise in prices brought about by the demand for commodities and the rise in the price of energy.
Secondly, the fall in output and employment was partly a response to the policies pursued by some countries, notably at
this stage the United States, Germany and Japan, to deal
with the accelerating inflation. Monetary policy was kept
tight or tightened in response to the inflation and the real
money supply was contracted, partly because of the inflation
itself and partly because of slower monetary growth. Thirdly, the rise in the balance of payments surplus of the oil-
producing countries initiated a recycling problem, the initial impact of which was deflationary. The sharp contraction
produced an impact on the inflation rate for the world at
large, and after the sharp downturn in 1975 the world
bounced back in 1976. Since then, however, despite a sustained period of growth in the United States, the industrial
world has not regained the growth path of the post-war
years.

In the United Kingdom, the inflationary situation after
the rise in the price of energy deteriorated rapidly. The
upswing in 1972/3 had been accompanied by a massive monetary
expansion, owing partly to the new competition and credit
policies that had been introduced in 1971, and partly to the
expansionary action taken by the government to stimulate
output and employment. At the peak the money supply was
growing at a rate of 30 per cent per annum. In 1973 the
pound was floated, and the combination of a floating exchange rate and monetary expansion was to superimpose a
major fall in the exchange rate on already accelerating inflation. British budgetary policy, aimed at stabilising output and employment in typical Keynesian fashion, fuelled the
inflation rate without succeeding in preventing rising unemployment and a sharp fall in national output in 1975. The
attempt to spend one's way out of the recession and to avoid
the impact of world recession served only to exacerbate the
inflationary situation. The fate of the United Kingdom at
this time was paralleled by the fate of Sweden at a later
date, and the anatomy of the problem was reflected in the
decline of the dollar and a rising rate of inflation in the
United States in 1978. All three suffered from the difficulties that arise when domestic monetary policy is excessively expansionary in relation to monetary policies being
pursued by other major countries.

So it was that in July 1976 the United Kingdom grasped again for the weapon of incomes policy to stem the inflationary tide. Wage restraint was sold to the trades unions as a substitute for government expenditure cuts and a contraction of the public sector deficit, which had been fuelling monetary growth. The social wage rather than take-home pay became the focus of attention. Paradoxically, the form that the incomes policy subsequently took, with £6 for all, was probably on balance inflationary insofar as it gave it to many for whom it would not have been negotiated in a free market. The familiar pattern of dividend controls and restrictions on the salaries of the 'higher paid' became the order of the day. However the steps already taken failed to prevent the much-needed control from being exercised over the public sector borrowing requirement and monetary growth. The brokers' men from the IMF were called in, and the United Kingdom was once again *pro tempore* in the international pawn shop.

The deflationary measures taken in the budget in November 1976 produced dramatic effects. Sterling had sunk to a low point of $1.57 against the dollar in 1976. In the first three months of 1977 monetary growth was reduced to virtually zero. Confidence in the pound rose sharply, and by the early weeks of the year it was clear that it was distinctly undervalued against external expectations. But both government and industry were obsessed with the need to maintain a competitive pound so that, rather than using the opportunity for an appreciation of the pound to assist in the anti-inflationary struggle, for nearly ten months the government chose to allow the undervaluation of sterling to be reflected in a major rise in the reserves. Money poured into London, and short-term interest rates came tumbling down. The improved position was thrown away without benefit either to the inflation rate or to the levels of output and employment. Policy benefited neither fish nor fowl. Given the intention to refuse to allow sterling to appreciate, there was no logic to tight monetary control. Maintaining the parity would have enabled faster monetary growth to be reflected in higher output and more jobs. Alternatively, given that inflation was the central target, an appreciation of the rate was clearly in order. The ultimate consequence was neither more output nor less inflation, but a major increase in reserves which on the next round provided a further basis for pressure on the growth of the money supply.

On top of this inflammatory material came tax cuts in November 1977 and further cuts in the Budget of 1978. By June of that year, it was clear that the consequences of these changes for the public sector borrowing requirement were in-

consistent with the avowed monetary targets adopted by the
authorities, which set the outlying growth of sterling M3
at 8-12 per cent. Restrictions on the commercial banks in
the form of the 'corset' (see Chapter 3 below) had to be
imposed, and interest rates started their inevitable climb
upward. The pound had finally been allowed to appreciate in
November 1977 when it was felt that the upward pressure
could no longer be resisted. But the delay, with its subsequent consequences when allied to tax cuts which stimulated
the largest consumer boom since the Second World War, had
laid the foundations for the total non-acceptability of the
5 per cent incomes policy introduced in the summer of 1978.
The arithmetic of the policy did not add up. With monetary
growth of 12 per cent and an output growth of the order of
2 per cent, a long-term inflation rate of 10 per cent seemed
on the cards. Against this background in July 1978 private
forecasters were looking for an earnings growth of around
at least 12 per cent in a relatively free market situation.
The uproar and unrest of the first quarter of 1979 did not,
as was commonly supposed by the foreign press, have its origins in the class war or a new peasants' revolt, but constituted a predictable free market reaction to the stance of
fiscal and monetary policy, coupled with the unwinding of
anomalies between the public and private sectors resulting
from the sustained application of incomes policy.

Thus on the crest of a further wave of inflation a Conservative government took office in May 1979, committed to both
reducing public spending and reducing taxation. The serious-
ness of the situation in inflationary terms was not realised.
The growth of the money supply was already out of control.
The tactical error of a major increase in value-added tax to
finance a modest reduction in the standard rate of income
tax added to the inevitable problems of securing rapid and
substantial cuts in public spending and led to the inevitable rise in nominal interest rates later in the year. In relation to their fiscal and monetary programme, virtually a
year was lost. In its own terms the major criticism of the
Conservative government at the outset was not that it was
monetarist, but that it was not monetarist enough.


PERSPECTIVE

This review of the past is no more than a sketch of the developments of the last century. It generates both themes
and questions which are germane to the problems that face
the United Kingdom and the world economies today. Throughout
we have emphasised the interaction between the United King-

dom and the external world, believing that the interpretation of Britain's economic problems must be set in an international context. The overall behaviour of the external
world had important consequences for British domestic policy-
making.

The focus has been on issues relating to stabilisation
policies affecting output, employment, inflation and the
balance of payments. Nothing has been said about economic
growth *per se*, a fuller discussion of which is reserved for
Chapter 5. Only in passing have we noted that the apparent
problem of slow real growth in the United Kingdom economy is
a problem which spans a century. The questions raised with
regard to growth unemployment and the balance of payments
have appeared before in the story, and attention will be
paid to them in succeeding chapters.

Considerable emphasis has been placed throughout on the
behaviour of the international monetary system in influencing the course of world output and trade. Difficulties with
international trade and payments are associated with the
difficulties of individual countries in achieving adequate
growth and employment rates, both in the inter-war period
and in the years of the seventies. Conversely, the period
before the First World War and the years of prosperity after
the second have been associated with international monetary
stability, formerly based on the role of the pound sterling
and latterly on the role of the dollar.

The lack of an efficient international monetary system
lends scope for de-stabilising monetary discretionary action
by individual countries, without regard to the consequences
for the rest of the world. At the end of the day both world
output and world inflation are affected by the sum total of
the policies pursued by individual countries. When in the
past one country has been as economically powerful as the
United States, the consequences of its domestic monetary
policies represent powerful influences on the world outside.
The enormous monetary contraction in the United States after
the slump profoundly affected the economic world of the
1930s in terms of trade, output and unemployment, while the
American dollar outflow of the late sixties and early seventies played a big role in the generation of world inflation.

At the time of writing the failure of the industrial world
to return to something like the growth path of the earlier
post-1945 period is hotly debated. It follows from our earlier discussion that some of the reasons are to be found in
the reversal of the particularly favourable set of factors
that accounted for the years of prosperity. Apart from the
disarray in the international monetary system with a lack of
coordination of fiscal and monetary policies between coun-

tries, there are severe doubts as to whether the industrial
countries can now count on a ready supply of cheap materials,
even apart from the steep jump in the price of energy which
is with us and from which the world as a whole sees little
respite. As we are aware, as far as energy is concerned the
United Kingdom is better off than most for a considerable
period at least.

A central question that faces us is whether there are
other real factors, below the monetary surface, which imply
that the years after the Second World War constituted a
norm to which we might expect to return, or an exceptional
period of industrial opportunity triggered off not only by
the war itself but also by a backlog response to the depressed conditions of the thirties. Ideas of this kind are
often derided as excessively pessimistic. Nonetheless, there
is evidence that the rapid underlying rates of growth of the
industrial countries outside the United Kingdom were slowing
down in the late sixties, long before the turbulent years of
the seventies were upon us. Those who do not share any fears
on this account tend to emphasise the role of economic
policy-making as being at the heart of our difficulties. In
some measure, they are. The persistent failure to eliminate
the imbalances between the deficit and surplus countries
stems from inappropriate international economic policies.
However there are those who see the problems of individual
countries almost entirely in terms of their own domestic
economic policies, believing in the capacity of those countries to take unilateral steps to restore employment and
growth, irrespective of the external world. As in the thirties, they seek to establish a splendid isolation within
which to operate, whether by tariffs or direct controls on
imports. On this reading persistent unemployment in Britain
becomes largely the consequence of inappropriate domestic
economic policies rather than part of a worldwide problem.

The events of the last decade have also produced a major
intellectual challenge to the ideas that have dominated
British economic thinking since the Second World War. The
challenge has been both intellectual and practical. At an
intellectual level there have been doubts as to whether the
Keynesian apparatus of thought did in fact provide us with
the means to ensure full employment unilaterally. To be
sure, it is widely recognised by all Keynesians that man
does not live by demand management alone, and that inflation
and the balance of payments have presented problems inhibiting the simple prescription of spending one's way back to
full employment. The practical challenge has been delivered
by the events of recent years, which have perplexed governments, previously sure in their qualitative if not their

quantitative assessment of how the economy works, and sure
of the principles within which fiscal and monetary policy
should be conducted. In the chapters that follow we shall
examine some of the technical considerations that bear on
answers to these questions.

# 3 Employment and Inflation

Unemployment was the central economic issue of the inter-
war period and, while relatively full employment was sustained in the industrial countries after the Second World
War, the problem of unemployment has become of increasing
concern in recent years.

The writings of Keynes suggested that unemployment was
caused by a general deficiency in the monetary demand for
goods and services which could be made good if governments
pursued the appropriate mix of fiscal and monetary policies.
It was well understood subsequently that policies aimed at
creating full employment could have undesirable side effects on both the rate of inflation and the balance of payments. Thus it seemed necessary to supplement such policies
with some form of incomes policy aimed at containing inflation, while the balance of payments might require a
floating exchange rate, periodic devaluation of the currency or some direct measures to restrain the growth of imports. Demand management by itself was clearly not enough.

In this chapter we consider the problems of inflation and
employment in the closed economy, that is to say an economy
without foreign trade. There are certain advantages in exposition in disregarding for the moment the complications
introduced by international trade, and concentrating on key
analytical issues that separate Keynesian thinking from its
critics. This will do no harm provided it is borne in mind
that the discussion of this chapter is only a stepping
stone to a more complete account of inflation trade and employment which will be put together in Chapter 4.

It must also be understood that this chapter and Chapter
4 have little to say about the underlying rate of economic
growth. We concentrate on the behaviour of employment,
prices and the balance of payments, along a growth path determined by the underlying growth of output and productivity in the medium and longer term. For the purposes of exposition it is helpful to distinguish between policies direc-

ted primarily toward cyclical fluctuations, and policies
directed toward fundamental shifts in the potential rate of
economic growth. For shorthand purposes we refer to the former
as *stabilisation* policies and the latter as *industrial* policies, bearing in mind that at the margin it may be difficult to draw such sharp distinctions.

Against this background we look at crucial factors that
affect the response of employment and inflation to policy
changes. It is necessary to digress and to present some
technical analysis of the determinants of the supply of money, the behaviour of labour markets, the determinants of
private expenditures, and the determinants of the rate of
inflation in the closed economy. But first we begin with a
review of the ideas of simple Keynesianism and some indica-
tion of the standpoint of the monetarist critics.

## SIMPLE KEYNESIANISM IN THE CLOSED ECONOMY

The Keynesian approach to the determination of output and
employment focusses on the relationship between national income and expenditure. Given the labour force and the stock
of capital equipment in the economy, the level of output
and employment in the short run is determined by the balance
between the flow of income and the flow of expenditure. Income is regarded as the most important determinant of expenditure. It reflects the value of output produced and its
division between profits and other forms of income. Output
produces income, income in turn determines the volume of expenditure and, provided these are all equal, the economy will
be in balance.

Confusion often arises because, in an accounting sense,
the income expenditure and output measures are all different
ways of measuring the gross national product. However, what
is important is not that they are equal in an accounting
sense, but that production plans and spending plans are consistent with each other. If plans to spend out of a given
income are less than the value of the goods produced (which
have generated the income), producers will be left with un-
sold stock, and production plans will be cut until a match
is achieved. If planned expenditures exceed the value of
goods produced, there will be pressure either for the volume
of output to be increased, or for prices and wages to rise.

The simplest form of the analysis assumes that prices are
relatively stable at high levels of unused capacity, so the
prime effect of any increase in demand is felt on output and
employment. In the absence of government, income is divided
between what people spend on consumption and what they save.
Expenditure is divided between consumption goods and capital

goods which represent investment. It follows that the equality of income and expenditure implies equality between savings and investment. Other things being equal, short period
equilibrium is determined by the equality of savings and investment. If individuals plan to save more than business
plans to invest, output will tend to fall and vice versa.

The utilisation of existing capital and labour resources
depends on the level of income at which planned investment
and planned saving are equal. Keynes' central point was that
this equilibrium could occur anywhere, not necessarily at
the level of income consistent with full employment. The behaviour of savers and investors could result in an equilibrium, or stable, level of output far below the full employment level. The economy could be stuck, and the failure to
achieve full employment would result from insufficient effective demand to employ all the resources.

So the policy problem became how to raise the level of expenditure and achieve a balance between income and expenditure at full employment. Given the existence of government,
total saving is equal to the production of private capital
goods and public consumption and investment. Saving is equal
to private investment plus government expenditure which suggests that, if excessive saving prevents full employment
from being achieved, public expenditure might be increased
to offset the failure of private investment to rise sufficiently with income.

At a stroke, it seemed one had been provided with a theoretical framework to justify public works as a means of reducing unemployment, which Keynes had been searching for. In
addition, private saving depends not only on income, but also on the proportion of income taken in tax. At any given
level of income, more private spending might be achieved by
cutting the tax rate and so shifting the economy upward. In
theory, the tax rate could always be cut to a level which
ensured the equilibrium of savings and investment at a level
of income consistent with full employment. More generally it
was argued that fiscal policy, comprising a suitable combination of tax cuts and public expenditure increases, could
ensure that the full employment of resources was achieved.
It seemed obvious therefore that action taken by government
in Britain in 1931 as described in the last chapter, in
which emphasis was placed on cutting public spending and
balancing the budget, was precisely the wrong way to go
about things. The removal of unemployment required more public spending and not less.

Three more features of simple Keynesianism are worthy of
note. The first is that, while income was regarded as the
dominant influence on expenditure, Keynes also discussed at

length the influence of interest rates, particularly on fixed investment.

Secondly Keynes had a particular theory of the determination of the rate of interest which focussed on the relationship between interest rates and the quantity of money.
According to this theory, the demand for nominal money
balances depended in part on a precautionary demand for
liquidity and in part on the need to hold money in order to
facilitate transactions. Both these reasons for holding money
were heavily influenced by the level of nominal income, although later work has suggested that the demand for money
on transactions account is also influenced by interest
rates. But, it was said, money is also an asset which com-
petes for a place in private investment portfolios. How
much money people will wish to hold will therefore depend in
part on interest rates which affect the opportunity cost of.
holding money and in part on expectations about future interest rates. When interest rates are high and bond prices
low, the opportunity costs of holding cash in interest foregone are high, and expectations are likely to favour a fall
in rates, yielding capital gains from the holding of bonds,
and vice versa when interest rates are relatively low. Consequently it was argued that, for a given level of nominal
income, there will tend to be an inverse relationship between the quantity of money and the nominal rate of interest.

As a result of empirical investigation it was believed
that lower interest rates were unlikely to have much effect
on business decisions and on business investment in particular. Low investment in the thirties was attributed to
expectations about demand which influenced the state of confidence about laying down plant. Moreover it was felt that
the effects of changes in interest rates would be asymmetri-
cal. High interest rates could choke off excessive borrowing,
but low interest rates would not necessarily encourage the
demand for loans. The horse could be made to stop by pulling
on the reins but not to gallop by pushing on them.

All this led those who came after Keynes, if not Keynes
himself, to assign very little role to monetary policy as
part of any attempt to establish full employment. The impact
of fiscal policy in the form of tax cuts and increases in
public spending was believed to be more direct and immediate.
The consequence of this was that the behaviour of fiscal
policy dominated British thinking after the Second World War
and monetary policy was for the most part assigned an accommodating and passive role.

The third feature is the set of assumptions that related
to supply, and the determination of wages and prices. The
crudest forms of Keynesianism after Keynes assumed that any

increase in demand resulting from an expansionary fiscal
policy would call forth a corresponding increase in supply.
Supply would be forthcoming up to a point which represented
the limitations of capacity, either in terms of labour or of
capital equipment, whichever came first. A rather more general analysis originally adopted by Keynes himself in *The
General Theory*, but abandoned later, supposed that as output
expanded there would have to be some increases in prices to
ensure the profitability of the output produced. This was
because, with a fixed stock of capital equipment, there
would be diminishing returns to the employment of additional
labour.

Nothing however was said about the effects of higher demand in increasing money wages. This particular aspect of
Keynes' analysis was not given much attention by those who
followed. A popular interpretation was that an increase in
nominal demand would be divided between increases in real
output and increases in prices, with the balance shifting as
full employment was approached. With unused capacity and
heavy unemployment, the prime impact of expanding nominal
demand was expected to be on output, while any attempt to
expand nominal demand at full employment would be reflected
in inflation.

It follows from these three further features that the
effectiveness of fiscal expansion on output and employment
depended on the answers to certain empirical questions. The
Keynesian analysis emphasised the role of fiscal policy in
raising levels of output and employment even if the quantity
of nominal money was kept fixed. It assumed that the effects
of interest rate changes on the demand for money were substantial, that effects on the rate of private business investment were low and that the major part of an increase in
nominal demand would affect output and employment rather
than prices until very near full employment.

To illustrate the consequences, suppose that the government keeps the nominal money supply constant, and increases
public expenditure, financing it by the sale of bonds to the
public. The expansion of public expenditure leads to a rise
in nominal income, which under conditions of high unemployment is primarily reflected in more output and employment.
The increase in nominal income also increases the demand for
transactions balances, and so with a fixed nominal supply of
money forces up interest rates. Other things being equal,
this has some dampening effect on investment, but this effect
was thought to be small, given the insensitivity of business
investment to interest rates. There would be some increase
in prices but it would be hoped that the resulting inflation
would be modest. Moreover, while the fixity of the nominal

supply of money was maintained, to illustrate the power of
fiscal policy to raise output and employment without any
increase in the money supply, there was no necessity in the
real world to hold it constant. By allowing some monetary
expansion, even the rise in interest rates and the dampening of investment could be offset.

We can summarise by separating the zero and non-zero inflation cases. If there is no inflation until full employment, a suitable combination of fiscal and monetary policies, achieved by expanding public expenditure to prime the
pump of demand and expanding the money supply to stabilise
interest rates, allows us to achieve full employment. The
consequences of monetary and fiscal expansion on output and
employment will be permanent. Even if there is no expansion
in the quantity of money, such effects will be permanent
although not so great due to the rise in interest rates.

If inflation takes place on the upswing, the expansionary
effects of fiscal policy on output and employment will be
permanent provided that the money supply is permitted to
rise sufficiently to accommodate the rate of inflation.
Notice, however, that it is only through its effect on nominal interest rates that inflation has any consequences for
real demand. The quantity of money has no direct consequences for the inflation rate, and the feed-back effects of
inflation on the real economy are weak. Inflation tends to
be caused by the pressure of real demand, rather than real
demand and employment being affected by inflation.


MONETARISM

Few sets of economic ideas have been so systematically mis-
represented in public debate in the United Kingdom as those
which have been lumped together under the general heading of
monetarism. In the sections that follow we attempt to determine some of the differences between those who are labelled
monetarists and those who are labelled Keynesians.

In many respects the labelling process is both futile and
misleading. The initial confusion in Britain starts from the
proposition that anyone who believes that monetary control
is important in its own right is a 'monetarist'. In addition, those who are classified as monetarists are accused of
believing that the control of inflation is clearly far more
important than reducing unemployment, that unemployment and
depression are permanently necessary in order to ensure
price stability, and more generally that monetarists believe
that the control of the supply of money is all that matters.
None of these propositions is in fact true.

Monetarism has been described as being policy-oriented and resting on certain empirical propositions. Monetarists tend to believe that monetary impulses are a major factor accounting for variations in output, employment, and prices, that movements in the money stock are the most reliable guide to the strength of such impulses and that, in the closed economy at least, the behaviour of the monetary authorities dominates movements in that stock. These propositions are empirical ones, and they are policy-oriented, insofar as they focus on the role of the authorities in determining the behaviour of the money supply and its consequences.

For our purpose the most useful starting point is to focus on the relationship between the real and the monetary economy. The nature of this relationship underlies the monetarist view about the way in which variations in the money supply affect the economy. It also leads the monetarist to dispute the effectiveness of fiscal policy, in direct contradiction to Keynesian thinking.

The monetarist believes that in the long run the consequences of changes in the supply of money are neutral as far as the levels of real output and employment are concerned. That is to say that changes in the supply of money do not affect *real* magnitudes such as the volume of output and jobs but *nominal* values such as the level of prices and the value of national income. As we shall see, there is much dispute as to how long the long run actually is. There are those who agree that over time monetary changes are neutral in this sense, but who believe that the period of time is so long as to make the proposition of neutrality irrelevant to short-term policy-making. But it is important to distinguish this position, which is an empirical one, from the analytical statement that neutrality implies.

Monetarism therefore to begin with draws a sharp distinction between real and nominal values in the economy. Money is said in the long run to determine money things. Money things are, for example, the price level, the value of the national income, the value of the government deficit and the current account of the balance of payments. Real things, for example, are the volume of national output, the number of people employed, and the volume of capital equipment installed in factories. Relative prices which reflect relative resource costs and productivities are also real things whereas the general price level is a money thing. Money in the long run is a veil that covers the reality of real resource allocation.

It follows from this that increases in government expenditure, financed by printing money, will in the long run primarily affect money things such as the rate of inflation rather than the level of output and employment. It is impossible to spend one's way to any arbitrarily selected level of employment by the creation of money. In one sense the monetarist position does not say that money is important. In real terms it is unimportant. Paradoxically, the significance of money for real changes in output and employment in the long run is due to Keynes, who argued that he had produced a theory which integrated the effects of monetary change with the real economy, therefore making it more, rather than less, important. The position of the monetarist is well summed up by John Stuart Mill when he wrote:

> There cannot be intrinsically a more insignificant thing in the economy of society than money. . . . Like many other kinds of machinery, it only exerts a distinct and independent influence of its own when it gets out of order.

Monetarists do not agree with the story told in the last section about the effects of fiscal expansion on output and employment. They deny that such effects are permanent. For this to be so, it is sufficient that the ratio of the value of the national income to the supply of money, which defines the so-called velocity of circulation, should be unaffected by changes in interest rates. If the money supply is held constant while fiscal expansion occurs through an increase in public spending financed by the issue of bonds, its ratio to national income must fall if output increases, and fall permanently if the increase in output is to be permanent. In the Keynesian analysis, this fall is brought about through the rise in interest rates, which makes people wish to hold fixed quantities of nominal money at the higher level of income. If, however, interest rates have no effect on the demand for nominal money, and the demand for money increases in proportion to the level of income, then the level of income cannot rise unless the supply of money also rises. Fiscal policy is not enough.

So, it is said, a crucial difference between Keynesians and monetarists concerns the way in which the demand for money is determined. However, as we shall see, while the assumption that the ratio of money to income is fixed in the short as well as the long run is *sufficient* to preclude any independent effects of fiscal expansion, it is by no means *necessary*. Moreover, monetarists in general would not deny that interest rates affect the demand for money in the short run. The dispute about the determinants of the demand for money is thus a red herring.

The most important feature of conventional monetarism is

that, compared with standard Keynesian thinking, it provides
a different explanation of the level of output. For a given
stock of capital equipment, a given set of technologies determining the productivities of the different factors of
production, and a given set of responses of labour to job
opportunities at different wage rates, there is - it is supposed - a most profitable level of output that firms will
wish to produce. Corresponding to this level of output, for
a given labour force there will be a rate of unemployment
which is sometimes called the 'natural' rate of unemployment,
a somewhat unfortunate appellation in many respects. This
natural or equilibrium rate of unemployment is assumed to be
stable, in the sense that a temporary demand shock which
disturbs it will be offset by market forces which will tend
to return it to its original position. Thus in the monetarist world, real output and unemployment are determined by
real factors such as equipment, technology and relative
prices rather than by the level of monetary demand *per se*.
Instead of being called 'monetarists', those who subscribe
to monetarist propositions might be called 'realists'. Real
things in the long run are determined by real factors.
Whereas the Keynesian emphasises the importance of money
*demand*, the monetarist emphasises the importance of decisions to *supply*.

   To illustrate the difference, suppose that the economy is
at its natural rate of unemployment with zero monetary
growth and zero inflation. The fact that the natural rate of
unemployment is what it is does not make it 'socially' desirable so the authorities might try to achieve a lower rate
of unemployment by expanding public spending financed by an
increase in the supply of money.

   The strong version of the story says that increases in
output will only be profitable if the expansion in the supply of money leads to inflation. The inflation reduces workers' real wages in the short run, and so makes it profitable
to employ more labour and produce more output. Thus in the
first round of the process the expansion in public spending
produces more output and more jobs. However the trouble with
the Keynesians, according to the monetarists, is that they
focus on these first-round effects only. As in the Keynesian
case there is some increase in output and employment and
some increase in prices.

   But, says the monetarist, there are important second-round
effects as workers realise that their real wages have fallen, and seek redress by demanding higher money wages. If
the increase in money wages is granted, then real wages rise
back toward their original level, so destroying the profitability of the extra output produced and the additional jobs

that were initially created. If the new jobs are to be permanently maintained, the authorities must keep the level of real wages at the new lower level, which they can only do by more public spending and monetary expansion generating faster inflation.

However, this process cannot continue indefinitely since, after a while, the inflation will come to be anticipated, and inflation will have to continually accelerate in order to maintain unemployment at the new lower level. Taken to its limit the result of the process will be runaway inflation and monetary collapse. Consequently the most likely outcome in practice will be a temporary increase in jobs, higher inflation and an eventual falling-back toward the natural rate of unemployment as the rate of money expansion is decreased. Moreover, if the rate of inflation is to be reduced and price stability restored, there will have to be a period during which unemployment runs at a higher than natural rate. Thus, the greater the initial expansion, the more painful the consequences if price stability is to be restored and expectations readjusted.

In the strong monetarist story it is only at the natural rate of unemployment that there can be a stable rate of inflation (not necessarily zero). If unemployment is below its natural rate inflation will tend to accelerate, and if it is above it will tend to fall. With a steady increase in the money supply, the economy will, if left to itself, settle at the natural rate of unemployment. The inflation rate will tend to be equal to the difference between the rate of growth of the nominal stock of money and the underlying real growth of the economy.

Monetary disturbance can exert a powerful influence in either direction. A sharp monetary contraction can produce depression, exerting downward pressure on wages and prices, while an excessive monetary expansion leads to accelerating inflation. Thus, while the Keynesians would explain persistent unemployment and falling prices in the slump of the thirties by the lack of effective demand, the monetarist would tend to see it in terms of an unnecessarily harsh monetary contraction or unnecessarily slow monetary growth. The depth of the recession in the United States would be seen as the consequence of excessively tight money superimposed on the 1929 downturn. By the same token the cuts in public spending made in Britain in 1931 could be criticised in terms of their effect on monetary growth.

If output is limited by supply, neither fiscal nor monetary expansion is capable of permanently reducing the unemployment rate below its natural level. If the expansion in government spending is financed by selling bonds rather than

by increasing the supply of money, the result will simply be
that interest rates have to rise until private spending has
been reduced by an amount equal to the real increase in government expenditure. The increase in public spending will
'crowd out' private spending until equilibrium has been restored. In this scenario there will be no effect on prices.
The assumption with regard to output leaves the supply of
money to determine money things, in this case the rate of
inflation, and in the long run the neutrality of money is
preserved.

We see that in this analysis the Keynesians and the monetarists are divided by two main issues. The first is the
nature of the determinants of supply and the second the nature of the inflationary process. The second has been somewhat glossed over in the discussion, but it is important
since an inherent part of the monetarist story requires that
an acceleration of the rate of increase of the money supply
will lead to an acceleration of the rate of inflation - a
conclusion that would be vehemently resisted by the Keynesians - an issue to which we will return at a later stage.

In contrasting these relatively simple versions of Keynesian and monetarist thinking we have left undefined the concepts of the supply of money and of full employment itself.
Moreover, to date, we have given only cursory attention to
the determinants of expenditures in the economy and it is to
these matters that we now turn.


THE CREATION OF MONEY

To begin with it is necessary to digress from the main
stream of thought and examine in outline the method of money
creation and in particular the relationship between government financing and the supply of money.

The quantity or the supply of money is usually taken to
include notes and coin in circulation, which represent legal
tender, and 'deposits' in 'banks'. Differences in money supply definitions depend on what we mean by deposits and what
we mean by banks. For our purposes banks consist of what the
Americans call commercial banks and excludes a variety of
other deposit-taking financial institutions such as building
societies, the National Savings Bank and the Trustee Saving
Banks. Sometimes the deposits of all these institutions are
added together to form some composite measure of 'liquidity', but it is usual to distinguish these from the supply
of money, for three reasons.

First, the deposits held in non-bank institutions are in
some respects less 'liquid' than most of those held in the

banks themselves. Secondly, non-bank financial institutions
have less power than the banks to create deposits. All financial institutions, including banks, are 'intermediaries'
between ultimate lenders and borrowers. They only lend what
they receive. But because deposits with the banks are actually used as a means of payment, via the cheque system, this
puts them in an advantageous position collectively. If banks
expand their lending, a relatively high proportion of the
funds spent will return to the banks as a whole as deposits,
through the very act of spending by borrowers, whose payments by cheque provide their recipients with deposit balances.

An individual bank expanding its lending will only regain
a correspondingly small proportion of the funds lent; but if
the banking system as a whole is increasing its lending,
banks as a whole will gain deposits. A reflux of deposits to
the building societies may also occur if the building societies lend more - the sellers of houses to building society borrowers may put part of their proceeds in building
society deposits - but the fact that building society deposits are not used themselves to finance payments means that
the ability of these institutions to create deposits with
themselves is less.

Such distinctions between the banks and other financial
institutions are largely differences in degree, and developments in payments 'technology' may cause them to become
blurred. But although in some contexts it is useful to aggregate deposits over a range of institutions, it remains
desirable today to distinguish between 'money', i.e. currency in circulation plus the deposit liabilities of banks,
from the liabilities of other financial institutions. This
will be so as long as there is a reasonably predictable relationship between 'money' and the subsequent behaviour of
total income, and this is likely to be the case in the absence of controls of one form or another which might dis-
tort the balance between banks and other intermediaries.

The third reason for disintinguishing between the deposit
liabilities of banks and those of other institutions is that
the former are under the closer control of the monetary authorities, i.e. the central bank. This is particularly the
case if the assets which the banks themselves choose to hold
to ensure their own liquidity are controlled by the central
bank. For good commercial reasons banks need to hold a proportion of assets which can be turned immediately into notes
and coin, to satisfy the possible demands of their deposi-
tors, plus balances which can be used to settle payments
from one bank to another. Notes and coin plus the commercial
banks' balances with the central bank are sometimes des-

cribed as 'high-powered money' in view of their part in the
money creation process.

The banks' balances with the central bank are today the
most crucial, as inter-bank settlements are more unstable
than the public's demand for notes and coin. For this purpose the 'clearing' banks, which dominate the money transactions system, hold balances with the Bank of England itself. These balances can be used to purchase notes and coin
from the Bank of England as well as to settle debts with
other banks.

If the main reserve asset of the commercial banks were
their balances with the central bank, the latter would be in
a strong position to control the level of the commercial
banks' deposits and, therefore, the money supply. For the
commercial banks' balances with the central bank represent
part of the latter's own liabilities, and the central bank
can always control its liabilities by means of operations
involving its own assets.

For example, sales of securities by the central bank would
diminish its assets and liabilities, including its liabilities to the commercial banks. The purchasers of securities
sold by the central bank would pay by cheques drawn on their
own commercial bank accounts, and the banks concerned would
discharge their ensuing debt to the central bank in turn by
writing cheques on their balances held with the central
bank. Unless they had 'excess' reserve asset balances, i.e.
above the required minimum, the commercial banks would then
have to respond by adjusting their own balance sheets. If
the banking system as a whole were under such pressure, the
banks could respond only by running down their holdings of
non-reserve assets, i.e. non-reserve securities and loans
to customers, by a multiple of the original loss of reserve
assets. This multiple would depend on the required reserve
asset ratio itself. The 'required' ratio might be a minimum
prescribed by the central bank, as in most countries, or
that chosen by the commercial banks on commercial grounds
alone.

In Britain the system of central bank control is not as
direct as this short account, which describes what is sometimes called a 'monetary base' system of control. Instead,
over the years the reserve assets of the banks have come to
include other assets besides their balances with the Bank
of England. Reserve assets prescribed by the Bank of England
have included Treasury bills and good quality commercial
bills (and money at call lent against them), together with
government stocks of up to one year to maturity.

Because such assets are also held outside the banking system and some, like commercial bills, can to some extent be

created by the banks and the private sector, the commercial
banks have been able to adjust to a potential shortage of
reserve assets by bidding them in from non-bank holders. To
this extent the supply of reserve assets to the commercial
banks has not been under the 'direct' control of the central
bank, and it has not operated to influence the level of bank
deposit liabilities through the deposit multiplier mechanism
described above.

Instead, in the past the reserve asset needs of the banks
have been used by the Bank of England to influence interest
rates, and it is mainly through this channel that the central bank has sought to control the quantity of money. A
system in which the central bank operated on the commercial
banks' reserves by directly controlling their quantity would
be one in which the monetary authorities would have to re-
nounce control over interest rates in general and short-term
interest rates in particular. This is true of all policies
aiming at close control over the quantity of money, as the
amount of money which people wish to hold depends, *inter
alia*, on the interest rates. In the last resort, therefore, if
the authorities wish to control the quantity of money they
have to surrender control over interest rates.

For some years the most vigorous supporters of monetarist
policies have been urging the replacement of the traditional
system of control by one in which the main reserve asset of
the banks would be their balances with the central bank and
that the latter should control these simply by buying and
selling securities in the market - i.e. by its 'open market'
operations - accepting whatever might be the consequences
for interest rates, especially short-term interest rates,
which have not been allowed to move freely under the traditional system. Some step in this direction, but a limited
one, is now in the making.

Whatever the exact system of control, the extent to which
money is created through the banking system depends on a set
of similar factors. Of these the most important are: the
willingness of the private sector to hold bank deposits rather than other financial assets; the demand for bank loans
by private and public sector borrowers; and the ability of
the banks to accept deposits, on the one hand, and re-lend
them profitably on the other. The private sector's desire to
hold bank deposits, given the level of income, will depend
very much on the pattern of interest rates; and this will
also influence the demand for bank loans, although perhaps
not as much as other aspects of the private sector's financial position, such as its desire to spend in excess of its
own cash flow. The terms on which the banks can obtain reserves assets will clearly affect the ability of the banks

to increase their balance sheets profitably.

The impetus to money creation can come from various
sources, and these will change according to the stage of the
business cycle and according to longer-term economic and
'technological' factors. In all this the behaviour of interest rates plays a central part, either in guiding the
path of money creation, as under the traditional system in
Britain, or as a consequence of it, as under a system of
more direct reserve control. But there is also another aspect of money creation that needs highlighting.

This is the public sector borrowing requirement, i.e. the
excess of public sector disbursements of all kinds over public sector current receipts. To the extent to which this is
financed by the public sector borrowing from the banking
system, the result is to increase the money supply. The
loans made by the banks to the public sector add to their
assets, and these are financed automatically to the extent
to which deposits are created as the beneficiaries of public
deficit spending place their receipts in their bank accounts.
Money is also created insofar as the public sector borrowing
requirement is financed by the issue of notes and coin; but
in most systems this is only of minor importance today.

It follows, in general, that if the authorities wish to
limit the effect on the money supply of a particular level
of public sector borrowing, they will have to place their
borrowing outside the banking system. Moreover, any such
borrowing outside the banking system will have to be in a
form that does not create reserve assets which the banks
could purchase on advantageous terms. This has effectively
required the authorities to limit the money creation effect
of a large borrowing requirement by selling large amounts of
relatively long-term government securities and various forms
of National Savings. The excess of the public sector borrowing requirement over sales of these to the public non-bank
sector is the measure of money creation due to the operations of the public sector; it is the full modern equivalent
of 'printing money' to finance part of the public sector's
spending.

The authorities may also seek to influence the growth of
the money supply by more direct means. In the past this has
taken the form of direct instructions issued to the banks
to limit their lending, or to call for special deposits with
the Bank of England. A particular method of doing this was
known as the 'corset' or the supplementary special deposits
scheme which, when imposed, required the banks to increase
their deposits with the Bank of England in line with their
lending.

Although in this chapter we are concerned with the closed

economy, it is convenient to complete the picture with regard to international influences on the supply of money. In
general the change in the money supply depends not only on
domestic circumstances but also on the inflow of money from
abroad. For our purposes it is sufficient to divide the total
change in the supply of money into a domestic component, referred to as the rate of domestic credit expansion (DCE),
and an overseas component, the increase in reserves, resulting from the combined transactions on current and capital
account of the balance of payments.

As we shall see in the next chapter, it is argued that under a pegged exchange rate the authorities cannot control
the supply of money, because they cannot control the balance
of payments and hence the reserve inflow. It is this that
accounts for the fact that monetary targets set for individual countries by the IMF tend to be expressed in terms of
DCE, over which the authorities are expected to exercise control, as opposed to the total money supply which is partially determined by the balance of payments. The precise consequences of a reserve inflow depend on the willingness or
ability of the monetary authorities to offset the inflow by
what is described as *sterilisation*.

If dollars flow in as a result of an excess of export receipts over import receipts, there will be a net gain in
dollars which can be exchanged for high-powered money with
the Bank of England, so increasing the monetary base. On the
other hand the authorities can try and offset this effect by
open-market operations. From time to time such external
monetary inflows have made control of the money supply problematical, particularly when they concur with a desire to
keep the value of the exchange rate stable. In some instances
the pressure on the domestic money supply has become so great
that it leaves little or no option other than to allow the
rate of exchange to float upward in line with expectations,
in order to cut off the excessive inflow.

Finally we may note the different definitions of the money
supply which are in common use. There is some debate as to
which is the most appropriate to use in defining the monetary stance in terms of a monetary aggregate. In the United
States it is more common to use M1, which is represented by
the current accounts of the private sector which are of
course non-interest bearing. M2 includes M1 plus deposit accounts which bear interest, while sterling M3 represents the
broadest definition, including M2 together with public sector accounts and accounts held by overseas residents in the
United Kingdom. In recent years in the United Kingdom sterling M3 has most commonly been the focus of attention, and
it is in terms of sterling M3 that monetary targets have

been set.


LABOUR MARKETS AND SUPPLY

We earlier identified a key difference between the Keynesian
and monetarist analysis with regard to the supply response
to an increase in monetary demand. There are two polar cases.
The first is the extreme position that an increase in monetary demand calls forth an increase in real supply of equal
magnitude, the price level being unaffected up to a point
of 'full capacity'. In the economists' jargon, supply is
perfectly elastic up to full capacity. The second polar case
is that of conventional monetarism, which postulates that in
the long run, starting from the natural rate of unemployment, the elasticity of supply of output is zero. Starting
from such a point the longer-run consequences of monetary
expansion are eventually fully reflected in prices with no
lasting effect on the level of output and employment.
    No Keynesian would take seriously the assumption of a
perfectly elastic supply of output, although it would normally be supposed that with 'high' unemployment the elasticity of supply would in fact be 'substantial'. More generally a rapid expansion of monetary demand, greatly in excess
of the underlying rate of growth of productive potential,
would be expected sooner or later to run into supply bottlenecks and shortages of capacity and skilled workers. It
might even be the case that such supply difficulties co-
existed with high unemployment by historical standards.
    The two important points that emerge from the Keynesian
discussion of supply are, firstly, that the limits on the
capacity of supply to respond to demand tend to be defined
in physical terms and secondly, that being the case, the
elasticity of supply is essentially an empirical question.
It may be that in a given instance and at a particular
time, supply will not respond to demand, but there is nothing in principle to prevent supply responding to increased
monetary demand without generating such a rate of inflation
that its effects on output would be offset. On the contrary,
some Keynesians argue that an expansion in output brought
about by an increase in demand might actually *reduce* inflation, although this position would be defended only by a
minority. This is not to be confused with the proposition
that, in the long run, faster growth of supply and productivity would not be a help in containing inflation. The
argument here relates essentially to the short period during
the cyclical upswing.
    The monetarist position on supply is logically quite dif-

ferent. Starting from the natural rate of unemployment, the reason why no more output will be produced is not that there are any physical limitations, but simply because it is not economic to expand it. The monetarist theory of output is rooted in the labour market. The demand for labour at any given level of real wages represents the most profitable level of employment given the availability of capital equipment and existing technology. The supply of labour is supposed to depend on the level of real wages. With diminishing marginal productivity, the demand for labour is expected to be inversely related to the real wage, and the supply of labour is expected to vary positively with the real wage, with more labour coming on offer at higher real wages. It is assumed not only that labour markets are relatively competitive, but also that the adjustment process toward equilibrium in the demand and supply for labour is efficient.

Equilibrium in the labour market, i.e. the equality of demand and supply, offers a market definition of full employment. If there is persistent unemployment, defined as an excess of labour willing to work at the ruling real wage over the demand for labour at that wage rate, then its persistence must be due to the real wage rate being stuck at an excessively high level. So it would seem that unemployment was due principally to a failure of money wages to be sufficiently flexible in a downward direction and this inflexibility was attributed to the monopoly power of trade unions.

Much of the debate in the thirties and after focussed on this issue. On the face of it it seemed nonsensical, with men standing idle on every street corner palpably prepared to do any kind of work if they could get it, that the recession could be blamed solely on the fact that powerful unionism was keeping money wages excessively high. On prima facie grounds the monetarist theory of the labour market appeared to be without credibility. However subsequent monetarist analysis makes it clear that it is unnecessary to invoke such an argument to explain events. The outcome is consistent with the idea that high and persisting levels of unemployment could be attributed to the inappropriateness of monetary policy which kept the actual rate of unemployment above the natural rate. This also explains the persistent decline in prices which occurred in the United Kingdom between 1925 and 1935. Moreover if, in the face of a dramatic recession, the process of restoring market equilibrium was slow, the recession could be accounted for without blaming intransigent trade unionism, or abandoning the idea of a market for labour which entailed the existence of something like the natural rate of unemployment.

Be that as it may, other specific objections to the labour

market theory were made by Keynes and by others later.
Keynes initially attacked the idea that there existed a
meaningful relationship between the supply of labour and the
level of real wages, at the national level. The argument
could easily be caricatured by picturing those in the dole
queue considering the average level of real wages in the
daily newspaper, and deciding that it had not reached a level
where it would be worth coming off the streets and going
back to work. While it was argued that workers would certainly resist a cut in their money wages, they were believed
to be willing to accept a reduction in their real wages,
through price increases, if this was necessary to ensure that
there were jobs. Those who were in this position were said to
be involuntarily unemployed i.e. they were prepared to work
at or below the going rate of real wages. This involuntary
unemployment owed its existence to the lack of effective demand. It was not real wages that determined output, as in
the monetarist story, but output that determined real wages.

In addition it was argued that this labour market theory
confused what might be valid at the level of the individual
firm or industry, and what was valid for the economy as a
whole. The criticism suggested that there was a confusion
between the supply of labour for a firm or an industry, and
the supply of labour as a whole. The supplies of labour to
firms and industries depended on relative wages, not the
average absolute level. Moreover, while the anti-Keynesian
case seemed to depend on the demand for a cut in money
wages, it was argued that although this might increase profitability and job prospects for a particular firm, a general wage cut across the board would do untold harm to total
demand since consumer spending largely came out of wages.

Much was made on both sides of the argument of wage and
price rigidities. Early attempts to reconcile Keynes with
his critics set great store by the downward inflexibility of
wages which could prevent clearing in the labour market, and
the Keynesian analysis was differentiated from more traditional analysis by that fact alone. Later writers tended to
draw the conclusion that the apparent rigidity and inflexibility of wages and prices in a downward direction were a
prima facie indictment of a market theory of the demand and
supply for labour, that relied on the assumption that both
the labour market and the economy were highly competitive.
On an extreme view no market existed at all, and real wages
and employment were treated as more or less totally independent of forces other than the level of effective demand.
A more balanced conclusion suggested a half-way house between this and the monetarist position, namely that the labour market worked in such a way that for given expectations

about the future rate of inflation, there would tend to be a
trade-off between real wages and the rate of unemployment.
Organised labour would accept lower growth in real wages in
return for more jobs.

But, just as it appeared that the simple theory of the labour market was rendered prima facie unsatisfactory by the
observed events of the thirties, so the events of more recent years have challenged the view that there is a trade-
off between real wages and unemployment in the long run.
Whether one accepts some form of competitive labour market
theory or not, the notion that those in work would make
material sacrifices, either in the level or rate of growth
of real wages, in order to employ those who are not, is
increasingly less plausible. Keynes' original idea that
organised labour was prepared to accept reductions in real
wages, or increases in profitability brought about by rising
prices, is simply not consistent with contemporary wage bargaining. It is quite possible that in the aggregate, the
average level of real wages may make it unprofitable to
employ people in certain sectors of the economy, with the
result that jobs will be extinguished, and through this process the marginal product of labour will tend to be brought
into equality with the real wage. Unemployment from this
source cannot be eliminated simply by expanding monetary
demand, since this will do little to reduce real wages so
making profitable what was not profitable before. There is
not simply money wage resistance but real wage resistance.

However it is important to emphasise that one must not
suppose unemployment of this kind is the only form of unemployment that we observe, or that unemployment in general is
somehow solely attributable to the intransigence of trades
unions. As has already been emphasised, unemployment may be
due to monetary disturbances coupled with relatively slow
adjustment in the labour market. Unemployment may also exist
because of the slow adjustment of relative wages to market
conditions which creates limits to expansion and shortages
of particular skills. Unemployment may persist, with slow
adjustment in the labour market, in part because unemployment benefit and supplementary benefits encourage longer
periods of job search. This is not a matter of scrounging
but is a rational response to the costs of search. The time
taken for equilibrium to be achieved in the labour market
may mean that, given the lack of flexibility due to the
fixity of contracts, the world might appear to be mislead-
ingly Keynesian in the short run, although in the long run
the profitability of employing labour will dominate the
short-run effects on employment of expanding monetary demand.

Moreover the lower the rate of profit coupled with extensive legislation to ensure job security, the more the employment of labour becomes an investment decision. The marginal costs of employing additional labour in response to an
increase in monetary demand, rather than increasing order
books and extending delivery times, may be high when account
is taken of the longer-term financial commitment that employment now represents. This suggests that Keynesian optim-
ism that expanding monetary demand will have major permanent
effects on real output and profitability is likely to be
less justified in current conditions, and that the steady
state level of unemployment (or the natural rate if you
wish) may well be substantially higher than one has been accustomed to. The problem of supply now becomes a major issue,
and the malfunctioning of labour markets a matter of concern.


## THE DETERMINANTS OF EXPENDITURE

The Keynesian emphasis on the income/expenditure approach,
and on the analysis of the components of demand in a national
income framework, has generated many valuable insights
into our understanding of the functioning of the economy. In
the closed economy, private consumption and private investment are the two principal components of demand on which attention is focussed.

In explaining private expenditures, the major weakness of
traditional Keynesian analysis, which in more recent times
has been remedied by many leading Keynesians themselves, has
been the failure to integrate the effects of changes in the
real value of wealth into the theory of expenditure. This is
necessary both in order to establish the appropriate time
dimension over which policy changes must be assessed, and in
order to understand how changes in the rate of inflation result in important feed-back effects on the level of demand.

The traditional Keynesian neglect of wealth and assets effects stems partly from a theoretical over-emphasis on the
importance of changes in income flows, and partly from certain empirical considerations. In the thirties some emphasis
was placed on the importance of the real balance effect in
automatically restoring full employment. The notion was that
private expenditures not only depended on the flow of income
but also on real money balances, that is to say money adjusted for the price level. Other things being equal, a fall
in prices would stimulate demand by increasing the real value
of money balances. But since money wages and prices were
regarded as sticky downwards the issue appeared to be somewhat academic.

Even those who supposed that the wealth effect existed took
the view that, from a policy point of view, it would take
time under the conditions of the day and was not to be relied on. As Samuel Brittan put it at a much later date, if
the real stock of money was regarded as too low, the proper
remedy would not be to reduce wages but to increase the supply of money.

> As a matter of practical policy it may well be better in
> such circumstances to adjust the money supply or the ex-
> change rate to the wage level rather than face the long-
> drawn-out agony of trying to depress the latter. Is it not
> better to adjust our watches for summer time than to ask
> everybody to get up an hour earlier?

Subsequent analysis of consumer spending based on data
following the Second World War suggested that variations in
consumer spending could be adequately explained in statistical terms without reference either to the real balance
effect or any other kind of wealth effect. These considerations relegated wealth effects to a back seat and, by the
same token, ignored the effects of changes in the quantity
of money and the rate of inflation on consumer spending. The
flow of private savings was firmly tied to the flow of income, without any notion that savings behaviour might be
affected by desired asset holdings. When combined with the
view that interest rates had little observed effect on real
investment, with the notable exception of private housing,
the unimportance of monetary policy and the supremacy of
fiscal policy for the behaviour of real demand were apparently confirmed.

The greater emphasis on wealth effects in recent years
stems in part from theoretical considerations and in part
from the empirical challenge posed by the need to interpret
economic events. From a theoretical point of view the exclusion of wealth effects is illogical since it implies economic behaviour by spending units that is prima facie implausible in the long run. In simple traditional Keynesian
economics the proportion of income saved is regarded as relatively stable, allowing for certain cyclical fluctuations.
But, if income is relatively constant for a considerable
period of time, this assumption implies that with positive
net saving, the ratio of personal net worth to income would
be continually rising without limit.

A more sensible assumption is that for any given level of
money income there is some desired ratio of wealth to income
beyond which it is not worth sacrificing current consumption.
Thus, in general, savings behaviour and so consumer spending

will be affected by changes in the real stock of wealth, and
by changes in the yields on assets of which it is composed.
It follows from this that we would expect, in the long run,
that a constant level of money income would imply that the
ratio of net saving to income would tend to zero. Correspondingly, if the ratio of wealth to income fell below the
desired ratio, the savings ratio would tend to rise. Failure
to discover such effects in early post-war data can be attributed to a lack of variation in the data observed, to a
more stable rate of change in money income at or near full
employment than that more recently experienced and to relatively stable expectations about the rate of inflation.

The empirical evidence which throws some light on the importance of wealth effects and the consequences of changes
in the real stock of money comes both from the experience of
the major industrial countries in recent years and from the
particular experience of the United Kingdom. As shown in
Figure 3.1, given the sharp fluctuations of the seventies,
there is a clear relationship between changes in the real
stock of money and changes in real output for the industrial
countries represented, with some evidence of movements in
the real stock of money leading the change in output by
something between a year and eighteen months. At the same
time, following the acceleration in the rate of inflation
during the boom of 1972/3 and afterwards, the proportion of
nominal income saved tended to rise in most countries. In
the case of the United Kingdom, which experienced one of the
fastest rates of inflation, the rise in the savings ratio
was particularly marked as shown in Figure 3.2.

Some have tried to explain this by reference to growing
uncertainty about the future, and lack of confidence. One
difficulty with this explanation is that in the past, the
savings ratio has tended to fall during depressions and rise
in booms, relative to the long run average, so that on past
performance it might be thought that depression with all its
uncertainties should result in a fall in the savings ratio
rather than an increase. The common link between past observations of a rising savings ratio in booms and the events of
recent years can be found in the rate of inflation. An unanticipated rise in the rate of inflation will falsify savings
plans aimed at maintaining a desired ratio of wealth to income. Other things being equal, the rise in the inflation
rate will reduce the real value of monetary assets in particular. Unanticipated inflation provides gains to borrowers
and inflicts losses on the holders of net monetary assets.
In this process, one of the main gainers is in fact the
state. The likely effect is that real wealth is depressed
below its desired level so that, in response, the proportion

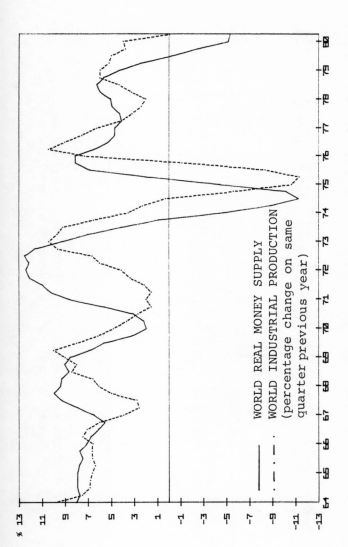

FIGURE 3.1 *World real money supply and world industrial production*

SOURCE World money stock index, 1975=100, *International Financial Statistics*; world whole-sale price index in world currency, 1975=1, formed at London Business School; world industrial production index. 1975=1, *Main Economic Indicators* (OECD).

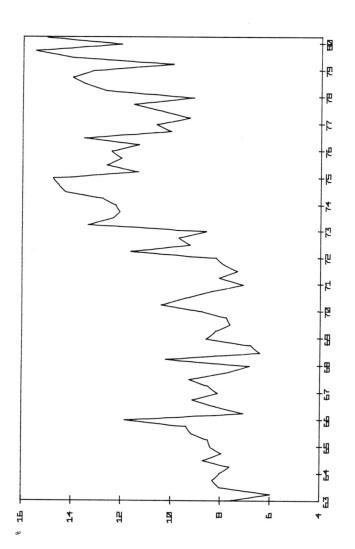

FIGURE 3.2  *The ratio of the UK personal sector savings to*
*disposable income (current prices, %, seasonally adjusted)*

SOURCE   CSO, *Economic Trends* (HMSO); CSO, *Financial Statistics* (HMSO).

of income saved rises in order to make good the deficiency,
a process which inevitably takes time. The greater the initial inflationary shock, the longer the savings ratio will
be kept at the historically higher rate.

But, it may be objected, to save proportionately more as
inflation increases is irrational. Surely the rational response is to switch out of monetary assets into goods? This
argument fails to take into account the importance of expectations. If, after the initial inflationary shock, the
rate of inflation is expected either to stabilise or to
fall, it is perfectly rational to attempt to restore the relationship between monetary assets and income. However, if
inflation is expected to accelerate continually without relief it would not be rational. Indeed, if it is regarded as
irrational to continue to accumulate monetary assets, this
implies that one is already in a state of expected hyper-
inflation and the inflationary game is completely lost.

It is a matter of some technical debate as to what should
be included in the definition of wealth for present purposes, which takes us beyond the scope of the present discussion. In some cases wealth is defined solely in terms of
the real stock of money, but even here there is some choice
as to whether bank deposits are included as part of the real
money stock for this purpose, or simply the stock of high-
powered money. There is also a debate as to whether the real
value of government debt should be included. On balance,
most analysts would tend to include it but there is an argument that says it should be excluded, on the ground that it
is offset by the present value of future tax liabilities
which arise from the necessity of servicing the debt. In addition there is the problem of what other real assets should
be included as part of personal wealth.

For the most part these are empirical questions upon which
one would hope that research might throw some light, but in
practice this is extremely difficult since the different
measures of wealth are highly correlated. This is not however of central importance for the purposes of the present
discussion. What is of importance is the idea that the savings ratio, and thence expenditure out of a given income,
are likely to be affected by the combination of changes in
the supplies of assets and the expected inflation rate. It
follows that, unlike the simple Keynesian expenditure model,
unanticipated shifts in the inflation rate can have very
material consequences for real expenditures. Through this
mechanism unanticipated shifts in the inflation rate have
consequences for the rate of unemployment, so that accelerating inflation rates are not merely important for their
own sakes.

As already pointed out, traditional Keynesian economics also largely discounted the effects of changes in the quantity of money and interest rates on private investment, although it must be said that this criticism is primarily true in the United Kingdom rather than in the United States. The exception to this is in the housing market, where it has been recognised that interest rates and changes in the flow of funds into building societies are of major significance.

Until recently, however, empirical investigations into investment behaviour both in stocks and equipment have suggested that financial factors such as interest rates have been dominated by changes in the level of demand. Again this may be the result of lack of variation in the historical data. For much of the period after the Second World War, in the United Kingdom nominal interest rates were often kept artificially low and the real rate of interest, i.e. the difference between the nominal interest rate and the rate of inflation, has often been negative. However the long-term decline in profitability, combined with the recession of 1975, produced a major liquidity crisis for British industry, so that monetary factors became of major importance. Inflation destroyed the balance-sheets of industry, and led to major problems of financing ongoing operations, let alone the effects on investment in expansion. Moreover, while interest rate effects may well have been minor for much of the period after the Second World War, their effect on industry in recent years has been material.

Two important conclusions follow from this analysis. The first is that even within the limits of the closed economy, changes in the quantity of money and in nominal interest rates are likely to be far more important in affecting both output and employment in the short run in the United Kingdom than has commonly been supposed. Secondly, unanticipated changes in the rate of inflation can have marked effects on the level of private expenditures, both on personal consumption and on investment. Thus the control of the inflation rate is an essential element in any set of policies designed to provide the kind of environment in which the stability of employment can be achieved.


INFLATION AND UNEMPLOYMENT

A more complete account of the inflationary process cannot be undertaken until Chapter 4, where we consider the consequences for inflation of exchange rate policy and changes in external prices. Nevertheless, even within the framework of the closed economy it is possible to isolate and discuss some of the important elements.

The simplest theory of inflation put forward by some is that it results from the monopoly power of trades unions. Independently of the general state of the demand for labour, it is said that unions have the power to enforce whatever general level of money wages they choose, with consequent effects on prices. This is an extreme form of what has been described as cost inflation. While trades unions might be so powerful as to enforce any level of money wages they choose, e.g., by the successful threat of some kind of general strike, there is no evidence that they have tried to do so or that the historical past could be explained in this way. This is not to say that trades unions are not powerful, although there is often confusion in relating the power of trades unions, which is something that exists at a point in time, to the inflation rate which is a rate of change.

The existence of trades unions affects the nature of the inflationary process, in particular by increasing the stickiness of money wages in adjusting relativities. Productivity gains therefore tend to result in higher money incomes rather than lower prices to the consumer. However, if the wide fluctuations in the inflation rate that have been recorded are to be attributed simply to trade union power, we also require a theory of why and how trade union power itself fluctuates. Since there are other plausible factors whose influence has in fact fluctuated in line with changes in the inflation rate, the search for such a theory is unnecessary.

Furthermore, the idea that trades unions can cause permanent shifts in the inflation rate runs into some difficulties with regard to the supply of money. Even allowing for interest rates to exert some influence on the velocity of circulation of money, the existence of a degree of stability in the relationship between the quantity of money demanded and the level of national income implies that a sustained inflation cannot occur without disastrous effects on the levels of output and employment, unless there is some increase in the supply of nominal money to finance it. It is certainly true that if the authorities are determined to maintain existing levels of output and employment at all costs, they may be prepared to create sufficient additional money necessary to reconcile any money wage level that the unions choose to insist on at that output and employment level.

In this case, we are on what has been described as a labour standard as opposed, say, to a gold standard. Monetary policy is purely accommodating, and the authorities are prepared to underwrite any inflation rate that organised labour

chooses. In this very limited sense it might be said that
trades unions can cause inflation. However, if the authorities refuse to expand the money supply in line with the increase in wages, then the consequences will be falling output and rising unemployment. By and large those who believe
that inflation is primarily caused by trades unions would
argue that, even with this scenario, the rate of inflation
will not stop until unemployment levels have become socially
totally unacceptable. For them the fact that rising unemployment might bring the inflation to a halt is purely academic.

Insofar as the rate of inflation is eliminated by a rise
in the unemployment rate, it is argued that provided the
monetary authorities stand their ground, trades unions do
not have the power to generate persistent inflation, but
they do have the power to generate persistent unemployment.
The description is a matter of taste. The important point is
that full employment and a high rate of inflation cannot in
general be achieved without monetary expansion on the part
of the authorities. In this sense it is said that governments and not trades unions are responsible for inflation.

Paradoxically, while trades unions often decry the effectiveness of monetary policy in reducing the rate of inflation, they also vigorously deny that it is the responsibility of trades unions. The resolution of the paradox stems
from the assumption that the level of money wages is not too
high, thus causing inflation, but that the level of productivity is too low, the responsibility for low levels of productivity being laid either at the door of management or,
due to a lack of demand and investment, at the door of government, or both. Given this analysis it is sometimes concluded that only incomes policy, which either statutorily
requires or persuades unions to accept wage restraint voluntarily, can possibly reconcile something like full employment with something like price stability. In this analysis labour markets effectively play no role in the inflationary process.

While elements of this kind occur in many people's accounts of the inflationary process since the war, much of
the analysis even in the Keynesian tradition has not been
so extreme. A more general presumption has been that tightening and slackening in the labour market, as measured
either by unemployment or vacancies or some combination of
the two, has had a discernible effect on wage settlements
and the rate of inflation, provided that proper account is
taken of inflationary expectations. According to this view,
other things being equal, some inverse relationship between
the unemployment rate and the rate of inflation is to be

expected. Indeed, as we have already seen in this chapter, this assumption is crucial to the idea that fiscal expansion will have permanent effects on levels of output and employment.

As already recorded, the spirit of this analysis suggests that the direction of causation is from output and employment to real wages since, given the absence of wealth and monetary factors already discussed, there is very little feedback from the rate of inflation to the level of real demand itself. On this theory there is therefore a trade-off between unemployment and the inflation rate. Lower unemployment can be permanently bought at the expense of higher inflation. The position the economy adopts is a matter of social choice.

Even this is not generally enough, insofar as there may be no combination of unemployment and inflation that is regarded as socially acceptable. In this case we are back again to the need for an incomes policy to ensure that the costs of controlling inflation through unemployment are not excessively high. In a nutshell this probably best represents the central post-Keynesian position with regard to inflation and its control, although in practice there is some difficulty in disentangling this position from the first.

There was a time in the 1960s in Britain when it was believed by some that stability in wages and prices could be achieved by what are, by today's standards, extremely modest levels of unemployment. The difficulty with this view, however empirically plausible it seemed at the time, is that it is highly implausible that modest levels of unemployment sustained permanently should radically alter trade union behaviour and expectations. While there was evidence of a cyclical relationship between inflation and the unemployment rate, there was no evidence on what would happen if the new higher rate of unemployment became the norm. It was more likely that the norm would be adapted to and that, in time, the inflation rate would tend to accelerate again.

Contrary to popular misrepresentation, it is not true that monetarist theories imply that control of the inflation rate is brought about through permanently higher levels of unemployment. The monetarist precisely denies that in the long run the rate of inflation has anything to do with the equilibrium rate or natural rate of unemployment, at which the economy is supposed to settle if left on its own. It is not unemployment but the growth of the nominal supply of money that is held responsible for the equilibrium rate of inflation. Inflation and the unemployment rate interact only when the economic system is in disequilibrium. If accelerating inflation is caused by monetary expansion aimed at keeping the rate of unemployment below the natural rate, then higher-than-average unemployment is part of the process through which inflation and inflationary expectations are reduced.

It is clear that disagreements between monetarists and others about the inflationary process turn critically on views as to how the markets for labour and goods actually function. As we have seen non-monetarists tend to argue that markets are either very inefficient or non-existent and that wages and prices are in the main determined by some *deus ex machina* which keeps the inflation rate suspended by its own bootstraps. Two issues in particular are often invoked as part of the explanation of why monetary expansion may have little or no effect on prices and wages.

The first depends on the view that money wages can be set arbitrarily by trades unions without reference to general market pressures, and this is said to be particularly true for wages set in the public sector. With regard to the public sector, the argument rests partly on an assumption which is highly dubious, and partly on confusion in interpreting events. The assumption is that the labour markets in the public and private sectors are completely independent. But this is not the case, in part because of the application of comparability in wage bargaining and in part because there is a margin of substitution between public and private sector employment. Both comparability and market forces establish links between public and private sector wages. The confusion stems from the misinterpretation of public sector behaviour during periods of prolonged incomes policy, during which such policies are often applied more rigorously in the public sector, so causing anomalies, lack of comparability and in the end strong resistance by the public sector to the erosion of its relative position. Stable wage behaviour in the public sector requires stable wage behaviour in the private sector. Excessively expansionary monetary policies make it easy to finance excessive wage claims in the private sector which, through market substitution and comparability, are translated into higher wage claims in the public sector. In this way it is not the rate of unemployment *per se* that is crucial in determining the rate of increase of money incomes, but the monetary stance.

The rate of increase in wages, however, is not directly determined solely by the rate of monetary expansion, but also by the expected rate of inflation in prices. This brings us to the second argument raised against the monetarist viewpoint, namely that industrial prices are themselves very little affected by changes in monetary demand since they are essentially cost-determined by mark up and full cost-pricing procedures. It may be true that industrial

prices are largely determined in this way but this does not
warrant the general conclusion that the price level is not
directly responsive to changes in monetary demand. While industrial prices may be sticky, flexible prices exist in primary markets for food and raw materials. These prices are
directly responsive to changes in demand relative to supply,
and it must be borne in mind that here we are dealing with a
closed economy in which, by assumption, food and raw material
needs are fully satisfied internally. As we have seen in the
seventies through the operation of flexible price markets,
which include not only food and  raw materials but also
housing, monetary expansion can directly affect prices,
which have important secondary effects both on industrial
prices and on the demand for money wages. There are thus major channels through which monetary expansion can affect
prices and the rate of growth of money incomes.

Does this mean that if monetary growth is restricted to
zero, equilibrium is possible, with the complete elimination
of inflation? In practice the answer is likely to be no. Relative wages are sticky and labour markets do not function
instantaneously. Nurses and policemen do not benefit from
increased industrial productivity by paying lower money
prices for industrial goods. Instead, they share some of the
benefit through increasing their own money wages in line
with increases in industrial money wages, so leading to
price increases in those sectors in which productivity increases have not taken place or are hard to measure. Labour
markets do not adapt quickly enough to prevent inflationary
pressure from this source. This has sometimes been described
as productivity inflation. To try and force labour markets
to deal with this problem is unnecessarily harsh and some
monetary expansion and modest inflation may be the best way
of dealing with it. For much of the post-1945 period there
has been creeping inflation of this type. By current standards therefore much of the inflation up to the late sixties
cannot be sensibly attributed to irresponsible monetary policies. In the longer run it may be more practical to live
with an inflation rate of something of the order of 3 per
cent than to attempt to squeeze it down to zero. When inflation is running in double figures, however, it is clear that
it is more than the stickiness of labour markets in the
short period that is creating problems.

# 4 The Open Economy

The analysis of the behaviour of the open economy, with
trade in goods and services and inflows and outflows of
capital, brings us closer to the typical problems of the
real economy. While the ideas discussed in the last chapter
might be applied to the world as a whole, important new
considerations now appear which affect the economic behaviour of one country among many. We have seen how views
about the determination of the supply of goods and services
affects the analysis of inflation and employment in the
closed economy. In the open economy, trade offers additional sources of supply which require that the stories
about employment and inflation be amended. Trade, capital
flows and changes in exchange rates create new transmission
mechanisms, through which economic change in one country
can be transmitted to another. Consideration of these relationships not only raises the need for a re-examination
of the effects of stabilisation policies on employment and
inflation, but also wider questions about the capacity of
an individual economy to pursue such policies independently
of the behaviour of the rest of the world.

In the United Kingdom both the intellectual tradition and
discussions of current policy have represented the balance
of payments as a constraint on desirable levels of employment and economic growth. For most of the period since the
Second World War, the current account of the balance of
payments has been seen as a problem, with a persistent
tendency to deficit which has required correction. It has
been said that if only the 'problem' of the balance of payments could be 'solved', this would open the way to the
pursuit of other policies to maintain full employment and
stable growth. In fact, the perception of a current account deficit as an unfortunate side-effect of otherwise
sensible monetary and fiscal policies has considerably de-
layed the acceptance of a wider and more integrated approach to the joint determination of output, employment,

inflation and the balance of payments.

Such an approach is needed to analyse the effects of North Sea oil on the exchange rate and employment levels. On the face of it the flow of oil is a benefit to the balance of payments yet, paradoxically, while for most of the post-war period the fear has been of a weak currency and a persistent tendency to current account deficit, there are now fears about a strong currency and a tendency towards surplus. Suddenly the 'problem' has changed. To deal with these matters we need a more general overview of the behaviour of the economy than seemed to be required when the difficulties arose year in and year out from recurrent periods of deficit.

For the purpose of exposition and analysis we can separate two main streams of thought. The first extends the Keynesian story of economic behaviour into the open economy, emphasising the lack of any automatic mechanism in the economy to generate full employment. While in the closed economy it appeared that equilibrium in the flow of planned saving and planned investment could occur at substantially less than full employment, the behaviour of the current account of the balance of payments is thought to present yet another source of difficulty. While the actual level of output could diverge from the full employment level, there might not be any economic forces leading to balance of payments equilibrium at the full employment level. Increases in public spending or tax cuts might seem appropriate solely from a domestic point of view but the effects of such changes in raising output and employment could lead to the deterioration of the current account.

Thus a distinction is drawn between the problems of internal and external balance at full employment, and the policy problem then becomes one of choosing the appropriate mix of policies that will jointly produce both. Like the problem of unemployment, the problem of the balance of payments was seen as requiring a deliberate set of fiscal, monetary and other policies, such as exchange rate policy or controls on imports, to lead to an acceptable outcome. As in the case of employment, little or no consideration was given to the possible influence of any automatic adjustments brought about through market forces to maintain balance of payments equilibrium. The current account of the balance of payments was seen as a problem and a constraint which, like unemployment, required deliberate governmental policies if the problem was to be solved.

The second mainstream of thought, by analogy with the story of the closed economy, emphasises the operation of market forces on the behaviour of the balance of payments, and in particular market forces brought about through

changes in the supply of money. This tradition of thought
has been described as the monetary approach to the balance
of payments. To a greater degree than in the case of the
closed economy, the monetary approach to the balance of
payments contains within it a variety of different emphases
and opinions about the way in which the economy actually
functions.

As in the closed economy case, the monetary approach presented by a variety of economists emphasises the longer-run
properties of the economic behaviour of the system, but
leaves much room for disagreement about its actual dynamics.
Some of the disagreements between those who espouse a version of the monetary approach to the balance of payments are
virtually as great as between the Keynesians and the rest.
There is a wide spectrum of analysis and opinion between the
crudest form of Keynesian analysis applied to the open economy and what is defined later as 'global monetarism'. This
makes it much more difficult to draw firm conclusions about
the working of the real world open economy, particularly
with regard to the conduct of stabilisation policies in the
shorter term. In analysing the open economy, the difficulty
of labelling particular points of view is exemplified by the
remark made by the American economist, Professor William
Branson:

> I am encouraged to wander in the no-man's land between
> the 'monetarist' and 'Keynesian' international schools
> since I am viewed by some of my professional colleagues
> as a 'die-hard Keynesian' and by others as a 'closet
> monetarist'.

KEYNESIANISM IN THE OPEN ECONOMY

We begin by tracing through the development of Keynesian
thought about the balance of payments, which influenced
and continues to influence thinking in the United Kingdom
today. As we have already noted, the perception of the current account of the balance of payments as a policy problem
for governments went naturally with the view that unemployment also was such a problem.

Early thought was set in the thirties in a period of considerable international monetary turbulence, of competitive
commercial policies and floating exchange rates. It assumed
the existence of money-wage rigidity together with a high
degree of responsiveness of the output of goods and
services to increases in monetary demand. Moreover, since
wages and prices were regarded as rigid in terms of domes-

tic currency, this drew attention to the possibility of altering the current account of the balance of payments by adjusting the exchange rate, a depreciation in the rate meaning that exports would be cheaper in terms of international currency, and imports more expensive in terms of domestic currency. There would be a tendency for a higher level of exports and a lower level of imports to be demanded. On the assumption that supply was very elastic, there was no problem in supplying the extra volume of exports, or the additional output which could result from import substitution. The only possible difficulty stemmed from the consequent changes in the terms of trade, i.e. the ratio of export to import prices. The change in the current account following the change in the exchange rate depended on the assumption of rigid money wages, a perfect elasticity of supply, and the price sensitivity of both exports and imports — in technical language, on the price elasticities of demand for both exports and imports. This approach focussed solely on the current account of the balance of payments and became known as the 'elasticity' approach to balance of payments analysis.

In later years much attention was paid to the size of these elasticities and to the debate on whether a devaluation would or would not lead to an improvement in the current account. Empirical work after the war seemed to suggest that the relevant elasticities might be rather 'low', so leading to what was described as 'elasticity pessimism'. There were then further debates on whether, if the elasticities were 'low', it might be a better idea to seek an adjustment to the current account through quantitative restrictions on imports rather than by exchange rate changes.

However, while in the thirties both unemployment and the balance of payments appeared to present problems, by the late forties full employment had been achieved. Under these conditions there were evidently no unemployed resources automatically available to provide the additional output that a devaluation might encourage. Understanding of this problem was made clearer by a shift away from the 'elasticity' approach to the analysis of the current account.

We may note that the current account of the balance of payments, $B$, is equal to receipts by residents from foreigners $R_f$, less payments to foreigners $P_f$, so we have

$$B = R_f - P_f$$

But receipts by residents from residents, $R_r$, are identically equal to payments by residents to residents, $P_r$, so that the current account can be expressed as

$$B = R_f + R_r - P_f - P_r = R - P$$

where $R$ represents total receipts by residents and $P$ total payments by residents. In more familiar terms the current balance is the difference between what the economy receives in total income $Y$ and what it spends in total $E$ so that

$$B = Y - E$$

This seems to imply that a deficit on current account occurs because the country as a whole is spending or 'absorbing' more than it receives, suggesting that the nation is living beyond its means. It followed from this 'absorption' approach that, since at full employment the level of domestic output was given, a successful devaluation had to reduce domestic absorption relative to productive capacity. A favourable devaluation did not depend on the price elasticities alone, but also on the inflation that resulted from devaluation effectively reducing absorption. This underlined the fact that, at full employment, adjusting the current account imposed a real burden on the standard of living.

If no automatic mechanism existed to bring about the reduction in absorption, then it was necessary for government to intervene, for example reducing domestic absorption by increasing taxation. This led to the important distinction between policies which are 'expenditure-reducing' and those which are 'expenditure-switching'. The simultaneous achievement of both internal balance (the maintenance of full employment) and external balance (establishing an appropriate current account) depended on putting together an appropriate mix of such policies, combining fiscal and monetary policy with devaluation or with some other expenditure-switching policy such as import controls.

The most general presentation of this form of analysis is due to James Meade, who provided a synthesis between the so-called elasticity and absorption approaches. In Meade's analysis, fiscal policy was used to ensure a balance between demand and capacity, so achieving full employment, while the exchange rate was adjusted in order to maintain the external balance. Monetary policy was thought of as accommodating to the level of interest rates desired. Through fiscal policy the appropriate overall level of expenditure could be determined, while the exchange rate set the appropriate relative prices between exports and imports. In addition the target level of interest rates could be set relative to foreign interest rates to ensure that there was no reserve loss stemming from capital movements.

While the absorption approach recognised the supply problem at full employment, the Keynesian analysis still depended on the assumption of rigid money wages in the face of
a devaluation. The subsequent experience of the post-war
period made it clear, however, that this assumption was not
tenable. The analysis implied that labour would have to suffer from money illusion, i.e., a failure to distinguish between nominal and real wages if the devaluation were to be
effective. Part of the subsequent debate, particularly in
more recent years, has therefore focussed on the extent to
which, under free collective bargaining, the effects of a
devaluation may be offset by wage claims, in response to
the increase in the price level brought about by the devaluation itself.

The response to this problem has led to something of a
split among those Keynesians who still think in terms of the
framework described. Some advocate the need for an effective
incomes policy to permit the exchange rate to do its work.
In practice this is equivalent to abolishing real wage rigidity in the face of exchange rate changes, either by statutory or voluntary means. As we are aware, the difficulties
of doing this in practice are, to say the least, considerable. Some other Keynesians, while adhering from time to
time to the possibility of an incomes policy, prefer the
alternative of controls of some kind over imports.

This could be argued on several different counts. A devaluation required to adjust the current account might be
regarded as 'too large', either because of its direct inflationary consequences or because it implied an unacceptable shift in favour of profits. In addition it might be
thought that current account difficulties stemmed from non-
price competition so that devaluation would bias the response towards commodity-type products rather than those
with higher value added. The implied assumption, in the
shorter run at least, that the supply response to import
controls would be sufficient to avoid inflationary pressure, is of course open to grave suspicion.

This general framework by and large dominated thinking in
Britain until the early seventies. The devaluation of the
pound in 1967 and the ensuing discussion is very much a
reflection of it, while the decision to float sterling in
1973, combined with an expansionary fiscal policy and a
statutory incomes policy, represents its climacteric. As we
shall see later in this chapter this standard Keynesian
theory has serious analytical and empirical weaknesses.

However, for much of the post-war period, their benign
neglect did little harm. While the theory was widely accepted for nearly twenty years, from the late forties to

the late sixties, the United Kingdom exchange rate was in
fact pegged against the dollar so that in practice the
search for an optimal fiscal policy/exchange rate mix was
ruled out. Indeed the failure to achieve this mix became a
growing target for criticism by many economists who, by the
time Labour came to power in 1964, were convinced that maintenance of the parity and the defence of sterling had prevented faster growth in Britain for nearly two decades. The
devaluation of 1967 was welcomed by many as a throwing-off
of chains. It was belatedly supported by tax increases, and
by the comparative success of the government's incomes
policy. The incomes policy eventually collapsed and, by the
early seventies, the benefit from the devaluation had been
eroded. The floating of the pound in 1972 on a wave of
monetary expansion, precariously offset by a fragile incomes policy, was carried on almost to the point of disaster. The subsequent events provided a practical challenge
to the standard Keynesian theory of the balance of payments
that had dominated thinking in Britain for nearly thirty
years.

THE MONETARY APPROACH TO THE BALANCE OF PAYMENTS

The monetary approach to the behaviour of the balance of
payments is rooted in the important distinction between
stocks and flows. The standard Keynesian theory of the
balance of payments is cast in terms of flows, the current
account of the balance of payments, and the effects on it
of changes in the flow of income and the flow of expenditure. However, such an analysis concentrates only on the
short-term equilibrium in which the plans of savers and
investors are being realised. But this tells us nothing
about whether there is stock equilibrium, i.e., whether
the stocks of money, other financial assets and real capital are themselves equal to what people wish to hold. Long
period equilibrium requires that both stock and flow equilibrium co-exist together. The examination of long-period
balance requires us to take into account these stock
effects which are excluded from the standard Keynesian
analysis.

In the Keynesian analysis it is *de facto* assumed that
there are no feedback effects from deficits or surpluses in
the balance of payments or the supply of money. If a current
account deficit or surplus results in the loss or acquisition of reserves, it is assumed that any effects on the
money supply will be offset by sterilisation as explained
in the last chapter. More generally, the analysis omits any

discussion of the effects of balance of payments flows on asset holdings. If a current account deficit is not accompanied by a reserve loss, it must be offset by a net capital inflow induced perhaps by high interest rates relative to the rest of the world. But such a situation will affect asset markets, since overseas investors will be bidding for assets in domestic financial markets. It follows that, in a more complete analysis of balance of payments behaviour, account must be taken of changes in wealth and financial stocks, rather than focussing exclusively on short period flows such as the current account.

The monetary approach to the balance of payments is macroeconomic in character. The behaviour of the balance of payments is not built up from a set of micro-responses to exchange rate and price changes reflecting the economic behaviour of individual exporters and importers. It does not focus on the myriad decisions affecting the flow of goods and the behaviour of invisible exports from tourism, shipping and similar items that enter into the balance of payments.

Indeed, at the outset it does not even distinguish between the capital and the current account. It starts by concentrating on the surplus or deficit in the balance of payments as a whole, as represented by the combined outcome of the two accounts taken together. If the balance of payments is in surplus overall, monetary reserves will be accumulated and vice versa when the balance of payments is in deficit. Consequently, without off-setting action by the authorities, the money supply in a deficit country will tend to fall and in a surplus country to rise.

If we start from a position of internal and external balance the emergence of a balance of payments deficit will produce monetary disequilibrium. In the surplus country the effect will be expansionary, and expenditures will tend to rise, so eliminating the surplus, whereas in the deficit country it will be contractionary, so reducing imports and reducing the deficit. So there will be forces that work automatically to eliminate deficits and surpluses between countries. In practice the period of adjustment required in some circumstance might not permit this mechanism to function, if the period of adjustment were long and reserves limited. The available reserves might be used up in financing the deficit before the adjustment could take place. Alternatively, adjustment might be inhibited by the monetary action taken by the authorities to offset the effects of the external account on the money supply. In a system of pegged exchange rates a balance of payments deficit could be sustained if overseas holders of the domestic currency of the deficit country were prepared to go on accumulating it in unlimited amounts, or to lend equal amounts in terms of gold or reserve currencies. It follows that the significance of the monetary approach to the balance of payments, when looked at in this way, rests on certain important empirical assumptions.

The first is that the period of adjustment is such that the automatic effect of the changes in the money supply is feasible. The second is that in practice either monetary inflows and outflows induced by the balance of payments cannot be sterilised, or at least they cannot be sterilised within a period that is relevant to policy-making. As an illustration of the problem, we may take the case of the United Kingdom in 1977, when a massive capital inflow was prompted by the belief that the pound was undervalued. For some nine months the authorities believed that the inflow could be neutralised, and that there was no need to allow the exchange rate to appreciate. Finally, however, the pound was allowed to find its own level, but too late to prevent the reserve inflow from presenting a serious problem for the authorities in subsequently managing the money supply.

Thirdly, the monetary approach to the balance of payments focusses on the effects on the stock of money and more generally on changes in the stocks held in asset markets. It is in this sense a long- rather than short-run analysis, whose practical relevance depends on how long the long run actually is. The implicit conclusion reached by the proponents of the monetary approach is that the stock effects induced by the balance of payments operate sufficiently rapidly to be relevant.

An alternative way of looking at the monetary approach is to start from the accounting identity that states that the liabilities of the consolidated banking system are equal to the domestic assets of the system, plus its foreign assets. Under a pegged exchange rate system, any divergence between the domestic demand for money (i.e., the liabilities of the banking system) and the willingness of the system to meet that demand by acquiring domestic assets must result in a change in the reserves. A key assumption in this analysis is that there is a stable demand for money to hold, which is dependent on real income and interest rates. It is stable in the sense that demand is largely and systematically determined by these factors. If the amount of money provided by the domestic banking system is less than the community wishes to hold at a given level of real income and interest rates, then more money can be obtained from an improvement in the balance of payments.

This gives rise to the proposition that, under a pegged

exchange rate, the authorities cannot control the supply of money, since it can be varied according to demand by increasing or decreasing the foreign component of the reserve base. What the authorities can control in principle, however, is the domestic component of the reserve base. In flow terms the authorities cannot control the rate of change of the money supply, but can control the rate of increase of domestic credit expansion which, as we saw in the last chapter, is the monetary variable on which the IMF concentrates when laying down conditions for loans.

In a system of floating exchange rates, the consequences of monetary change are different. In the long run floating rates in theory ensure that the overall balance of payments deficit will be zero. Monetary disequilibria will not be reflected in reserve changes but in changes in exchange rates. If the real stock of money is higher than the community wishes to hold at existing levels of real income and interest rates, and the nominal stock of money is fixed by the authorities, the result will be a fall in the exchange rate and a rise in the price level, until the demand for the real stock of money is equal to that supplied. The authorities can now control the supply of money since reserve changes are prevented by exchange rate changes. It may be noted that this conclusion is more general than might appear. The assumption of a stable demand function for real money is central. However, the conclusion is consistent with more than one explanation of how the inflation adjustment is brought about.

A conventional monetarist argues that the excess supply of nominal money acts directly on wages and prices to produce inflation since the economy is supply-constrained at the natural rate of unemployment. However, the result is also consistent with a weaker version of the story which attributes the inflation to the fall in the exchange rate itself. The argument that changes in the relative supplies of money between countries have implications for exchange rate behaviour, roots the determination of exchange rates in a floating system in asset markets. Flows such as the current account of the balance of payments represent asset changes, so that in the long run exchange rates are determined by stocks rather than flows. Both nominal exchange rate changes, and the observed balance of payments flows, are attributable to a common stock adjustment process. Other things being equal, changes in the demand for and supply of money will therefore be reflected in the long run by changes in nominal exchange rates. While in principle floating rates enable the authorities to control the supply of money, they are a mixed blessing since there is an important connection

between changes in the money supply, exchange rates and inflation.

It was the failure to see this connection after the pound
sterling was floated in 1972 that contributed to the dramatic rise in inflation in Britain relative to the rest of the
world, although both suffered the consequences of the rise
in commodity prices and in the price of oil. The importance
of the relationship between the money supply and exchange
rates shifts attention away from the idea that the nominal
exchange rate is an *instrument* of economic policy, to the
idea that it is a *consequence* of fiscal and monetary policy.
Under a pegged exchange rate system, monetary policy is determined by the objective of maintaining the pegged rate.
In a floating rate system the situation is reversed. It is
monetary policy that determines the rate. Tying the pound
to the dollar for nearly twenty years after 1949 obscured
the importance of this distinction and encouraged the
implicit assumption that money did not matter. It was a poor
preparation for dealing with the situation that arose after
the pound was floated.

It is important not to confuse the monetary approach to
the balance of payments with monetarism, either in the form
in which it was presented in the last chapter, or in the
form of 'global monetarism', which has been of such intellectual importance as to warrant a separate section below.
The monetary approach focusses on the importance of incor-
porating stock, as well as flow, behaviour into the analysis
of the balance of payments, and in particular stresses the
way in which the supply of money interacts with it. This
implies that issues such as devaluation cannot be adequately
discussed other than in a macroeconomic framework. The approach emphasises the importance of nominal exchange rates
as relative prices of national monies, so that they are determined in the long run by demands for assets rather than,
as often in the past, simply by flows of foreign exchange,
determined by events in the markets for goods and services.

The behaviour of asset stocks in balance of payments
analysis underlines the importance of the distinction between short- and long-run effects of policy changes and exogenous disturbances that affect the economy. The monetary
approach is consistent with considerable divergence of views
about other related issues. While it emphasises the importance of the monetary implications of the balance of payments, and recognises the impact of monetary disequilibrium
on the behaviour of reserve changes, it leaves open as an
empirical question whether or not monetary shifts have in
fact been the prime causes of balance of payments disequilibria in the industrial countries. Those who believe that

monetary disturbances are primarily responsible for such difficulties tend, therefore, to describe the balance of payments as essentially a monetary phenomenon. Moreover while
acceptance of the monetary approach to the balance of payments implies, in both theory and practice, that money 'does
matter', it does not by itself carry any implications either
as to the wisdom or the futility of fiscal and monetary intervention in the international economy as part of a programme of stabilisation. To reach a conclusion on that matter
requires far more than simply a recognition of the importance
of money and its interrelation with the balance of payments.

But, as Marina von Neumann Whitman has put it, the insights
that the monetary approach have generated, at least outside
the United Kingdom

...are so widely accepted as to be considered obvious, and
they are incorporated into virtually every model analysing
the balance of payments, the exchange rate, or indeed the
impact of a wide variety of policies in an open economy.
As a result it is difficult to draw the line - to tell
where the 'soft monetarists' leave off and the 'eclectic
Keynesians' begin.

This cannot be said either of the analysis or the assumptions
promoted by what has been described as 'global monetarism' to
which we now turn.


GLOBAL MONETARISM

Global monetarism could be regarded as an extreme form of the
monetary approach to the balance of payments, but it makes
certain assumptions that are not necessarily acceptable to
those who are sympathetic to that approach. In addition, unlike the monetary approach to the balance of payments, it
leads to strong policy conclusions and its proponents generally believe that attempts to actively pursue fiscal and
monetary stabilisation policies as a matter of course are at
worst undesirable and at best unnecessary.

Global monetarism starts from the monetary approach to the
balance of payments by assuming that, within the relevant
policy period, surpluses and deficits arising from the combined effects of the current and capital accounts will result
in changes in the holdings of foreign assets, whose effects
on the supply of nominal money cannot be offset by sterilisation - for example, by selling government securities to the
non-bank public. For a time a country may prolong the adjustment of a balance of payments deficit by depleting its for-

eign exchange reserves. Alternatively, it may attempt sterilisation, but eventually this will exhaust its stock of domestic credit assets or promote further problems by the excessive creation of its own debt. As in the case of the more
general monetary approach, it emphasises the importance of
the existence of a stable demand function for money but, unlike some other analyses within the monetary framework,
places almost complete emphasis on the role of changes in
the real stock of money in the adjustment process, to the
exclusion of the effects of changes in other forms of private wealth holdings.

The second key feature of global monetarism is its acceptance of the existence of the natural rate of employment as
discussed in the last chapter. Real output is determined by
supply and demand in the labour market and this ensures that
the effects of changes in the money supply on output are
neutral, at least in the long run. The argument that for the
purposes of balance of payments analysis, the level or the
rate of growth of real output may be treated as given independently of the monetary variables, is justified by most
global monetarists in terms of conventional monetarism,
which implies that in the long run equilibrium will tend to
be restored through changes in prices and wages. This implies that the economy is not only inherently stable, but
also that fiscal policy is incapable of affecting any real
aspect of the economy as well as the price level in the long
run.

It was argued at one time that since full employment existed for much of the post-war period, it was reasonable
prima facie to assume it as the starting point of the analysis. In the light of the events of the seventies, this particular argument would be regarded as implausible by many.
The acceptance of the natural unemployment hypothesis would
seem essential to the global monetarist case, rather than
any general appeal to the existence of full employment as a
post-war norm.

The third assumption that is central to the global monetarist analysis concerns what is described as the 'law of
one price'. This postulates that in the world as a whole, in
the absence of artificial barriers to trade, perfect commodity arbitrage will ensure that the prices of similar goods
measured in terms of a common currency will tend to equality. While it might be accepted that this is a plausible
assumption for certain goods at the microeconomic level
which are virtually identical and so highly substitutable
for one another, the force of the global monetarist assumption is that it is assumed to apply to average price levels
rather than to the price levels of particular goods. It

follows from this that inflation rates between countries will tend to equality under pegged exchange rates. Only if exchange rates are changing can such rates of inflation diverge.

Under pegged rates, inflation becomes a world problem and not one generated by the behaviour of individual countries in isolation. The world level of inflation will be determined by the behaviour of world money relative to the world's supply of output. Moreover, since the behaviour of the money supply under pegged rates is determined by the aggregate outcome of the relationship between what an economy earns and what it spends, the actual composition of that output between traded and non-traded goods appears to be irrelevant. This re-emphasises the view that, while relative prices affect the composition of expenditures, it is the average or general price level which is central to balance of payments analysis, since it is this that affects real stocks of money and debt and real interest rates. Thus for analytical purposes real output and the rate of inflation can be dealt with in highly aggregate terms. While world inflation depends on the total world money supply, that total money supply is distributed between individual countries through the mechanism of balance of payments deficits and surpluses. Those with an excessive share of world money will run deficits, and those who have insufficient will accumulate more through running surpluses.

Although it is denied by the proponents of global monetarism, the law of one price is sometimes said to rest on the so-called small country assumption. This suggests that a country that is small relative to the rest of the world will be a price taker, and a follower in international markets for goods and capital. Consequently for an individual country under pegged exchange rates, both the rate of inflation and the rate of interest are determined from outside and, since domestic output is set by equilibrium in the labour market, output, prices and interest rates are in the long run independent of balance of payments behaviour. Starting from a position of equilibrium a monetary expansion engineered by the authorities will have no long-term effects on output prices and interest rates. The monetary expansion will raise the real money stock above the desired level and equilibrium can only be restored by running a balance of payments deficit. This process will continue until the monetary loss has been sufficient to return the nominal money supply and the real stock of money to its original position, so reducing the rate of expenditure to a level that is consistent with both internal and external balance.

In the case of a one-off devaluation of the currency, the

initial impact of the fall in the exchange rate is to raise
the rate of inflation *vis-à-vis* the rest of the world and,
in the absence of any offsetting action by the monetary authorities, the real stock of money will fall and with it
the real rate of expenditure. This leads to a balance of
payments surplus and the accumulation of money from overseas, so restoring the real money stock to its original
level. Expenditure increases and the surplus is ultimately
eliminated. The devaluation does not result in any permanent shift in the balance of payments, but in a higher price
level in terms of domestic currency after the process of
adjustment has been completed, and in an accumulation of
foreign exchange reserves during the adjustment process.
Thus, for the global monetarists, devaluation is not concerned with balance of payments policy but with reserve
policy.

It is sometimes claimed that global monetarism only explains what happens to an individual economy under pegged
exchange rates and offers no theory about what happens under
floating rates. Global monetarists would strongly deny this,
asserting that under a system of perfectly floating exchange
rates the overall balance of payments will tend to equilibrium. Starting from a position of internal and external
balance, with floating rates, monetary expansion will not be
reflected in the balance of payments but in a fall in the
exchange rate and a rise in the inflation rate. If the monetary expansion is a one-shot affair, the result will be a
permanent increase in the price level in terms of domestic
currency. The difference between the pegged and floating
exchange rate cases is sometimes said to be that, under
pegged rates, the inflation rate is the world rate and the
supply of money cannot be controlled by the authorities,
although through the control of domestic credit the balance
of payments is affected. Under floating rates, it is argued,
the authorities regain control of both the money supply and
the domestic rate of inflation.

It has been said that the most significant implication of
global monetarism is its rejection of the standard Keynesian argument that monetary and fiscal policy can be directed
toward the domestic level of economic activity, while the
exchange rate can be used to maintain external balance.
For the global monetarist, it is only in the case of pegged
exchange rates that the balance of payments can be an object of policy at all, since in this case surpluses and deficits will be determined by the behaviour of domestic credit expansion. In the case of floating rates the balance of
payments will remain in equilibrium, unaffected by monetary
policy which will instead determine the behaviour of the

exchange rate and the rate of inflation. If this is indeed the central point of global monetarism, it is perhaps less shattering than might at first appear, since it is possible to adduce other explanations of balance of payments behaviour which utilise some, if not all, of the assumptions of global monetarism in reaching similar conclusions.

The apparent iconoclasm of global monetarism does not arise simply because it calls for a rejection of standard Keynesian balance of payments analysis, but because it is inconsistent with one important aspect of conventional monetarism. This concerns the question of whether or not the monetary authorities can control the supply of money under fixed or pegged exchange rates. Conventional monetarists advocated the use of floating exchange rates to offset the divergence between the national monetary policies of individual countries, on the ground that this enabled them to choose lower rates of inflation if they wished, and shield themselves from excessively expansionary monetary policies in other countries. However global monetarists argue that balance of payments disequilibria will be automatically eliminated even under fixed exchange rates, which are regarded as more desirable from a welfare point of view since they permit the benefits to be gained from the existence of stable international money. The distinctiveness of global monetarism lies in the belief in the automaticity of the elimination of surpluses and deficits under fixed rates, rather than in asserting that exchange rate adjustments will have no permanent effect on the balance of payments.

An equally important belief of global monetarists is that the longer-run consequences of changes in fiscal and monetary policy will come through quickly enough to offset any apparent advantages in the shorter term that the authorities seek through the exercise of such policies. In this respect their stance is similar to conventional monetarists. For global monetarists the economy is inherently stable, so attempts to interfere with it will either be de-stabilising or unnecessary. Some take a more reserved position by saying that while the short run is of significance, we do not know enough about the dynamics of the short run to interfere with any confidence. Moreover both global and conventional monetarists tend to assume that disturbances in the economic system are of a monetary nature, which highlights the importance of monetary policy for external balance under pegged exchange rates and for price stability under floating.

With regard to policy, and the distinctions between the long and short run effects of policy changes, the parties can be divided as follows. There are those who, like the global monetarists, believe that the long run properties of

the economic system are important. There are those who dis-
cern that these properties exist, but who regard the long
run as too long to be relevant to current policy-making.
This group emphasises that the real world does not in fact
start from some position of equilibrium and adjustment processes are so long as to require government intervention to
help them out. Finally there are those who would reject the
monetary approach in general and have no belief that the
monetary tendencies discussed in this section have any
significance at all. These questions are discussed later in
this chapter and again in Chapter 7.

## SOME MODIFICATIONS TO GLOBAL MONETARISM

As we have seen, part of the package that is presented as
global monetarism is the so-called 'law of one price' which
has received considerable attention and criticism. At the
simplest level the critics have focussed on the prices of
those goods which are traded and have sought to establish,
often correctly, that at any given point of time there may
be considerable differences in prices in terms of a common
currency. Moreover it is clear that there are distinctions
between traded and non-traded goods, so that for example
there is no apparent tendency to equalise the prices of non-
traded goods such as haircuts in Tokyo and haircuts in London.
   We may note at the outset that the so-called law of one
price is not new, but is a special case of what has been
described in economics as 'purchasing power parity'. Some
thirteen years before the publication of *The General Theory*,
Keynes himself wrote,

   If therefore the difference from the preexisting equilibrium is mainly due to monetary causes (for example different degrees of inflation and deflation in the two
   countries) *as it often is* [my italics], then we may reasonably expect that purchasing power parity and exchange
   value will come together before long

- a sentiment that could well be expressed by a global monetarist today.
   There are two versions of the purchasing power parity
theory, sometimes called the 'strong' and the 'weak' versions. The strong version seems to accord with the law of
one price and asserts that, through profitable arbitrage,
the prices of goods in the two countries will come together
in terms of a common currency. As we have seen, this propo-

sition runs into immediate difficulties with regard to non-
traded goods, such as haircuts and personal services in general. The price of haircuts will be governed by the wage
rate for people with equivalent skills, employed in industries which are subject to external competition. If the market for industrial goods is competitive and prices of traded
goods tend to be equalised between countries, then wage
rates in countries with high levels of industrial productivity will be high relative to countries with low industrial
productivity. Hence services such as haircuts will be relatively expensive in countries with high industrial productivity as the possibility of an equivalent increase in productivity in cutting hair is limited. Unless individual countries have similar levels of industrial productivity, it is
unlikely that the absolute price level for all goods and
services will be equal. Accordingly the strong version of
purchasing power parity has been found wanting irrespective
of whether traded goods have a high degree of substitutability or not.

The weak version of purchasing power parity does not as-
sert that *absolute* prices will be equated but that *relative*
price levels between countries will be the same when expressed in a common currency. It is argued that, while it is
not generally in order to compare absolute price levels, it
is sensible to compare price indices between countries
through time. As far as traded goods are concerned, the weak
version of purchasing power parity does not assume that perfect substitutability holds. However the problems raised by
the distinction between traded and non-traded goods remains.
The average price of all goods will tend to rise faster than
the price of traded goods, since the general price level
will reflect services, where the possibilities for productivity growth are less than in manufacturing industry. The
more inefficient the non-traded goods sector relative to the
traded goods sector, the greater will be the disparity between the growth of export prices and the average domestic
rate of inflation. This explains why, for some part of the
post-war period, domestic inflation in Japan was relatively
high while export prices remained competitive in world markets. It follows from this that, under the law of purchasing
power parity or the law of one price, the exchange rate is
supposed to equal the ratio of the absolute prices between
countries, so that the absolute rate of inflation will be
the same everywhere.

When we cast purchasing power parity in relative terms,
and allow for differential rates of productivity growth, a
stable exchange rate will require a certain ratio of the inflation rates between countries. To see this, suppose that

the average rate of inflation in the world is constant.
Then, if its average inflation rate *vis-à-vis* the rest of
the world is the same, for a fast growing economy such as
Japan - with relatively high productivity growth in traded
goods - its traded goods costs will be falling relative to
its competitors and so there will be pressure on the nominal
exchange rate to rise. To put the matter the other way
round, under these conditions, for the yen to be stable relative to other countries in the long run, during its period
of exceptionally fast growth Japan needed to have a faster
overall rate of inflation than the rest of the world, which
indeed was the case.

The significance of this conclusion is that, under a pegged
exchange rate system, inflation rates will not be equalised
between countries, but there will be a determinate relationship between them. The law of one price is thus a special
case of a more general theory of purchasing power parity
which implies that there is a unique set of inflation rates
in relative terms that is consistent with pegged exchange
rates, in the long run. The essential analytical importance
of the law of one price is thus largely preserved. Under the
revised theory, for given rates of growth of productivity,
the average rate of inflation for the world as a whole can
still be determined by the world's money supply relative to
output with the revised theory of purchasing power parity
distributing that average rate between countries.

Notice that the revised theory leads to the concept of
what has been described as the productivity adjusted real
exchange rate. This highlights the fact that changes in relative inflation rates as a result of monetary disturbances
are not the only reasons for shifts in the nominal exchange
rate between two countries. Shifts in the exchange rate can
also come about as the result of real changes in the economy. So we can add the other half of the quotation from
Keynes given earlier, which says that if there are changes
taking place in the

> ... behaviour of the services and products of one country
> and those of another, either on account of movements in
> capital or reparation payments, or changes in the relative
> efficiency of labour or changes in the urgency of the
> world's demand for that country's special products, or the
> like, then the equilibrium point between purchasing power
> and the rate of exchange may be modified permanently.

Global monetarism focusses only on the monetary causes of
changes in exchange rates, whereas more generally changes
may also be due to real changes in the economy. The revised

theory is consistent with the conclusion of the global monetarists namely that, without such real changes, devaluation
will eventually be fully offset by inflation. In the short
run the productivity-adjusted real exchange rate will fall,
but the subsequent inflation will tend to restore it to its
former position.

The conclusions of global monetarism also require modification with regard to the issue of sterilisation. As we have
seen, it assumes that inflows and outflows of money cannot
be prevented from affecting the domestic money supply, at
least within the relevant policy period. Attempts to invalidate this argument have largely depended on empirical inves-
stigations to see whether in fact countries have succeeded
in sterilisation or not, and the evidence on this is mixed,
both as between countries and between periods of time. This
is an important question, which affects the conclusion of
whether or not an individual country can control its money
supply under pegged exchange rates. In the case of Germany,
for example, evidence seems to suggest that changes in the
domestic money supply have shown a high degree of dependence
on the external balance while, in the case of Japan, the
evidence suggests that the Japanese have been very successful in preventing the domestic money supply from being affected by her trade surplus. The reason for this depends
partly on the fact that the German capital market is relatively open to the rest of the world whereas the Japanese
market is not.

However the critics of global monetarism on this score
are often in danger of throwing out the baby with the bath-
water. The fact that certain countries do achieve a high
degree of sterilisation in no way implies that such sterilisation is desirable. On the contrary it may be part of the
explanation of why balance of payments disequilibria continue to exist. The fact that they do persist often leads to
the call for controls and direct intervention to adjust the
flows of trade, when the proper policy is to allow the monetary adjustment mechanism to take its course. In the case of
Japan, for example, the proper procedure to correct a persistent Japanese trade surplus is not to forbid the export
of Japanese cars but to open up the Japanese capital market
and prevent the sterilisation of monetary flows being carried out.

However there is a further difficulty with the global
monetarist argument, regarding sterilisation, that derives
both from the size and the role of certain currencies as reserves. These problems apply particularly to the United
States. The American money supply is so large relative to
the rest of the world that it has tended to affect the world

without being much affected by it. Whereas the behaviour of
the money supply in Germany may seem to have been consistent
with the propositions of global monetarism, the money supply
in the United States has not, and conforms more closely with
the traditional view that a country's money supply is controlled by domestic monetary policy.

The role of the dollar as a reserve currency has meant
that the exports of dollars became monetary reserves in the
hands of the recipients. The export of dollars, other things
being equal, need not result in a decline in the American
money stock but simply in an increase in the foreign liabilities of the United States. Countries with large claims in
terms of dollars may be unwilling to cash them in since this
would result in a devaluation of their existing reserves, so
putting pressure on the American exchange rate. To a lesser
extent this has also been true of the United Kingdom in the
past, although it has become less important with the relative decline in sterling as a reserve currency. The status
of the dollar as a reserve currency has therefore led to the
criticism that this gave the United States the privilege of
running a large balance of payments deficit without the necessity of adjusting it, and of exporting inflation to the
rest of the world. The empirical evidence therefore is
clearly not consistent with the view that in practice sterilisation has been systematically impossible throughout the
world, not forgetting however that it may not have been
desirable.

Global monetarism has also been criticised for its relatively exclusive focus on changes in the real stock of money
in the process of balance of payments adjustment. In part
this stems from a belief that the importance of changes in
interest rates on demand for money have been neglected.
Moreover, just as the law of one price is not regarded as
holding for an individual country, neither can it be assumed
that its interest rate is pegged to the world rate. Evidence
on this point is not clear although it is sometimes argued
that individual countries' interest rates can diverge for
substantial periods from average world levels. However it
seems clear that interest rates in the major financial cen-
tres of the world are closely related. Moreover as a matter
of analysis it is easy to show that including interest rates
in the demand function for money does not necessarily invalidate the long-run conclusions of global monetarism.

A more general criticism is that the focus on the real
stock of money ignores the behaviour of other asset markets
than the market for money. Thus it is sometimes said that
global monetarists distinguish only between the banking system and the real sector of the economy, while a more general

approach would distinguish between the real sector and the financial sector as a whole. However, more general definitions of wealth, including for example government debt, do not affect the long-run conclusions in a variety of plausible models of balance of payments, although the question remains a matter of central dispute among economists in some quarters.

As we have seen, the apparent simplicity and elegance of global monetarism rests on the assumptions that, in analysing the process of balance of payments adjustment for an individual country, there is no sterilisation; that under pegged exchange rates the price level and interest rate are determined in world markets, while the level or rate of growth of domestic output is determined by the behaviour of the labour market and by real forces affecting technology and productivity. As in the case of the closed economy, this latter conclusion is central not only to the proposition that in the long run monetary changes are neutral in their effect on the real economy, but also to the policy conclusion that fiscal and monetary intervention is either de-stabilising or unnecessary. It is a matter of concern to what extent the main conclusions of global monetarism are dependent on the existence of the natural rate of unemployment. As has already been pointed out, the monetary approach to the balance of payments must be distinguished from the particular assumptions of global monetarism. The monetary approach recognises the monetary implications of surpluses and deficits in the balance of payments and also recognises that the behaviour of exchange rates must in part be related to money markets and to the behaviour of asset markets as a whole. The question is therefore to what extent are the more traditional conclusions about balance of payments adjustment and economic policy-making modified, by combining the monetary approach to the balance of payments, with the view that the concept of the natural rate of unemployment is irrelevant.

In the extreme case, under pegged exchange rates, assume that there is a perfectly elastic supply of output, implying that up to full employment the general price level is constant. Starting from a position of relatively high unemployment, monetary expansion will stimulate an increase in domestic output and a deterioration in the balance of payments, the balance between the two being determined by the nature of the demand for imports as domestic output increases. The extent of the deterioration in the balance of payments in this case will not, as in the case of global monetarism, be exactly determined by the rate of domestic credit expansion but by the change in the composition of expenditures.

With fixed prices the increase in monetary demand will be divided between imports and domestic output. Since, in the global monetarist case, the equilibrium level of output is given independently of the rate of monetary demand, in the long run the division of expenditure is irrelevant. In the present case, which is typically Keynesian, the division between the two does matter. Thus it appears that the stop/go phenomenon of the United Kingdom economy after the Second World War was associated with monetary expansion followed by a deterioration in the balance of payments and would have been predicted by both global monetarists and Keynesians. The difference between them is that for the global monetarist all the increase in monetary demand would ultimately be reflected in the balance of payments, whereas for the Keynesians it would only be partial.

This mirrors a similar outcome in the closed economy where the Keynesian would say that an increase in monetary demand would be divided between increases in output and increases in prices, whereas conventional monetarism would argue that, in the long run, all the increase in monetary demand would be reflected in prices and none in output. This leads to the global monetarist idea that with a fixed level of output and pegged exchange rates, by analogy with the closed economy, a balance of payments deficit could be interpreted as the export of inflation. Since domestic output is fixed, additional output is obtained from abroad, but with no effect on the domestic price level. However even in the Keynesian case, if only part of the increase in monetary demand with elastic supply finds its way into the balance of payments, the deficit so created will - other things being equal - cause a drain on the domestic money supply. Either a reserve outflow will be taking place, so reducing the domestic money supply, or there must be an offsetting capital flow on private or official account.

Given the monetary approach to the balance of payments, the nature of the problem is similar to that which arises under global monetarism. The two differences are that the increase in monetary demand is only partially, rather than fully, reflected in the balance of payments and that, as a matter of language, since there is by definition no supply constraint on the increase in output, it seems possible to say that the balance of payments is an obstacle to the attainment of full employment. The crucial difference that emerges is therefore not so much in the method of analysis but in the policy conclusion. In the typical Keynesian case where the balance of payments is a constraint, the fact that it will automatically resolve itself is small comfort, since it means that the balance of payments equilibrium is

achieved at less than full employment. With global monetarism there is no conflict in the long run between internal
and external balance. For the Keynesian however there remains the problem of reconciling internal and external balance at full employment.

The abandonment of the natural rate hypothesis under
floating exchange rates is not by itself crucial to the validity of the proposition that, in the long run, changes in
the exchange rate as exemplified by a devaluation will have
no permanent effect on the balance of payments. To see this,
we may combine the assumption of a highly elastic supply of
output with a theory of monopolistic wage bargaining to replace the natural rate hypothesis. In the case of perfect
monopoly, the real wage will remain fixed in the long run so
that, in the face of a devaluation, money incomes and prices
will rise in the same proportion as the currency is depre-
ciated. The nominal supply of money will also rise in the
same proportion, leaving the real stock of money unchanged
in the long run. There will be a temporary improvement in
the balance of payments to be adjusted by the devaluation,
real income and so real expenditure must fall. But if the
community's collective bargaining power is sufficiently
great, the adjustment process will be frustrated, the competitive advantage will be bargained away, and in the long
run the economy will exemplify the property of neutrality
that characterises the analysis of global monetarism.

Thus, paradoxically, both the pure market theory of real
wage determination and the extreme bargaining theory can
lead to the same result. Moreover the result in the extreme
bargaining case is quite consistent with a model of the economy in which expenditures are largely determined by flows
in a traditional Keynesian way rather than also through
changes in asset stocks. In the case of purely floating exchange rates, the effects of an expansion in public spending
financed by the creation of money will be to lower the exchange rate and result in inflation. Since under floating
rates the balance of payments must remain in equilibrium,
the rate of inflation must be sufficient to reduce expenditures to ensure that this is so. This will require the general price level to rise without limit if the increase in
public spending is to be maintained, and the exchange rate
to fall continuously. In practice this will mean that the
initial increase in public spending will be cancelled and
the money supply brought under control again.

It follows that those who are wedded to a theory of monopolistic wage bargaining as an integral part of the inflationary process must either argue that the temporary reduction in real wages is sufficient to achieve the objective

of devaluation or that the community is prepared to permit
its real income to be reduced permanently and sufficiently
to make devaluation an important policy option. It is arguable that the latter is unlikely to be the case. This implies that the conclusion that exchange rate changes will
have only transitory effects on the balance of payments is
in fact quite robust with respect to different assumptions
about the determination of wages and the inflationary process. The case for devaluation or floating exchange rates
turns on the question of whether they have a role in speed-
ing up adjustment in periods of temporary disequilibrium
and of how long the long run is. Notice that the argument
does not necessarily imply that a devaluation is never justified, but simply asserts that in the long run its effect on
the balance of payments will be nullified.


PERSPECTIVE

Where from a practical point of view does all this lead us?
In the first place, it leads us to reassess the importance
of monetary policy in the analysis of the behaviour of the
balance of payments and of any policies associated with it.
At the very least, the monetary approach to the balance of
payments, in its more modest form, tells us that money does
matter and, moreover, that monetary policy assumes central
importance in a free market economy when exchange rates are
relatively flexible and are allowed by the authorities some
freedom to respond to market forces. When exchange rates are
flexible, changes in the quantity of money - other things
being equal - can play an important role in the inflationary
process, even under circumstances when money, wages and
prices in domestic terms appear rigid downwards, and labour
markets take relatively long periods to adjust. Balance of
payments problems are problems of disequilibrium but, in understanding the nature of disequilibrium and the process of
adjustment, it is important to integrate stock and flow behaviour. The analysis of exchange rate changes and exchange
rate policies cannot be understood solely in terms of balance of payments flows, as reflected in the current account,
but must be rooted in the behaviour of financial asset markets.

   As far as the extreme version of the monetary approach to
the balance of payments is concerned, so-called 'global
monetarism', it is easy to see why many find it difficult to
swallow either its particular analysis or its policy prescriptions whole. Its assumptions about sterilsation are
by no means precisely fulfilled, nor is the law of one price

in its extreme version widely acceptable. Nonetheless, it focusses our attention on the interdependence of monetary policies and inflation rates in a fixed exchange rate system, even if the relationships are not as precise as the theory suggests. On the policy side, its recommendations are limited by the implicit assumption that disturbances to balance of payments equilibria are predominantly of a monetary nature, and that the long-run behaviour of the system should almost completely dominate shorter-term thinking about balance of payments problems.

The monetary approach to the balance of payments by itself tells us nothing about the wisdom or feasibility of monetary and fiscal intervention in the economy as far as exchange rates and the balance of payments are concerned. There are two issues here. The first is whether there are automatic forces which tend to adjust balance of payments disequilibria. Given the perceptions and insights of the monetary approach, this is a proposition to which many would now readily accede in comparison with the past, although there would still be much argument as to whether such an equilibrium would also tend to coincide with what might be described as a position of full employment.

There is, however, much wider disagreement as to how relevant such long-run equilibrium analysis actually is for the purpose of policy-making in the shorter term. An eclectic view on these issues would perhaps be something like the following. A clear view of the nature of the longer-run implications of monetary and exchange rate changes is important. This is because, while full equilibrium in all markets may seem to be a long way away, many markets for goods, money and foreign exchange do respond quickly enough to changes so that a study of medium-term consequences is relevant to current policy-making. Even if the restoration of full equilibrium took ten years, it is still very important to look at consequences over, say, five years, which is the life of a Parliament.

If it is decided to take action in the short run, the choice of the best course to take is not independent either of the arbitrary time horizon over which one is looking, or of the basic direction in which the system is tending. For these reasons the long run outcome is important and, in the case of the balance of payments, the monetary approach has done us a service in turning our attention away from an excessively short-term Keynesian perspective and drawing our attention to the second-round and perhaps third-round consequences of short-term shifts in the direction of policy. The validity of this proposition is not upset by the observation that events occurring in the short term may affect

the long-term outcome, so that in a sense we are continually looking at a moving target. Long-term analysis of the
economy, as in the case of long-term planning in business,
does not carry with it the presumption that the long-term
future is fixed. It simply says that current information
about the long term is relevant to making the best decision
we can here and now. It does not preclude the necessity of
changing direction in the future if the information alters.

# 5 Economic Growth

In the previous two chapters we have examined some of the
issues relating to stabilisation policies, focussing particularly on the effects of changes in fiscal and monetary
policy on inflation, employment and the balance of payments.
For the sake of exposition we have assumed that the underlying growth potential of the economy was given, and that
concern was with employment levels, inflation and the balance of payments along the growth path. Here we turn to a
consideration of the determinants of the underlying rate of
economic growth, and the nature of the interrelationship between short-term economic management and long-term economic
development.

It was a popular view in the 1960s that the principal
reason why Britain did not grow as fast as other countries
was that demand was never allowed to grow fast enough, or
long enough, to induce the rate of investment required to
launch the economy on to a higher growth path. Part of the
argument suggested that successive periods of stop/go were
unsettling from the point of view of investment planning, so
that a smoother and more predictable trajectory for output
would induce confidence. For some a more modest but steadier
initial growth of demand seemed to be required, while others
emphasised the importance of sustaining a high degree of
pressure on productive capacity. For the latter the lack of
sustained demand held an important clue to long-term growth
performance.

It was this idea that underlaid the so-called Maudling
experiment of 1963/4 which exemplified the 'dash for growth'
theory. The conventional wisdom at the time was that attempts to manipulate demand by monetary and fiscal policies,
so raising the underlying growth rate, were frustrated by
the persistent tendency of the balance of payments to dete-
riorate and the inflation rate to rise as the rate of growth
of monetary demand gathered pace. In simple terms, the Maudling dash for growth rested on the belief that while a sus-

tained increase in the growth of demand would indeed create
initial pressure on the inflation rate and a deterioration
in the current account of the balance of payments, these ad-
verse effects could eventually be offset by the induced rise
in investment, which would both improve export performance
and increase the rate of growth of productivity, so revers-
ing the process. The problem was seen as one of breaking into a virtuous circle of growth and investment. In the short
run the inflationary consequences had to be lived with, although the main concern was with the behaviour of the current account of the balance of payments, which it was
thought could be dealt with by borrowing from abroad.

In the event the pressure on the balance of payments was
regarded as too severe and there followed a reversal of the
process, although not early enough to prevent the devaluation of sterling in 1967. While the experiment must be
deemed a failure, for good reasons that will figure in the
later discussion in this chapter, there are still those who
regard it as nearly coming off and who believe that it might
well have done the trick had it been allowed to continue.
The more lasting consequences however of this, and later
episodes, was to convince many that it was the by-products
of inflation and a deteriorating current balance of payments
that prevented the expansion of monetary demand from inducing the investment response that was required.

In particular, it gave rise to the view that growth would
have to be 'export-led', a thesis that was elegantly propounded by Lord Kaldor (following Wilfred Beckerman) in
1971. Government, it was said, was in error in having used
fiscal and monetary policies to expand the economy during
relatively slack periods, which stimulated private and public consumption so in turn inducing an excessive level of
imports. Leaving the issue of inflation on one side (which
was a serious error) the focus of attention was on output
and the balance of payments. In future, it was said, fiscal
and monetary policy should not be aimed at the level of demand and output, but at sustaining an appropriate pressure
of demand that just kept the current account of the balance
of payments in balance. Meanwhile, the exchange rate should
be used to ensure that exports grew at least in line with
world demand, so stimulating domestic output to grow at
least at the average world rate. The floating of the exchange rate in 1973 could be seen as a welcome development
given this line of argument. However, both subsequent analysis and the course of events strongly suggested that such a
strategy under free collective bargaining was doomed to
failure, since in practice changes in the real exchange rate
designed to promote a desired share of world exports could

not be permanently brought about by a change in the nominal
rate. To put the matter another way, changes in the nominal
exchange rate could not bring about the permanent changes in
the terms of trade that were needed to reconcile internal
and external balance.

Not everyone has given up hope on this score, and there
are those who argue that even if the gain in competitiveness
brought about by falling exchange rates is not permanent in
the long run, the short-run gains might be sufficient to enable a dash for growth and entry into the virtuous circle of
high investment and high growth. The most recent version of
this story has combined the use of the exchange rate to
eliminate what is regarded as the balance of payments constraint, with an incomes policy of some form to ensure that
the appropriate adjustment in real incomes takes place, although the more simplified analyses have been complicated
by the consequences of North Sea oil. However, disenchant-
ment with the exchange rate as an instrument of growth became widespread although no doubt we have not heard the last
of it. For some the emphasis has shifted away from the exchange rate and the problem of exports to import penetration and the problem of imports. In their view the effects
of export growth on total output growth have been offset by
import penetration, and it is the reduction of imports by
quotas or tariffs that should occupy the centre of the
stage.

All these analyses of growth focus on the limitations of
expanding monetary demand in inducing higher investment
and growth, imposed by the behaviour of the current account
of the balance of payments. They tend to suggest that low
growth is brought about by inadequate monetary demand and
that adequate demand cannot be brought about until the
balance of payments problem is 'solved'. Strictly speaking,
it is not the balance of payments as such which is the
centre of concern, but the consequences for the rate of
growth of domestic output and employment resulting from a
given export performance. Import penetration is seen as
preventing a given export performance, accompanied by appropriate Keynesian demand management policies, stimulating
growth as it should. They mostly reflect ways of modifying
conventional Keynesian thinking so that fiscal and monetary
policies can be directed toward raising employment levels
and the rate of growth.

There is little doubt that despite the obvious poor performance of the United Kingdom economy over the last twenty-
five years or so, the supply side of the economy has been
substantially neglected. It is true that as far back as the
early 1960s it was recognised that to improve the underlying

rate of growth, demand management – however important a part
in the process it might be thought to play – was not enough.
The creation of the National Economic Development Office under the Conservatives and the Department of Economic Affairs
under Labour both reflected attempts to come to grips with
structural and industrial factors that were thought to influence growth potential.

Another of Lord Kaldor's many contributions focussed attention on the importance of the manufacturing sector of the
economy, on the argument that productivity growth was fastest in the manufacturing sector so that the overall growth
rate of an industrial economy would be determined by the
share of manufacturing in total output. This led to the
invention of the Selective Employment Tax as a device for
influencing the distribution of employment between manufacturing and the non-manufacturing sectors. More recently,
attention to the problems of the manufacturing sector was
reflected in the industrial strategy of the Wilson-Callaghan
government, and by the arguments set out by Bacon and Eltis
which emphasise the importance of the distinction between
the marketed and non-marketed sectors of national output.
Despite differences in diagnosis, there has been widespread
agreement that the decline in the manufacturing sector is a
key element in understanding British growth performance. The
consequences of North Sea oil for this view are examined in
Chapter 8.

Over the last two decades much ink has been spilt over the
problem of growth in Britain. The management of demand
apart, there is no shortage of possible explanatory factors
that have been adduced to account for the existence of slower growth in Britain relative to other countries, although
the weight to be attached to each is problematical. They include the behaviour of government, trades unions and management, the inadequacy of the education system, excessive
taxation, inadequate investment, exclusion from the EEC,
entry into the EEC, being an early starter, labour shortages
in the earlier years and an outdated initial capital structure. And the list could be extended. The bewilderment that
such a plethora of possible explanations produces tempts one
to search for some *deus ex machina* to account for all these
things, in terms of such concepts as the conservative nature
of the British people, or the psychological national disturbance caused by loss of Empire and world importance, or
to conjure up a conspiracy theory of disruption caused by
the behaviour of transnational companies.

This is not to imply that none of the factors may have ex-
erted some influence on economic performance since the Second World War. But it is important to begin with an attempt

to structure the analysis in economic terms, and to draw at least a rough distinction between economic factors on the one hand and the institutional and behaviour structure in which they are embedded. Before it is necessary to resort to some *deus ex machina* or other to account for events, an attempt must be made to examine performance in terms of the behaviour of the economic markets which make up the economy and which include the markets for goods and services both here and abroad, the labour market, the markets for real capital assets, and the markets for money and financial assets. There is no reason to start from the presumption that the laws of economic behaviour as reflected in markets have been suspended in Britain as opposed to elsewhere.

The central focus of this chapter is therefore on the supply and demand for goods and services, and their behaviour over time initially in terms of basic economic concepts. For this purpose we continue to use the term demand in its conventional macroeconomic sense as representing monetary demand expended on goods and services. Demand can, of course, be interpreted in a microeconomic sense as reflecting the desirability of purchasing a particular service or good. If a good is available for purchase, but no one wishes to buy it because it is regarded as inadequate for its purpose, it could be said that there is a lack of demand for it. In such cases, however, the lack of demand could be said to originate from the behaviour of the supplier in failing to meet market needs. In such cases as bad design or a faulty product, no increase in monetary demand may persuade customers to buy it. Alternatively, it may be ineffectively marketed or poorly distributed. For the purpose of this chapter we shall regard such problems as supply problems. Demand problems arise from a deficiency or an excess in overall monetary demand and, while the distinction is not wholly watertight, it should be borne in mind. We are concerned with the overall interaction between aggregate monetary demand and the supply of goods and services with consequent results for the rate of growth of output overall, the balance of payments and the rate of inflation.

Explanations of the rate of growth in economic terms should satisfy a number of criteria. They should in principle be verifiable from empirical observation. They should be capable of providing a first-hand explanation of the behaviour of the economy over a considerable period of time. The danger of *ad hoc* explanations dominated by contemporary events is always with us. They should also be capable of providing a reasonable explanation of differences in performance between industrial countries. The temptation toward parochialism is also one to be resisted. As emphasised in

Chapter 2, there has been a persistent failure to integrate
explanations of economic behaviour in Britain with countries
elsewhere, subject to many of the same economic pressures
that are shared out across the trading world. Finally, it
should be emphasised at the outset that providing an 'explanation' of events does not necessarily imply that the ob-
server can actually do anything about them. If a man wishes
to commit suicide by driving a car over a cliff at sixty
miles an hour one might try and persuade him to a different
course of action by explaining the consequences of his action on his family and his insurance company. All that may
be left in the end is to tell him to fasten his seat-belt
and hope he survives.


GROWTH AND DE-INDUSTRIALISATION

Facts do not speak for themselves; statistics even less so.
Statistical information is open to wide difference as to its
interpretation as we shall see subsequently. As emphasised
above, it is not simply the statistics of British economic
performance that we need to focus on, it is also its performance relative to other countries. This creates further
problems of statistical comparability between countries
particularly since, in order to be manageable, it is frequently necessary to resort to aggregate measures of one
kind and another. However, bearing these reservations in
mind, we present in this section as neutrally as possible a
number of major facts about the United Kingdom and its competitors which serve as a background to some later discussion.
    In Table 5.1 we set out summary statistics relating to the
economic performance of nine major industrial countries between 1953 and 1976. These figures illustrate certain well-
known features of British economic performance over this
period relative to its major competitors. The rate of growth
of total output in Britain is clearly at the bottom of the
list, although the figure is more affected than the others
by the low rates of growth generally experienced after 1973.
Between 1953 and 1963 the average annual rate of increase
was just over 3 per cent and is virtually the same between
the peak years of 1964 and 1973.
    On average over the period, by comparison with other coun-
tries the UK was in proportionate terms a high consumption/
low investment economy. Public and private consumption accounted for some 82 per cent of national output, a figure
that is exceeded by the USA with no less than 84 per cent,
and close to Sweden, also a relatively slow growing country,

TABLE 5.1 *Comparative statistics for nine countries, 1953–76 (averages of yearly figures)*

| | % change, money GNP | % change, narrow money supply | % change, real GNP | % change, consumer prices | Public and private consumption as a % of GNP | Investment as % of GNP | % change in export volumes |
|---|---|---|---|---|---|---|---|
| USA | 6.9 | 3.9 | 3.2 | 3.3 | 84.1 | 14.5 | 5.9 |
| West Germany | 9.2 | 9.4 | 5.0 | 3.4 | 72.3 | 23.7 | 10.0 |
| Netherlands | 10.3 | 8.3 | 5.0 | 4.7 | 73.2 | 23.7 | 9.4 |
| Sweden | 8.9 | 6.8 | 3.7 | 4.8 | 79.3 | 23.0 | 7.2 |
| France | 10.7 | 10.7 | 5.0 | 5.1 | 75.7 | 21.9 | 8.8 |
| Italy | 10.4 | 14.0 | 5.0 | 5.4 | 78.4 | 20.9 | 12.1 |
| Belgium | 8.5 | 5.8 | 4.1 | 3.8 | 78.0 | 20.0 | 9.2 |
| Japan | 14.7 | 16.3 | 8.6 | 6.1 | 66.0 | 30.2 | 16.2 |
| UK | 9.0 | 5.2 | 2.7 | 5.9 | 81.6 | 17.3 | 4.5 |

SOURCE  D. Kern, 'An International Comparison of Major Economic Trends 1953–76', *National Westminster Bank Review*, May 1978.

with 79 per cent. These figures may be contrasted with figures of 72 per cent for West Germany, and only 66 per cent
for Japan. In both the USA and the UK the shares of national
output invested come at the bottom of the list with only
14.5 per cent invested in the USA and 17.3 per cent in the
UK. There is little doubt that specific country factors affect the dispersion in investment ratios that is observed,
but there is an evident association between higher rates of
growth and higher investment ratios, with Japan investing no
less than 30 per cent of its national output. At the same
time the average rate of inflation in Britain is second
only to that of Japan, although the figures are again much
affected by Britain's disastrous inflation performance
after 1973. The Japanese inflation is marked by the wide
disparity between the rate of increase in Japanese domestic
prices and Japanese export prices due to major differences
in efficiency between the traded and non-traded goods sectors.

Leaving on one side the generally poor economic performance as reflected in Table 5.1, attention has been focussed
in recent years on the specific performance of the manufacturing sector. The general thesis starts from the presumption that United Kingdom performance in the manufacturing sector has been particularly bad, with serious consequences as far as the growth rate is concerned, in view of
the argument that the manufacturing sector has been the en-
gine of growth for the industrial countries. This particular problem has been referred to as to the problem of 'de-
industrialisation'. It has often been supposed that with
economic growth the demand for services outside the manufacturing sector, as a proportion of income, would tend to
increase, which has led a number of writers to talk about
the inevitability of the 'post-industrial' society and its
economic consequences. Whatever the general situation in the
world as a whole, however, it has been argued that de-
industrialisation has been a particular problem for the
United Kingdom. The questions that arise immediately are
what is meant by de-industrialisation and what evidence is
there that this problem is particularly acute in Britain.

The confusing of the idea of de-industrialisation with
that of the post-industrial society, induced by change in
the long-term pattern of world demand, would seem to suggest
prima facie that changes were taking place in the observed
pattern of employment and output. In the United Kingdom
special emphasis was placed initially by Bacon and Eltis on
the shift of labour out of British manufacturing, which was
interpreted as a sign of the erosion of the industrial base.
At the same time employment in the public sector was ob-

served to increase, and the two trends were associated together in their familiar thesis that employment in manufacturing was being 'crowded out' by employment in the public sector, a thesis that is discussed in a later section
in this chapter.

The basic data shows that in 1966 total employment in the
United Kingdom reached a peak and that in the following decade there was a net decline in people at work of over
700,000. Over that period, employment in activity covered by
the industrial production index fell by nearly 2m and employment in the public sector, excluding public sector industry, grew by something less than 1.5m. However, it has
been estimated that of the increase in employment in the
public sector, something of the order of two-thirds of the
increase reflected the employment of women. Employment of
men in the industries covered by the index of industrial
production fell by nearly 1.5m, while increased employment
in the public sector rose by only 370,000. In fact the increase in the total labour force from 22.8m in 1951 to 25.9m
in 1976 is virtually wholly accounted for by the entry of
women into the labour force, with participation rates for
married women being among the highest in the industrial
countries. Given these figures the implication would seem to
be that a substantial proportion of the jobs reflected in
the fall of 15.6 per cent in manufacturing over this decade
disappeared. This amounted to about a half, or some 700,000
jobs. From the figures in Table 5.2 it may be noted that
male employment in the rest of the private sector also fell
by nearly 400,000. The fall in manufacturing employment is
not in doubt, but what remains in doubt is the interpretation of the mechanism through which the fall came about.

As Table 5.2 shows, the fall in manufacturing employment
as a proportion of total employment has not been confined to
the United Kingdom over the period since 1960. While international comparisons must be treated with caution, the evidence in Table 5.3 suggests a diversity of experience. It
suggests that 1970 provided something of a turning point for
most countries. With the exception of France, Sweden and
Italy, all countries exhibited a fall in the share of manufacturing in total employment although it can be seen that
the decline was particularly marked in the case of the United States, the United Kingdom, and the Netherlands. Moreover, even as late as 1975, the proportion of the labour
force employed in manufacturing in the United Kingdom was
exceeded only by West Germany and Italy. In terms of simply
looking at the employment proportion there would, on the
face of it, seem to be less concern expressed about the num-
bers actually employed in manufacturing industry than about

TABLE 5.2   *Changes in United Kingdom*
*employment, 1966-76, (000s)*

|                                   | Males      | Females       | Total    |
|-----------------------------------|------------|---------------|----------|
| Index of production industries    | -1 438     | -   536       | -1 975   |
| Other industries                  |            |               |          |
| (a) private sector                | +   385[a] | +   213[a]    | -   171  |
| (b) public sector                 | +   367[a] | +1 065[a]     | +1 432   |
|                                   | -1 456     | +   742       | -   714  |

[a]Estimates.

SOURCE   A.R. Thatcher, 'Labour Supply and Employment
Trends', in F.T. Blackaby (ed.), *De-industrialisation*
(Heinemann/NIESR, 1979).

TABLE 5.3  *Proportions of manufacturing employment in total employment,*
*1950-77 (per cent)*

| | 1950 | 1960 | 1970 | 1973 | 1974 | 1975 | 1976 | 1977 |
|---|---|---|---|---|---|---|---|---|
| United Kingdom | 34.7 | 35.8 | 34.7 | 32.3 | 32.3 | 30.9 | 30.2 | 30.4 |
| Belgium | 32.7 | 33.5 | 32.7 | 31.8 | 31.5 | 30.1 | 29.1 | 28.1 |
| France | – | 27.9 | 27.9 | 28.4 | 28.4 | 27.9 | 27.5 | 27.1 |
| Germany | – | 34.7 | 37.4 | 36.4 | 36.6 | 35.8 | 35.8 | 35.8 |
| Italy | – | 36.9 | 39.7 | 39.4 | 39.4 | 39.3 | 38.5 | 38.7 |
| Netherlands | 30.2 | 28.6 | 26.2 | 24.7 | 24.5 | 23.8 | 22.9 | 22.3 |
| Japan | – | 21.3 | 27.0 | 27.4 | 27.2 | 25.8 | 25.5 | 25.1 |
| Sweden | – | 32.1[b] | 27.6 | 27.5 | 28.3 | 28.0 | 26.9 | 25.9 |
| United States [a] | – | 33.1 | 34.4 | 33.2 | 32.5 | 30.7 | 30.9 | 30.9 |

[a]These figures refer to industrial employment

[b]1961 not 1960

SOURCE  OECD, *Manpower Statistics* and *Labour Force Statistics*

the efficiency with which these are used. If the decline in
the proportion becomes a matter of concern, it is arguable
that prima facie a simple parochial explanation is not
enough. If we take the period 1960-73, so leaving out the
effect of the later years affected by energy crises, the
simple fact is that the United Kingdom experience is not
that unique, and it is by no means the worst, its proportion
declining by 10 per cent compared to a similar figure for
Belgium, 14 per cent for the Netherlands and 15 per cent for
Sweden. Clearly there is some association between the behaviour of this employment proportion and the growth perfor-·
mance of output over the period. The critical issue to be
resolved, however, is whether changes in the proportion of
labour employed in manufacturing are simply another symptom
of poor growth performance in manufacturing or whether this
has in itself any independent significance. This is a matter
for later discussion.

Examination of the behaviour of manufacturing output presented in both real terms and in value terms as a proportion
of the gross domestic product is set out in Table 5.4. This
throws up further difficulties of interpretation. In real
or volume terms, the United Kingdom alone failed to register
a material increase in the share of manufacturing output between 1960 and 1973. However the value figure shares indi-
cate clearly that across the industrial countries as a
whole there has been a marked deterioration in the manufacturing terms of trade, i.e. prices in manufacturing relative
to the rest of the economy. In the case of France, the shift
is quite dramatic. The value share in the United Kingdom
also falls sharply to an extent exceeded by France and the
Netherlands and paralleled by the United States. Taking the
employment and output figures together, it is only in terms
of the output share of manufacturing in real terms that the
United Kingdom is unambiguously at the bottom of the list,
as far as behaviour over time is concerned. It seems a fair
judgement that the United Kingdom performance overall has
been poorest although there are other countries with similar
profiles, notably the Netherlands and the United States.

However, it has been argued that 'de-industrialisation'
should not be measured by changes in either the share of
manufacturing output or employment. Even if the share of
manufacturing in output were increasing, 'de-industrialisation' might be taking place. The appropriate question, it is
argued, is whether the manufacturing sector is efficient
enough to meet the needs of consumers at home, and is able
to sell enough abroad, to meet import requirements at socially acceptable levels of employment and exchange rate.
The key statistics in this case then become the share of

TABLE 5.4 *Manufacturing output as a proportion of GDP 1960-73*

| | 1963 prices (%)[a] | | | Current prices (%)[b] | | |
|---|---|---|---|---|---|---|
| | 1960 | 1970 | 1973 | 1960 | 1970 | 1973 |
| United Kingdom | 31.0 | 31.7 | 31.5 | 36.1 | 32.4 | 31.0 |
| Belgium | 26.0 | 30.3 | 31.7 | 30.5 | 32.1 | 30.5 |
| France | 35.0 | 38.0 | 39.6 | [c]40.3 | 31.3 | 30.6 |
| Germany | 39.9 | 44.5 | 44.6 | 42.2 | 42.7 | 41.1 |
| Italy | 25.5 | 31.2 | 32.0 | 27.2 | 28.8 | 28.7 |
| Netherlands[c] | 36.6 | 41.7 | 42.3 | 34.5 | 29.0 | 28.5 |
| Canada | 24.2 | 26.4 | 27.1 | 26.7 | 23.5 | 23.2 |
| Japan | .... | 41.9 | 41.8 | 28.9 | 35.9 | 35.0 |
| Sweden | 27.7 | 31.9 | 32.5 | 26.8 | 26.8 | 26.9 |
| United States | 27.4 | 27.9 | 29.2 | 28.4 | 25.7 | 24.9 |

[a]GDP at market prices, except for Italy and Canada, at factor cost.

[b]GDP at market prices, except for the UK, Italy and Canada, at factor cost.

[c]Manufacturing plus other smaller sectors.

SOURCE  C.J.F. Brown and T.D. Sheriff, 'De-industrialisation, a background paper' in F.T. Blackaby (ed.), *De-industrialisation* (Heinemann/NIESR, 1979).

manufactured exports in world trade and the behaviour of net exports of manufactured goods, which also reflects import penetration.

Data on the UK share in world manufactures is given in Table 5.5 which illustrates the familiar story of the decline in the UK share over the last quarter century. Apart from the decline in the UK share, the most dramatic features of Table 5.5 are the sharp fall in the share of the USA and the sharp rise in the share of Japan. At the same time between 1960 and 1976, as shown in Table 5.6, the share of imports in manufacturing sales in total in the UK rose from about 8 per cent in terms of both volume and value to 21 per cent, while exports of United Kingdom manufacturing production rose from 15 per cent to 25 per cent. This degree of import penetration in manufactured goods has apparently accelerated during the 1970s with the result that between 1970 and 1977 net exports in manufactures fell from £6000m to about £1000m.

In some respects it is peculiar to refer to these phenomena as reflecting a process of de-industrialisation. It is certainly not what has been in the minds of those who have been concerned with the post-industrial society. However, that is partly a matter of taste. The central purpose is to demonstrate the long-term decline of the competitiveness of British manufacturing industry relative to other countries, with consequent effects on the rate of growth of the economy as a whole. The simple and obvious fact is that Britain did not keep pace with the average performance of the major industrial countries which may be taken as evidence of competitive failure. The crucial issue is whether the explanation of that decline can be attributed to certain factors such as the specific behaviour of government, or to an insatiable appetite for foreign goods, or whether relative economic failure is rooted in the internal workings of the economy. None of these possible explanations are necessarily mutually exclusive, but it is important subsequently to attribute some kind of weighting to each of them.


DEMAND AND SUPPLY

As we have seen in the last two chapters, different perceptions of the nature of the interrelationship between aggregate monetary demand and the real supply of goods and services lie at the heart of much of the disagreement about economic behaviour in the short term. Various brands of Keynesianism attribute an independent role to aggregate monetary demand not only in the short run, but also in the medium

TABLE 5.5 *Shares in the value of 'world'[a] exports of manufactures[b] 1950-79 (per cent)*

|  | 1950 | 1960 | 1965 | 1970 | 1975 | 1978 | 1979 |
|---|---|---|---|---|---|---|---|
| United Kingdom[c] | 25.5 | 16.5 | 13.9 | 10.8 | 9.3 | 9.5 | 9.7 |
| France | 9.9 | 9.6 | 8.8 | 8.7 | 10.2 | 9.8 | 10.5 |
| Germany | 7.3 | 19.3 | 19.1 | 19.8 | 20.3 | 20.7 | 20.8 |
| Italy | 26.6 | 5.1 | 6.7 | 7.2 | 7.5 | 7.9 | 8.3 |
| Others[d] |  | 21.0 | 21.8 | 23.3 | 21.4 | 21.4 | 21.3 |
| Japan | 3.4 | 6.9 | 9.4 | 11.7 | 13.6 | 15.6 | 13.6 |
| United States[e] | 27.3 | 21.6 | 20.3 | 18.5 | 17.7 | 15.1 | 15.9 |

[a] 'World' defined as the countries covered by this table.

[b] Arms excluded except in 1950.

[c] Re-exports included from 1960; figures adjusted for under recording from 1965.

[d] Belgium, Luxembourg, Canada, Netherlands, Sweden and Switzerland.

[e] Special category exports excluded.

SOURCE  C.J.F. Brown and T.D. Sheriff, 'De-industrialisation, a background paper', in F.T. Blackaby (ed.), *De-industrialisation*, updated by *National Institute Economic Review*, May 1980, No. 92.

TABLE 5.6  *Import penetration and export-sales*
*ratio for United Kingdom manufacturing,*
*1955-76 (per cent)*

|  | Import penetration[a] | Export-sales ratio[b] |
|---|---|---|
| 1960 | 8 | 15 |
| 1965 | 9 | 15 |
| 1968 | 12 | 17 |
| 1970 | 13 | 18 |
| 1973 | 18 | 20 |
| 1974 | 19 | 22 |
| 1975 | 18 | 23 |
| 1976 | 21 | 25 |

[a]Import/(Sales + imports - exports).

[b]Exports/Sales.

SOURCE  C.J.F. Brown and T.D. Sheriff,
'De-industrialisation, a background paper' in
F.T. Blackaby (ed.), *De-industrialisation*
(Heinemann/NIESR, 1979).

term, with permanent effects on levels of output and employment. Such ideas lead naturally to the view that 'demand management' represents an important dimension of economic policy-making. Those of a monetarist persuasion, on the other hand, believe that variations in monetary demand brought about by government fiscal and monetary policies will not have such permanent effects.

In this chapter we are concerned with the determinants of aggregate supply in the economy and with long-term growth potential. In this context there are analogues to the kind of disagreements already referred to. Arguments about growth policy also depend in part on the role assigned to aggregate monetary demand, and on views of the relative efficiencies of the markets for factors of production. Conclusions (or assumptions) on these matters determine the analysis of the interaction between stabilisation and longer-term growth policies.

Keynesian approaches to the analysis of economic growth at the macroeconomic level start from the assumption that market forces are generally inadequate to ensure that the economy will grow at a rate that is sufficient to employ fully all the available resources. This puts in a growth setting the problem of unemployment that we have already discussed in the short and medium term in Chapter 3.

Assume for the moment that in the closed economy the overall rate of growth of output at full employment is given. This will be equal to the rate of growth of labour productivity plus the rate of growth of the supply of labour. The Keynesian analysis then typically identifies two problems. The first is the idea that 'equilibrium' growth requires a rate of growth of demand that generates a volume of investment sufficient to absorb the volume of planned saving and such a rate of growth may not be attainable. Such a rate of growth of output is sometimes referred to as the *warranted* rate of growth, while the maximum growth rate at full employment is referred to as the *natural* rate. The second is that even if demand and supply are growing at the warranted rate, there are no market forces that ensure that the warranted rate is equal to the natural rate. Steady growth at full employment requires that the actual, warranted and natural rates are all equal.

If the warranted rate of growth exceeds the natural rate of growth the consequence will be chronic depression. This is because since in the long run the actual rate of growth cannot by definition exceed the natural rate, then the actual rate in the long run must lie below the warranted rate, i.e. the rate of growth of demand can never be high enough in real terms to induce the rate of investment necessary

to absorb full employment savings. Vice versa if the warranted rate lies below the natural rate, and the actual rate
of growth is equal to the natural rate, there will be chronic inflationary pressure since the demand for investment
will tend persistently to outstrip the supply of savings.
The economy, other things being equal, is poised on a knife
edge between the Scylla of depression and the Charybdis of
inflation. In the absence of efficient market forces it is
only by accident that the three growth rates will be equal.
    Notice that, by definition, this does not provide us with
a theory of the growth potential of the economy since the
natural rate of growth is given. On the face of it, it simply provides a rationale for demand management or other
forms of government discretionary action in a growth setting. Market forces, it is argued, will not ensure that the
economy will realise a growth potential which is created by
technological possibilities and the available supply of labour. Moreover, as it stands, the analysis deals with a
closed economy without foreign trade and, from a Keynesian
point of view, the introduction of foreign trade introduces
further complications. In addition, we have referred only
briefly to inflation.
    In the closed economy demand management might not be able
to ensure acceptable price stability at the natural rate of
growth so that, in the absence of some *deus ex machina* such
as incomes policy, inflation might exercise a constraint on
the realisation of the economy's growth potential. Furthermore, in the open economy demand management might also not
be 'enough' because of problems arising from the balance of
payments. In a pegged exchange rate system, it was argued
that balance of payments equilibrium might be inconsistent,
other things being equal, with the natural rate of growth.
A persistent tendency to run balance of payments deficits at
full employment growth could exercise a constraint on the
realisation of growth potential. Such a view of the British
economy has re-emerged repeatedly since the Second World
War, and has been particularly associated with the periods
of stop/go experienced during the fifties and sixties. Demand, it was said, was prevented from growing sufficiently
rapidly by the state of the balance of payments. In theory,
under a fully floating exchange rate regime, balance of payments equilibrium in money terms is maintained.
    However, there remains the possibility that the required
rate of growth of monetary demand would result in a depreciating exchange rate and in consequence, yet again, an unacceptable rate of inflation in a world of free collective
bargaining. Such analyses led once more to the familiar
calls for demand management coupled with incomes policies,

exchange rate management and protectionism to secure equilibrium between the actual warranted and natural rates of
growth.

   As already noted, all this represents nothing more than a
restatement of the problems of stabilisation policy in a
growth setting. It tells us nothing about the natural rate
of growth itself. Insofar as subsequênt Keynesian thinking
has something to say about the relationship of the growth of
monetary demand to the natural rate of growth, it is to be
found in rather imprecise ideas that characterised some of
the thinking of the sixties and after. The central idea was
one of a virtuous circle of events resulting from a demand-
led expansion promoted by monetary fiscal and exchange rate
policies which, through higher investment and productivity,
would raise the natural rate of economic growth towards the
levels achieved by other nations. At the same time it would
break through the apparent constraints imposed by the balance of payments by increased efficiency and competitiveness. In some versions of the story a faster rate of growth
was also seen as part of the answer to securing greater
price stability through higher productivity and higher real
wages at lower rates of nominal wage increase. Later versions of the story shifted the emphasis from demand-led
growth to export demand-led growth, and later still to protectionism, to be used to buy time to get into the virtuous
circle and to raise the natural rate, perhaps with the further weapon of direct government intervention in a variety
of forms. All these analyses are rooted in the common idea
that expanding monetary demand is the key to expanding real
supply and it is this that gives them their particularly
Keynesian caste.

   Whereas, in the analysis of stabilisation and growth policy we have been describing, the emphasis is on market failure and constraints on the rate of economic growth requiring
government intervention in various forms, the monetarist and
neo-classical approach to economic growth relies essentially
on market success, at least in the long run. In the case of
the closed economy the presumption is that labour markets
'work' so that, to begin with, real wage movements will tend
to equilibrate the demand and supply for labour and capital
markets will tend to equilibrate the demand for capital
goods and the supply of savings. In general, prices and interest rates will play an important role in the adjustment
process, particularly in the longer run, so that for the
monetarist the disequilibrium between the actual and the
warranted rates of growth will be temporary and not chronic,
as in the extreme versions of the Keynesian-type story. In
the longer run monetary growth will tend to dominate the

behaviour of prices rather than output and employment.
Given the existence of a natural rate of unemployment, attempts by the authorities to pursue monetary demand-led
growth will simply result in inflation, either in the case
of the closed economy or - in the case of the open economy - with floating exchange rates. With fixed exchange
rates, monetary-led growth will be dissipated in a balance
of payments deficit which will eventually require remedial
action. On this analysis, inflation and balance of payments
problems are seen not as unfortunate side effects of demand
management or as 'constraints' to achieving the full utilisation of the real growth potential of the economy. They
are seen as emanating from a common cause, namely a low
elasticity of supply which is determined independently of
the rate of growth of monetary demand. For the monetarists
there is no problem in the longer run in reconciling the
actual and the warranted rates of growth.

This is not to say that shifts in fiscal and monetary
policy do not have any effects on the short period behaviour
of output and growth. On the contrary, the actual observed
path of an economy through time may be materially affected
by them. Demand shocks which occur may lead the authorities
to incorrect action which exacerbates such shocks rather
than reduces them. Attempts to launch the British economy
into the virtuous circle of growth through demand-led policies had clearly-observed effects, however much they may
have been regarded by monetarists as counter-productive and
inflationary. An unstable financial environment associated
with unanticipated shifts in the rate of inflation is likely
to be highly inimical to steady economic growth. To this extent a stable financial environment can be seen to be an essential part of the process of realising the underlying economic growth potential.

Neither Keynesian nor neo-classical (monetarist) theory
has anything of great analytical significance to say about
the natural rate of economic growth itself. It is the essence of monetarism that money is 'not enough', since monetarism *qua* monetarism offers us no searching perceptions
about the determinants of economic growth. To some extent it
goes beyond the Keynesian analysis previously discussed, in
that it not only offers mechanisms that bring about equality
between the actual and the warranted rates of growth, but
also in certain rather special cases gives an account of how
the warranted rates and natural rates of growth are recon-
ciled, the details of which are not central to this or our
subsequent discussion. Suffice it to say that further analysis tells us little more than that the natural rate of
growth of the economy depends on the rate of capital accumu-

lation, the rate of increase in the labour supply and the behaviour of the productivities of the two factors, which will depend in part on extraneous 'technical progress' and in part on change induced by the rate of accumulation itself.

At this level we have description rather than analysis and the rate of growth is left suspended by its own bootstraps. Monetarism offers us a particular analysis of the way in which monetary demand and the real supply of goods and services interact and the Keynesian-type analysis offers us another. Much beyond that they do not go. To take matters further it is unfortunately necessary to hunt for scraps of illumination. Small wonder that there is a persistent search for some overriding explanation of comparative growth rates and it is to two widely canvassed candidates for this honour that we now turn.

## THE ROLE OF GOVERNMENT EXPENDITURE

In recent years attempts have been made to discriminate between the growth performance of different countries by reference to the comparative behaviour of public expenditure. In some sense excessive public expenditure is regarded as inhibiting to economic growth, and it is important to examine the different elements in this proposition in some detail.

At the outset we must take care to define what such terms as 'government expenditure' and the 'public sector' mean. The definitions vary from country to country and this also affects the measurement of the public sector borrowing requirement. The simplest definition of government expenditure is its share in total national expenditure in flow terms which reflects the government's claim on real resources for public consumption and for public investment, and the figures in Table 5.7 show that for the United Kingdom this proportion has risen substantially since 1950.

However, international comparisons on this basis are difficult to make, since definitions of the public sector are not the same. The comparative shares of public consumption alone in gross national product are given in Table 5.8 for the period 1953-76. These tend to show a somewhat weak negative correlation between the share of public consumption and the real rate of economic growth although, as we shall see later, there are other economic variables whose perceived correlations with the rate of growth are greater. The correlation is dominated by the United States for whom the share is particularly large mainly because of high

TABLE 5.7  *Government*[a] *final consumption*
*plus investment as a percentage of GNP*
*at factor cost and current prices*

| 1950 | 1960 | 1970 | 1975 | 1976 | 1977 | 1978 | 1979 |
|------|------|------|------|------|------|------|------|
| 21.9 | 22.1 | 26.0 | 29.7 | 28.8 | 27.2 | 26.1 | 26.8 |

[a]Government as defined by the Central Statistical Office
as General Government, i.e. Central Government and Local
Authorities, but excluding public corporations.

SOURCES   CSO, *Economic Trends Annual Supplement*, 1980;
   CSO, *Economic Trends*, Oct. 1980; CSO, *Monthly Digest of
   Statistics*, Aug. 1980.

TABLE *5.8* *Public consumption as percentage of GNP,*
*current prices and real GNP growth, 1953-76*
*(averages of yearly figures)*

|  | *Public Consumption/GNP* | *Real GNP growth* |
|---|---|---|
| United States | 21.0 | 3.2 |
| West Germany | 15.6 | 5.0 |
| Netherlands | 15.4 | 5.0 |
| Sweden | 19.1 | 3.7 |
| France | 13.4 | 5.0 |
| Italy | 13.0 | 5.0 |
| Belgium | 13.2 | 4.0 |
| Japan | 9.4 | 8.6 |
| United Kingdom | 17.6 | 2.7 |

SOURCE   D. Kern, 'An International Comparison of Major
Economic Trends 1953-76', *National Westminster Bank
Review*, May 1978.

defence spending, and by Japan for whom the share is dramatically small.

It has been argued however, with much justification, that for many purposes this way of measuring the 'size' of public expenditure is not appropriate. A wider definition of public expenditure would also include what the national income statisticians define as transfers between one sector of the population and another, for example old age pensions, unemployment benefit, subsidies of one kind or another and the interest payments on the national debt. An increase in pensions, for instance, paid for by additional taxes, takes money out of some people's pockets and puts it into others'. On the face of it such a 'transfer' does not affect the government's overall claim on real resources, although as we shall see there are arguments which suggest that such transfers may not be neutral in their overall effects on output and economic growth. When measured in this way, as we can see from Table 5.9, the size of public expenditure relative to national output is substantially changed. It is this larger figure that has most relevance to the behaviour of the government borrowing requirement and to the tax policies that the government pursues. Simply measuring the direct claims of government on resources as a share of national expenditure does not take us far enough.

There is, however, a third concept relating to public expenditure that has been made a key feature of the analysis of economic growth by Robert Bacon and Walter Eltis. In their view, the important distinction is not so much between the public and private sectors, but rather between what is described as 'marketed' and 'non-marketed' output. The public sector includes activities such as those of the nationalised industries which sell goods and services in the open market place like any private industrial concern. To the extent that such activities are seeking to price their goods and services so as to cover their full costs, they may be regarded as operating in the marketed sector. In practice they may be partly in and partly out, to the extent that their costs are subsidised as a matter of government policy. Non-marketed activities of government in general include the services supplied by local authorities, the health service and the national system of education, together with the whole range of subsidy payments which result in a supply of goods and services to the public at less than their full cost. Some measure of the size of non-marketed output relative to marketed output in the United Kingdom, as measured by Bacon and Eltis, is given in Table 5.10. Their central thesis is that the root of the British growth problem lies in the excessive size of the non-marketed relative to the

TABLE 5.9  *A comparison of two definitions of government[a] expenditure - as a percentage of GNP at factor cost and current prices*

|      | Total expenditure[b] | Final consumption plus investment |
|------|------|------|
| 1967 | 47.3 | 26.0 |
| 1970 | 47.5 | 26.0 |
| 1975 | 54.5 | 29.7 |
| 1976 | 52.2 | 28.8 |
| 1977 | 49.2 | 27.2 |
| 1978 | 49.8 | 26.1 |
| 1979 | 52.3 | 26.8 |

[a]Government as defined by the CSO as General Government, i.e. Central Government and Local Authorities, but excluding public corporations.

[b]As defined in *National Income and Expenditure*, CSO.

SOURCES   CSO, *Economic Trends Annual Supplement*, 1980; CSO, *Economic Trends*, Oct. 1980; CSO, *Monthly Digest of Statistics*, Aug. 1980; CSO, *National Income and Expenditure Book*, 1980.

TABLE 5.10   *Share of the non-market sector purchases[a] in net total final sales of the market sector percentage 1955-75*

| 1955 | 1960 | 1965 | 1970 | 1975 |
|------|------|------|------|------|
| 33.3 | 33.1 | 34.5 | 37.5 | 45.7 |

[a] i.e. consumption from subsidies and from non-market sector incomes, plus non-market purchases of materials and investment.

SOURCE R.W. Bacon and W.A. Eltis, 'The Measurement of the Growth of the Non-Market Sector and its Influence: Reply to Hadjimatheou and Skouras', *The Economic Journal* 89, June 1979.

marketed sector for goods and services. Since the non-
marketed sector is substantially embraced by the wider definitions of public expenditure at both a local and a national level, we shall for the purposes of analysis confine
our definition of the public sector to the non-marketed sector.

In analysing the importance of the size of the non-
marketed sector, one must distinguish between what has happened in an historical sense, what might happen and what
ought to happen. We are concerned with what evidence there
is, if any, that a relatively large non-marketed sector has
been a factor inhibiting economic growth in Britain. The
question of what ought to happen is deferred to a further
discussion of the determination of public expenditure in
Chapter 8.

In dealing with this issue, it is useful to distinguish
further between the direct resource effect of changes in the
relative size of the non-marketed sector, and the secondary
effects on the prices of goods and services, the prices of
the factors of production and the real rate of return on investment. We should also bear in mind that while the concept
of the marketed sector includes marketed services as well as
goods, the mainstream of public discussion has focussed on
the relationship between the size of the public sector and
the performance of manufacturing industry.

The Bacon and Eltis thesis has sometimes been dramatised
under the banner of 'too few producers'. Suppose that the
marketed sector produces 'bread' and 'capital' which is sold
in the market place, and that the non-marketed sector administered by the government supplies 'health', which is freely
available to all. Suppose further that the government balances its budget so that all the expenses of supplying
'health' are met out of taxation. Labour is employed either in
producing 'bread' and 'capital', or in supplying 'health'.
To simplify matters further, assume that productivity growth
takes place in the bread and capital sector, but is zero
with respect to the supply of health.

In this simple world the amount of health supplied is limited by the capacity of the bread workers to generate a surplus over their own consumption, to support those engaged in
health and the producers of capital. In addition, the overall rate of growth depends on how labour is distributed, assuming that labour is freely interchangeable between the
sectors. A benevolent dictator with power to impose taxes
and to allocate labour would take a view as to the welfare
of the community and so determine the rate of growth of the
economy and the relative sizes of the sectors in terms of
employment. As a matter of arithmetic, the overall growth

rate would be a weighted average of the growth rates in the
two sectors. Given our benevolent dictator, the only sense
in which the non-marketed sector might be regarded as too
large is simply that it absorbs amounts of labour and capital which are inconsistent with the dictator's overall target growth rate. The problem is one of the physical availability of resources. With a given labour force, more labour
in the health sector means less labour, and so additional
output foregone, in the marketed sector. In this sense the
non-marketed sector could be over-expanded, limiting the
availability of labour and capital for the marketed sector,
and so reducing the overall rate of growth of output below
what might otherwise be the case.

Returning to the United Kingdom economy, the initial question is whether the expansion of the non-marketed sector
has in fact deprived the marketed sector of physical resources, so accounting for the United Kingdom's poor growth
performance in historical terms. When put in these terms
the answer to this question is 'no'.

While, as already seen in Table 5.2, there has been a substantial fall in employment in manufacturing industry in
Britain and a substantial rise in employment in the public
sector, it is clear that this does not represent simply a
transfer of labour from one to the other. The major proportion of jobs lost in the production industries are related
to male employment, whereas the major proportion of the increase in the public sector relates to female employment.
Moreover, it is difficult to attribute the primary cause of
slow growth in Britain to labour shortage, given the observed degrees of overmanning and low productivity relative
to our principal competitors. As shown in Table 5.3, the
decline in employment in manufacturing industry has been
shared by Belgium, Denmark, Germany, Holland, the USA and
Sweden, although not by France, Ireland, Italy and Japan,
and the proportion of the labour force employed in manufacturing is still higher in the UK than all the countries referred to except Germany and Italy. In comparative terms,
labour shortage due to an excessive expansion in the public
sector does not directly offer a major reason for slow
growth in manufacturing. With regard to the supply of capital there is ample evidence submitted to the Wilson Committee that the availability of finance has not been a problem.

Does this mean, therefore, that the size of the non-
marketed sector has been of no consequence, or that the total of public spending including transfers has not been excessive? The answer to this question is 'not necessarily'.
To see this, let us return to our simple world of health,

bread and capital and drop the idea of our benevolent dictator. Assume firstly that health continues to be paid for out
of taxes, to which the community may respond. Problems arise
on two counts.

Firstly, the size of the non-marketed sector at which the
government is aiming may require a tax burden which is inhibiting to enterprise and to the development of new business.
Secondly, those employed in the marketed sector may be un-
happy with the extent to which they have to surrender real
earnings through taxation in order to provide for those employed in the non-marketed sector. Accordingly they may seek
to redress the balance by demanding higher nominal wages in
an attempt to restore their real private incomes to a level
that they regard as satisfactory. However, they may well
vote for an increase in the size of the non-marketed sector
although in a sense they may not be prepared to pay for it,
or they may believe that there is some other group in society who are capable of doing so. This is plainly an empirical question, since it is possible that the division of
their total welfare as between health and bread may be
agreeable to them. Insofar as it is not, they may demand
higher money wages, the consequences of which will depend on
the monetary policies pursued by the authorities. If monetary policy is accommodating, inflation will result while,
if it is tight, there will be a tendency either for unemployment to emerge in the marketed sector or for the rate of
return on capital to fall.

Given the size of the marketed sector in absolute terms,
the larger the non-marketed sector the greater the claims on
the marketed sector's output will be, unless the relative
sizes of the two sectors happens to reflect the welfare
trade-off between the two. That is equivalent to saying that
one can have the size of non-marketed sector one likes provided the community is prepared to pay for it. In practice
this raises a whole set of new problems about community
choice. Expectations about what government should do in expanding the non-marketed sector may be inconsistent with
private behaviour. The belief that something may be had for
nothing may be pervasive. This may stem from the view that
there is a minority, the rich, who could and should be made
to pay through taxation for an expanding non-marketed sector. It may also stem from the fact that political parties
rarely present in a coherent way the real costs of public
spending policies. Electoral promises to expand public
spending have rarely been accompanied by explanations as to
where the real finance is coming from. In a world in which,
unlike that of years gone by, taxation is a reality for the
vast majority of income earners, the possibility of serious

incompatibility between private behaviour and public aspirations increases. Such incompatibility, when allied with an overall burden of taxation that is regarded as excessive, presents further problems for governments. As we have seen in earlier chapters, if tax revenues fall short of public spending, governments may borrow in the capital markets or they may create money. This is not necessarily undesirable. On the contrary in an expanding economy there is likely to be an increased demand for liquid assets, including money itself and other securities issued and guaranteed by government.

If the aim of financial policy is to preserve the stability of prices and interest rates along some path of real growth, limits are imposed on the overall size of the public sector deficit in the longer run and on the mix of claims (money and securities) that the government issues to finance the deficit. If there are no changes in the technical conditions underlying the use of money in financing transactions, price stability requires that the nominal money stock should grow roughly in line with the real rate of growth of the economy. If attempts to expand the non-marketed sector are made without any willingness of either the government or the community to meet the additional costs out of increased taxation, the upshot will be either an excessive creation of money or government securities or both. The consequences of this will be inflation and high nominal rates of interest.

Such attempts to expand the non-marketed sector will be financially de-stabilising, with feedback effects on the observed rate of growth through unanticipated inflation and high nominal rates of interest which will increase risk and squeeze company liquidity in the private sector. The non-marketed sector always has to be paid for out of taxation. The only question is what form the taxation takes. There is no such thing as something for nothing. The non-marketed sector may be paid for out of conventional tax revenues, it may be paid for through an inflation tax resulting from an excessive creation of money, or it may be paid for through an interest rate tax arising from an excessive creation of government securities, or some mix of these three. In the worst of all possible worlds the burden of taxation is excessive, the rate of inflation unacceptable and nominal interest rates too high. This unfortunate set of circumstances is prima facie evidence that the size of the non-marketed, relative to the marketed, sector is excessive.

To what extent has an excessive expansion of the non-marketed sector been inhibiting to the rate of economic growth in the United Kingdom? Leaving on one side the direct resource effects, has the growth rate been affected in the

long term by taxation and financial instability, resulting
from the size of the non-marketed sector?

With regard to taxation, hard empirical evidence is difficult to come by. Critics of the view that taxation in Britain has been excessive point to the fact that the British
rate of growth was always relatively slow, even when the
burden of taxation was much lower than it has been in recent
years. It is a fact, however, that the tax-paying public has
been much enlarged and that the payment of taxes is something that affects the behaviour of the community at large.
On the face of it there is a popular view that taxation has
been excessive, despite the beliefs that there are others
who should pay more.

In considering the effects of taxation it is important to
distinguish between the forms in which taxation is raised,
the total burden of taxation and the relationship between
the average and marginal tax rates. By international standards, Britain has raised a larger-than-average proportion
of her taxation in the form of income taxation, and it is
arguable that greater incentives would result from a shift
from direct to indirect taxation. By international standards, however, the total proportion of national income
taken in taxes in the United Kingdom is by no means at the
top of the league, as can be seen in Table 5.11. It is possible to argue that highly taxed countries such as Sweden
also exhibit some of the economic deficiencies found in
the United Kingdom. On balance, however, it is difficult
either to state categorically that the overall burden of
taxation in the United Kingdom relative to other industrial
countries has been excessive, or to quantify its effect.

It is a fact that marginal rates of income tax in Britain
have in the past been high, both at the top and the bottom
of the income scale. They have been out of line with the
majority of other countries, and it is difficult not to believe that they have exercised a disincentive effect on persons and on the small business sector. In addition, capital
taxes have both penalised savings and inhibited business development, although to what extent must remain speculative.
The argument is sometimes advanced that taxation has had
little or no effect on business enterprise because rates of
return before tax are low and for a variety of other causes.
But this is to miss the point. Those who bear the burden of
taxation are not necessarily those on whom the taxes are le-
vied. To the extent that employed labour shifts forward the
burden of direct taxation, pre-tax rates of return may be
reduced.

It must be concluded that it is difficult to be sure that
the overall burden of taxation in the United Kingdom was in

TABLE *5.11  Taxes including social security*
*contributions as a percentage of GNP*
*at factor cost and current prices*

|                | 1971 | 1974 | 1976 | 1978 |
|----------------|------|------|------|------|
| Belgium        | 39.7 | 41.7 | 44.7 | 47.4 |
| France         | 39.6 | 41.0 | 44.2 | 43.6 |
| West Germany   | 39.8 | 43.0 | 43.9 | 44.6 |
| Italy          | 30.9 | 30.5 | 33.0 | 36.2 |
| Japan          | 22.2 | 24.8 | 23.6 | 24.5 |
| Netherlands    | 46.7 | 49.3 | 50.5 | 52.3 |
| Sweden         | 51.1 | 49.6 | 58.0 | 60.2 |
| United Kingdom | 40.6 | 39.9 | 40.0 | 39.1 |
| United States  | 32.2 | 34.2 | 33.3 | 33.5 |

SOURCE   K.J. Newman, 'International comparisons of
   taxes and social security contributions, 1971-8',
   *Economic Trends,* (CSO, Dec. 1980).

itself a major influence on the relatively slow growth rate. On the other hand, it is prima facie clear that the structure of taxation, and the relationship between average and marginal rates, together with the nature of the capital taxes imposed, did not provide a system within which individual and corporate enterprise was encouraged. The direct effects on growth are virtually impossible to quantify. The long-term effects of an overtly disincentive tax system cannot simply be measured in terms of output foregone. Some succeed in spite of the system, through ways which hitherto would have been regarded as socially unacceptable. When the tax system begins to make rogues out of honest men the form of that system must become suspect.

While there may be doubt and debate as to whether the attempts to expand and maintain the non-marketed sector resulted in an excessive average rate of taxation, the form that taxation took meant that the disincentive effect at the margin may have been significant. There is less uncertainty as to the financial difficulties brought about by the expansion and maintenance of the non-marketed sector. Even here some care must be taken to distinguish between the initial period of some twenty years after the Second World War and subsequent events dating from the end of the 1960s.

In the earlier period, monetary discipline was substantially guaranteed by the pegged exchange rate system when sterling was tied to the dollar. By present day standards, inflation was modest and the rate of unemployment by historical standards extraordinarily low. On the face of it it is not obvious that,up to the Maudling experiment of 1963/4, the relatively slow growth experienced by the British economy could be attributed to excessive public expenditure, to an oversize non-marketed sector and to monetary indiscipline. The problem of accounting for slow growth over this period in other terms remains. Whatever the subsequent problems arising from the treatment of the non-market sector, there were forces at work.

However, having said that, there is little doubt that subsequent events, from the middle sixties onwards, bear witness to problems arising from the growth of public expenditure and the non-market sector. They started with the expansion of 1963/4 and a rapid growth in public expenditure, the consequence of which led to the devaluation of sterling in 1967. This was followed by a period of sharp retrenchment during which fiscal and monetary control was re-established. As unemployment rose in the early seventies, a further massive expansion was undertaken, imposed in conjunction with a floating exchange rate, and this continued in the face of the oil price increase and the subsequent world recession.

Government underwrote the real level of activity in the non-market sector and the burden of adjustment fell on the marketed sector, and in particular on private industry. The non-market sector continued to expand. The result was a clear imbalance between the non-market and market sectors, which continued the trend begun in the middle sixties, when there was a major increase in employment in the non-market sector as has already been described. This did not result from a deliberate attempt to expand the non-market sector as such, but from the use of public expenditure to absorb the perceived excess supply of labour. The general character of events could be described as the maintenance of an excessive volume of public expenditure financed by an inflation tax, and *de facto* taxes on interest rates in the absence of sufficient tax revenue to meet the cost of the non-market sector.

The principal conclusion from this analysis is that the main effect of the imbalance that emerged from the sixties onwards, between the non-market and market sectors, was reflected not so much in the direct pre-emption of resources by the public sector as in the financial consequences for inflation and the behaviour of interest rates. Financial instability results in damaging cyclical behaviour, and financial stability is certainly a necessary if not sufficient condition for the maximisation of the economy's growth potential. However, the experience of the first two decades after the war should warn us that financial stability and proper control of the balance between the market and non-market sectors is not in itself a magic cure for other problems that are discussed later in this chapter.


THE BALANCE OF PAYMENTS


The predominant concern of the fifties and sixties was not so much a concern with the rate of taxation or with the size of the public sector, however much such concerns preoccupied a convinced minority. Considerable emphasis was placed from the war onwards on the state of the balance of payments as a constraint on the rate of economic growth, which has been carried into the present day in the form of demands for protectionism. Notice that in the short run the argument for protectionism is not that it is required to 'solve' the balance of payments problem, but that it would enable a higher level of employment to be enjoyed with a given state of the current account. The argument is that a combination of inadequate export performance plus a strong appetite for imported goods prevents the expansion of domestic demand to a point consistent with what might be described as full employment. Protectionism is seen as a device for switching expenditure from imported to domestically-produced goods. In Chapter 6 we concern ourselves with some of the wider international issues relating to protectionism and free trade. Here we confine the discussion to the arguments that have been advanced in the United Kingdom as part of the explanation of its rate of economic growth.

In the 1960s the perceived problem of a balance of payments constraint on the rate of growth of the economy focussed attention on the sterling/dollar exchange rate, and to a lesser extent on the possibility of import restrictions. The maintenance of the exchange rate at its 1949 parity attracted increasing criticism, and while the act could hardly be described as one of free choice, the devaluation of sterling in 1967 was hailed by many as a throwing-off of chains, as was the later decision to float the pound in 1973. For a period of time the devaluation of 1967 appeared to 'work', at least in as much as an improvement in the current account was forthcoming, aided by an incomes policy administered under the auspices of the Prices and Incomes Board and by a tight fiscal policy. However, in 1969 world inflation accelerated and the consensus between the government and the trades unions collapsed. By the early 1970s the competitive advantage in price secured by the devaluation had largely vanished as domestic inflation took hold.

The ultimate failure of the 1967 devaluation did not destroy the belief that the exchange rate could be used to escape from the balance of payments constraint. The next phase was characterised by the phrase 'export-led growth', an idea that persisted until the decision in late 1977 to allow the exchange rate to float up. The idea was that the stop/go periods since the war had been in error, in that faster growth and falling unemployment had been consumption-led, either due to increases in private consumption resulting from tax cuts and relaxations of hire purchase controls, or from increases in public consumption. The revised theory was that fiscal policy should not aim at expanding domestic demand but at maintaining a pressure of overall demand that was consistent with controlling imports and keeping the current account of the balance of payments in equilibrium at a given rate of growth of exports. This left the exchange rate free to be used as a weapon to stimulate the growth of exports, which would then lead to the desired rate of growth of total output. From the summer of 1976 onwards a similar idea manifested itself in the combination of an incomes policy allied to a 'competitive' pound, which was supposed to encourage sufficient export expansion to offset the cuts

in public spending, shifting the balance between the public
and private sectors and increasing the rate of growth. This
attempt to produce the sought-after economic miracle and to
enter the virtuous circle of growth and strong balance of
payments failed in the face of a massive inflow of reserves
during 1977, which eventually forced the authorities to allow sterling to float up.

The central weakness of this analysis stems, as we saw in
Chapter 4, from the assumptions that the exchange rate can
be manipulated independently of market forces and that
changes in the nominal exchange rate will have material and
lasting effects on the real rate of exchange. In practice,
unless some effective form of incomes policy can be permanently maintained, the competitive effects of changes in
nominal exchange rates tend to be offset by the domestic
rate of inflation. However, even given an inability to manipulate the growth rate by altering the nominal rate of exchange, the idea of the importance of export-led growth has
not died and has been restated by Professor Thirlwall.

As emphasised earlier in this chapter, the neo-classical
approach to the study of comparative rates of economic
growth focussed on the supply side of the economy, reflecting the growth and production. As we noted, this does not
tell us why the growth of factor supplies and productivity
differs between countries. To answer this question Professor
Thirlwall argues '...some would say that a more Keynesian
approach is required which stresses demand. For the Keynesian, it is demand that "drives" the economic system to
which supply within limits adapts'. The thesis presented is
that the differences between the growth of economies are derived from different rates of growth of monetary demand and
that in an open economy the dominant constraint is the balance of payments.

To illustrate his point Thirlwall starts from the assumption of a current account balance in the balance of payments
which implies that

(1) $P_x X = P_m ME$

$\quad X$ = volume of exports of goods and services
$\quad M$ = volume of imports of goods and services
$\quad P$ = price of exports in domestic currency
$\quad P^x$ = price of imports in domestic currency
$\quad E^m$ = nominal exchange rate.

It follows from (1) that the rate of growth of export volume is equal to the rate of growth of import volume, plus a
term reflecting the percentage rate of change in relative

prices multiplied by the exchange rate. Thirlwall himself considers a more sophisticated form of analysis which allows for price effects on the volumes of exports and imports but for present purposes it is sufficient to make three simple assumptions.

The first is that the rate of growth of exports is related to the rate of growth of world export demand. Secondly, the rate of growth is a constant proportion $b$ of the rate of growth of total domestic output. Thirdly, in the longer run, either relative prices and the exchange rate are constant, or on average changes in relative prices and the nominal exchange rate are offsetting. On these assumptions it follows from (1) that the rate of growth of exports must in the long run equal the rate of growth of imports, if the current account is to remain in balance, and since the rate of growth of imports is a proportion   of the rate of growth of output we can write

(2) $G_x = bG_y$

where $G_x$ = growth of exports and $G_y$ = growth of output. Dividing through by $b$ the rate of growth of output is equal to the rate of growth of exports, divided by what can be defined as the income elasticity of demand for imports i.e. the per cent increase in imports resulting from a given per cent increase in output. So we have,

(3) $G_y = \dfrac{G_x}{b}$

In Professor Thirlwall's terms the growth of output given by the simple formula (3) is defined as the balance of payments equilibrium growth rate. It purports to tell us how fast the economy can grow for a given rate of export growth and, still on the assumptions made, ensure that the current account of the balance of payments is in balance.

To put empirical content into the analysis it is necessary to obtain some estimates for the income elasticity of demand for imports for different countries. A set of such estimates, together with a record of actual growth rates, is given for 19 countries in Table 5.12. The last column gives an estimate of the balance of payments equilibrium growth rate for each of the countries concerned, obtained by dividing column 2 by column 3. Professor Thirlwall concludes that applying formula (3) to this data

...gives a remarkable approximation to the growth experience of many countries over the last twenty years and *ipso facto* provides an explanation of why growth rates differ.

*Money and Employment*

TABLE 5.12 *Calculations of the growth rate consistent with balance of payments equilibrium 1953–76*

|  | % change of real GNP | % change in export volumes | Income elasticity of demand for imports | Balance of payments equilibrium growth rate |
|---|---|---|---|---|
| United States | 3.2 | 5.9 | 1.5 | 3.9 |
| West Germany | 5.0 | 10.0 | 1.9 | 5.3 |
| Netherlands | 5.0 | 9.4 | 1.8 | 5.2 |
| Sweden | 3.7 | 7.2 | 1.8 | 4.1 |
| France | 5.0 | 8.8 | 1.6 | 5.4 |
| Italy | 5.0 | 12.1 | 2.3 | 5.4 |
| Belgium | 4.0 | 9.2 | 1.9 | 4.8 |
| Japan | 8.6 | 16.2 | 1.2 | 13.2 |
| United Kingdom | 2.7 | 4.5 | 1.5 | 3.0 |

SOURCE A.P. Thirlwall, 'The Balance of Payments Constraint as an Explanation of International Growth Rate Differences', *Banco Nazionale del Lavoro*, Mar. 1979.

It might almost be stated as a fundamental law that, except where the balance of payments equilibrium growth
rate exceeds the maximum feasible capacity growth rate,
the rate of growth of a country will approximate to the
ratio of its rate of growth of exports and its income
elasticity of demand for imports.

The caveat is intended to apply to cases such as Japan.
Professor Thirlwall goes on to conclude that

> The simple policy conclusion for most countries is that,
> if they wish to grow faster, they must first raise the
> balance of payments constraint on demand. And that the ex-
> planation of growth rate differences must lie primarily in
> difference in the rate of growth of demand, and the major
> constraint on the rate of growth of demand in most coun-
> tries is the balance of payments. Our model and the em-
> pirical evidence lends strong support to the advocates of
> export-led growth.

Formula (3) has also been used to make a point about the
role of imports in impeding growth. Over the period 1953-64
exports of goods and services in the UK grew at an average
rate of 3.3 per cent and the average rate of growth of output was similar. Over the period 1964-73 the rate of growth
of exports averaged no less than 6.3 per cent whereas the
rate of growth of output remained virtually the same. The
reason for this is the increase in the apparent elasticity
of demand for imports. In terms of formula (3) $b$ rose. Thus
it is argued that increased import penetration largely nullified the good export performance observed during the second period. Observations of this kind underly the case for
some form of protection in order that imports should be constrained to grow more slowly relative to output.
It is of major importance to distinguish between the proposition that, if the rate of growth of exports had been
faster, so would a country's overall rate of growth, and the
proposition that the balance of payments acted as a constraint on the rate of growth of domestic demand. As we saw
in the last chapter, the monetary approach to the analysis
of the balance of payments suggests that, under a pegged exchange rate system, the emergence of an overall balance of
payments deficit is a reflection of excess monetary demand
relative to supply. Under a floating exchange rate the overall balance of payments will not be in deficit as appropriate adjustments will occur in the rate.
It is a curious and misleading use of language to describe
the balance of payments in either case as a constraint on

the growth of domestic demand, since deficits in the fixed
rate case and inflation in the floating rate case both originate from the constraint imposed by domestic supply. Part
of the confusion arises from the failure to distinguish between the economic and physical definitions of supply. Physical capacity both in terms of capital and labour may appear unused and so capable of producing goods. However, the
goods will not be produced and sold in the long run unless
it is profitable to do so and unless the goods are acceptable to the buyer. In the absence of either or both of these
conditions, there is a problem of supply which it is quite
incorrect to describe as a lack of demand.

Moreover, it is equally incorrect to assign the behaviour
of imports solely to the behaviour of import demand, independently of conditions of competitive supply. To put the
matter another way, it is not clear that we can make the
assumption that in formula (3) it is the rate of growth of
output that is the dependent variable. If a once-and-for-
all increase in the rate of growth of exports is not offset
by a faster growth of domestic capacity, imports will be
brought in to fill the gap. Imports can be determined by
supply rather than demand. In this case protectionism would
lead to excess demand and domestic inflation rather than to
a major permanent increase in the level of output and employment.

The conclusions that can be drawn from these data are in
fact very limited. They do not support the view that the
balance of payments is the major factor accounting for differences in growth rates between countries. Taken across the
board they reflect two phenomena. The first is the rapid
growth over the period in traded goods relative to non-
traded goods in the industrial world. In all the countries
listed, the rate of export growth exceeded that of output,
and in this respect the relationship for the period as a
whole between export growth and output growth for the UK is
not particularly unusual. The traded goods sector has been
the fast-growing sector. Secondly, obviously and not sur-
prisingly, the fast-growing countries have been those who
have most successfully exploited the fast-growing sector
i.e. those with rapid export growth.

As far as Britain is concerned, the conclusion that must
be drawn is not that growth has been constrained by the balance of payments, but that it has been unable to sustain its
share of expanding world demand. In the broadest sense it
has been uncompetitive, the reasons for which must be found
in the supply side of the economy and to this extent the
Cambridge 'school' of thought must be right in focussing on
the decline in Britain's share of world trade as the key in-

dicator of performance.

From there it is important not to make the jump to identi-
fying the balance of payments as a *cause* of slow growth,
which focusses attention back on demand rather than supply,
and leads to calls for protection which would only treat the
symptoms rather than the underlying lack of competitiveness.
In this context the concept of export-led growth can be dan-
gerously misleading since, as Professor Thirlwall correctly
states, it implies that variations in growth rates are explained principally in the long run by variations in rates
of growth of monetary demand. It sustains the idea that demand can create its own supply in the long run, a proposition on which we have sought to cast doubt in Chapters 3 and
4. The so-called balance of payments constraint merely reflects the lack of ability to implement demand-led growth.
But, on a monetarist view of the world, such attempts are
bound to fail even in the closed economy. To demonstrate
that the balance of payments is a real constraint on economic growth, it is necessary to demonstrate how it prevents
the occurrence of exogenous shifts in productivity and competitiveness on the supply side of the economy. So far no
one has explained how and why this may occur.


COMPARATIVE RATES OF ECONOMIC GROWTH

Arguments about the importance of public expenditure and
the balance of payments reflect the search for some *deus ex
machina* that may be prayed to for an explanation of the absolute rate of economy growth in the United Kingdom over the
post-war period, and the relative rates of growth of the industrial countries generally. Britain's own performance has
been attributed to inefficient management, recalcitrant
trades unions, excessive taxation, failure to join the Common Market, lack of competition, too much competition, an
inadequate rate of investment, and a loss of Empire. The
central issue is the extent to which its history of economic
growth reflects a basic supply failure rather than some particular reason or set of reasons that have prevented it from
realising opportunities of technical advance and world market exploitation.

The period from the end of the war up to the late 1960s
may be regarded as something of a golden age for the industrial countries. Stability in the international monetary
system was guaranteed by the stability of the dollar and the
conservatism of American financial policy. Cheap raw materials and energy favoured rapid industrial development.
From a secular point of view, the war stimulated technologi-

cal development in which the United States was the acknow-
ledged leader from the outset. The gap in living standards
between the United States and the rest of the industrial
world offered opportunities that some took and some did not.
The United States was the world leader in terms of both
standards of living and implementation of the best technology. The potential for growth for the rest of the industrial
countries was that much greater, insofar as they had the opportunity to exploit the advantage of a greater proportionate advance in moving closer to the frontier of best
practice. The brand leader was vulnerable to competition in
product design and efficient production, which resulted in
an increasing market share for those countries which were
capable of responding to the challenge. Low productivity
was not a disadvantage in itself. In terms of comparative
disadvantage, the United Kingdom was not in a worse position than the other major industrial countries. The simple
fact of the matter is that, over the period from the end of
the Second World War until the late 1960s, the United Kingdom was less successful than its competitors in closing the
gap between itself and the United States.

In the international market place the decline in Britain's
share of world trade in manufactures is a measure of competitive failure. When attention is focussed on the supply
side of the economy, the most general index of the health of
its manufacturing industry is to be found in the behaviour
of the rate of return on capital employed. The dismal story
of the decline in the rate of return in manufacturing industry is set out in Table 5.13. In absolute terms the decline
in the pre-tax rate of return coincides with the other problems of the economy, including the trend rate of increase in
the unemployment rate from one cycle to another. In comparative terms it is clear that in the United Kingdom the decline in the rate of return began earlier than in other
countries, and fell faster during the 1970s in the face of
the world recession that followed the rise in the price of
oil in 1973.

While it is clear from Table 5.13 that the rate of return
in the United States did not exhibit the same fall as in the
United Kingdom, its association with a relatively slow rate
of growth overall simply reflects the position of the United
States as the technological leader. The gap between the
United States and the rest of the world created opportunities for a period of faster growth for the remainder as they
caught up with the market leader.

One may compare the responses to this challenge on the
part of the United Kingdom on the one hand and West Germany
on the other. In this context we may note the observations

TABLE *5.13* *Net rates of return in manufacturing (per cent) 1960-76*

|  | 1960 | 1965 | 1970 | 1972 | 1973 | 1974 | 1975 | 1976 |
|---|---|---|---|---|---|---|---|---|
| United Kingdom | 18.1 | 14.4 | 9.6 | 9.3 | 7.6 | 4.8 | 2.9 | 2.8 |
| United States | 30.3 | 40.9 | 22.0 | 26.9 | 27.6 | 22.2 | 25.4 | 30.8 |
| Japan | 35.0 | 23.9 | 28.1 | 20.2 | 15.7 | 13.1 | 13.9 | - |
| Germany | 25.7 | 20.4 | 18.2 | 13.4 | 12.9 | 12.7 | 10.0 | 11.4 |
| Italy | 14.7 | 9.7 | 11.5 | 9.9 | - | - | - | - |
| Sweden | 14.2 | 12.2 | 14.6 | 9.8 | 13.3 | 16.9 | 11.7 | 8.2 |

SOURCE T.P. Hill, *Profits and Rates of Return* (OECD, 1979).

made by David Stout.

> The two main differences in the performance between indi-
> vidual industries in Britain and their counterparts in
> Germany are the difference in speed with which it has
> proved possible in German plants to improve techniques
> (and raise direct labour productivity for any given scale
> of production) and their continuing success in designing
> and selling within most product groups increasingly ex-
> pensive products, the demand for which tends to increase
> more sharply over time than does the demand for cheaper
> alternatives.

To put the matter simply, the key differences are direct
productivity and product quality allied to effective mar-
keting. To these we may add a third element, namely the proportion of national resources devoted to productive investment as opposed to consumption.

The evidence is by now widely accepted that non-price competitive factors play a key role in accounting for the weakness of British industry both at home and abroad. The notion
that British competitive difficulties arose from an inappro-
priately valued exchange rate can hardly account for the
growth differentials that were observed. Moreover, it must
be borne in mind that, other things being equal, a shift in
the exchange rate will have some effect of a once-and-for-
all nature, but it is not clear how this can permanently alter the rate of growth. In addition, attempts to stimulate
growth through changes in price competitiveness only further
emphasise the production and sale of goods of a commodity
nature rather than focussing on goods with higher value
added closer to the industrial technological frontier. In
this context the connection between product quality and productivity is important in several respects.

Firstly, observed productivity is in part dependent on
product quality. In this respect, product 'quality' has two
important dimensions, the first reflecting the perceived
value in use by the buyer and the second a high degree of
value added in production. The productivity of capital invested will depend not only on product quality but also on
direct labour productivity. Secondly, this implies that
productivity *ex post*, or comparisons of capital productivity
levels between countries, will reflect a mix of these factors. Thirdly, it is manifestly more agreeable from labour's
point of view to secure productivity increases through increases in product quality rather than through increases in
the productivity of direct labour, the one appearing to
sustain employment and the other to destroy it.

To quote David Stout again,

> ...The fact that over a long period the rate of growth of
> industrial productivity in Britain has been close to that
> of the technical leader, the US, suggests that British in-
> dustrial performance may have been overtaken not because
> it has dropped progressively behind best practice techni-
> ques, but because equivalent industries in rival economies
> have taken advantage of the existence of a technological
> gap to grow unusually fast in the process of narrowing it.
> In the course of realising some of this potential they
> have moved around a well-known virtuous circle, where suc-
> cess removes some of the obstacles to further advance.

In the main this was associated with markedly higher investment ratios as a proportion of Gross National Product
(GNP), and managed in such a way as to yield a productivity
of that investment similar or better over the period to that
of the United States.

Some crude figuring that makes the point is given in Table
5.14, which shows the overall investment ratios of selected
industrial countries, and their average rates of growth over
the period 1953-76. Dividing the growth rate by the investment ratio gives a crude approximation of the overall marginal productivity of investment. From these calculations it
can be seen that, in this respect, all countries did better
than the United States, with the exception of the United
Kingdom, for whom in addition the proportion of output invested was among the lowest. As a matter of arithmetic it
may be noted that, other things being equal, Britain would
have grown roughly as fast as Germany if either the proportion of output invested had been as high as that of Japan,
or if the actual proportion invested had been accompanied by
the marginal productivity of Japan's investment.

Further explanation of the process of the virtuous circle
that goes beyond simple description must inevitably be complex, due to the interrelated character of the variables
with which we are dealing. To say that the United Kingdom's
performance has been poor because investment has been low,
or that the problem with its industry has been low profitability, is simply to raise the question of why this has been
the case. In Mr Stout's view, the fundamental points of entry into the virtuous circle are product quality and direct
labour productivity. Clearly there are major feedback effects to both from investment. Whatever point of entry one
chooses the fact is that higher rates of investment and profitability must be associated in some explicable way with
shifts in product quality and direct labour productivity.

TABLE 5.14   *Investment ratios and marginal productivity of investment 1953–76*

*(average of yearly figures)*

| | % change in real GNP | Investment as % of GNP | Marginal productivity of investment |
|---|---|---|---|
| United States | 3.2 | 14.5 | 0.22 |
| West Germany | 5.0 | 23.7 | 0.21 |
| Netherlands | 5.0 | 23.7 | 0.21 |
| Sweden | 3.7 | 23.0 | 0.16 |
| France | 5.0 | 21.9 | 0.23 |
| Italy | 5.0 | 20.9 | 0.24 |
| Belgium | 4.0 | 20.0 | 0.20 |
| Japan | 8.6 | 30.2 | 0.28 |
| United Kingdom | 2.7 | 17.3 | 0.16 |

SOURCE   D. Kern, 'An International Comparison of Major Economic Trends 1953–76', *National Westminster Bank Review*, May 1978.

This raises the question of whether the behaviour of the system is rooted in behavioural patterns of both management and labour, or whether institutional and structural changes might be encouraged. Advocates of exchange rate depreciation and protection do not explain how they will change the working of the system. Investment incentives as such offer no immediate guarantee that the investment will be productively made rather than that it will lead to further subsidisation of low quality products and inefficient processes.

The argument is also relevant to the contention that a low rate of investment and a low rate of growth have been associated with the form and behaviour of the financial system. The issues have been dealt with at length in evidence to the Wilson Committee and in his 1975 Stockton Lecture by Professor Harold Rose. There is no clear evidence that the rate of investment in the United Kingdom has been the result of a shortage of finance, nor is it clear that, on an international basis, relative success has been associated with a particular form of financial system. In addition to domestic sources of finance, access has been available to international capital markets. The most important factors are the nature and profitability of investment projects rather than a shortage of finance – unless this is a convoluted way of saying that there has been no money to pay for the maintenance of unprofitable business.

It is clear that a higher rate of investment is a necessary but not a sufficient condition for faster economic growth and higher standards of living. Simply investing in existing lines of business and increasing their efficiency may be part of a process of ensuring their survival, but the increased efficiency is more likely to be reflected in reduced costs and less employment than in market expansion. It is largely defensive in character. A healthy basis for future growth and higher living standards requires investment in new business and market creation, where the key lies in the general state of enterprise and business creativity. If that is lacking, no amount of available finance will ensure the achievement of the nation's objectives. If it is lacking, the rate of investment will continue to be low, manifesting itself as a symptom of the underlying difficulties rather than as a result of a lack of financial resources.

# 6 The International Trade and Monetary System

The economic and financial interdependence of countries has never been greater than it is today. Since the Second World War there has been a remarkable rise in the ratio of traded to non-traded goods. The growth and widespread operations of transnational businesses have blurred the distinction between exports and domestic production so that many manufactured goods have assumed the nature of commodities, derived from multiple sources and traded in the generality of world markets. Trade liberalisation and the progressive freeing of restrictions on the movement of capital have played a key role in increasing interdependence, accompanied by the rapid advance in communications and an explosion in international travel.

Such increasing economic interdependence must, however, be set against a background of politically independent nation states, each with its own set of values and specific objectives. Interdependence in an economic sense imposes constraints on the abilities of individual countries to unilaterally pursue what they see as their own economic destinies. The desire to do so may, on occasions, lead to serious problems when the external constraints are ignored. It may also lead to isolationism, through various forms of protectionism, as witnessed by the chaos of the 1930s.

The international monetary and trading system constitutes the framework of trading rules, payments procedures and international credit provision within which individual countries operate. Its efficient operation has profound implications for all trading nations. Its many and varied problems, discussed in this chapter, arise from the inherent potential conflict between national and international interests stemming from this political independence in an interdependent world. An inefficient trading system will prevent the overall exploitation of the world's productive potential and limit the spread of economic welfare. A malfunctioning international monetary system will not only interfere with the

148

development of trade and investment between countries, but
will also make it difficult to adjust to economic shocks
that, from time to time, take place within the system, whether it be the US depression of 1929 or the dramatic rise in
the oil price in 1973. The functioning of the international
monetary system has implications for the general level of
employment in the trading world and for the world's underlying rate of inflation. Such issues cannot be simply contained within the narrow frameworks of individual country boundaries. Trade itself, through its effect on the balance of
payments, has monetary consequences as described in Chapter
4 and these in turn feed back on trade itself. An efficient
system is not in itself a sufficient condition for a sustained increase in general economic prosperity, but it is
certainly necessary.

In this chapter we shall concern ourselves primarily with
the problems of the international trade and monetary system
from a world viewpoint. In Chapter 7 we focus more specifically on the implications of the behaviour of the international system for domestic economic policies. At the international level an efficient system depends on the way in
which it deals with three major concerns.

The first of these concerns is the correction of imbalances, commonly referred to as the *adjustment problem*. The
inter-war period focussed attention on unemployment and, in
particular, on the undesirable consequences of enduring high
unemployment as part of the process of maintaining external
balance. This means that in an efficient international system it should be possible for equilibrium, in a balance of
payments sense, to be brought about between countries with
acceptable overall levels of employment. The second concern
is the arrangements that exist between countries for the
settling of transactions, the media through which international debts are dealt with and the credit arrangements on
which trade is based, which may be described as the *payments*
problem. Thirdly there is the mechanism through which international reserves are created and find their way into the
portfolios of individual countries. The second problem re-
fers to the need for international finance and credit facilities in order to conduct international economic transactions, reflecting the domestic analogue of the role of
money as a means of transaction. But countries, like individuals and companies, also require money balances as a store
of value for precautionary purposes, and as part of a diver-
sified portfolio of asset holdings. This need for reserves
reflects what we may describe as the *liquidity* problem.

The history of the development of the international monetary system since the Second World War reflects attempts to

come to grips with these several problems, although the emphasis on each of them has shifted from period to period. Moreover, the underlying economic problems with which the system has had to deal have also changed. For the first two decades after the war, the prime emphasis in discussion was on the apparent problem of reconciling balance of payments problems with growth and employment together, particularly in the 1960s, with the problem of supplying adequate reserves in the right form to sustain the post-war boom in output and trade. The disturbances of the late sixties and early seventies, on which the rise in the real price of energy was superimposed, shifted immediate attention to the problem of international inflation. The problem of the sixties was thought to be a possible shortage of international liquidity, whereas by the mid-seventies, the emergence of world inflation raised the question of whether liquidity was excessive rather than deficient.

The rise in the real price of oil posed new problems for the international system, because of its inflationary impact across the world as a whole, and because of the danger of a major world collapse as funds were sucked out of the system by the surplus position of the oil-producing countries. The task of 'recycling' the surplus of the oil-producing countries was accompanied by a new concern as to the volatility of large liquid funds owned by the oil-producing countries in the world's financial markets. To many, the existence of the mountain of these petro-dollars constituted a serious potential threat to the stability of international financial markets and orderly exchange rates.

Rather than dealing with the various problems that have arisen in an abstract setting, it is more helpful to deal with them as they have arisen in the course of events. Consequently the first three sections of this chapter deal with the historical development of the international monetary system, following the style of Chapter 2. In the course of historical description it is easier to pick out and exemplify the problems of payments, international adjustment and liquidity. In the two final sections, we focus attention on the problem of balance of payments adjustment and exchange rate regimes, and the issues raised under the heading of 'managed trade'.

THE EARLIER YEARS : 1944-59

We begin with some description of the international system between 1944 and 1959. The period begins with the celebrated agreement concluded at Bretton Woods in 1944 and ends with

the move to full currency convertibility with regard to current transactions in 1959. It reflects, by the standards of
the period following the Great War, a remarkable transition
from war to peace and the economic recovery of Europe and
Japan.

   Peter Oppenheimer and the late Fred Hirsch have written
that

   Major wars normally mark a break in economic and financial
   evolution. World War II did not. It marked rather a con-
   tinuum in the subordination of finance to economic management, which had begun in the 1930s.

This comment reflects the apparent shift from the domination
of 'sound finance' in the years following the Great War,
much influenced by the precepts of good financial and banking principles, to more direct governmental concern and desired influence over the general behaviour of real output
and employment. In the United Kingdom, the influence of
Keynes was dominant, and it was Keynes himself who led the
British negotiations at Bretton Woods. His prime concern
was the creation of an international economic system which
would be compatible with full employment, and which imposed
minimum constraints on the freedom of domestic action to ensure that this objective could be met without undue international strain. His concern was universally shared. But in
practice the negotiations had to take into account the particular dependence of the rest of the world on the United
States.

   The British approach to the design of the post-war monetary system had two distinctive elements. As far as the adjustment process was concerned, there was a belief that
greater exchange rate flexibility should be a key ingredi-
ent. This arose from a fear of the fixed exchange rate system based on gold and, in particular, from the view that the
gold exchange standard operated by Britain after 1925 was a
key factor accounting for the prolonged depression of the
twenties. Thus, rather than adjustments in the balance of
payments taking place through changes in domestic incomes
and prices with a fixed exchange rate, it was the exchange
rate that should be used to achieve external balance. As far
as the liquidity problem was concerned, Keynes had advanced
a scheme for the creation of liquidity at a world level by
the use of a new reserve asset which would be controlled
centrally.

   However, the concern of the United States was not simply
with the question of the relationship between external and
internal policy, but with its own particular position. The

United States was the major creditor at the end of the war, a position that was likely to continue for some time. In this situation, she was concerned that discriminatory action might be used against her, either through competitive depreciation at some stage or, more probably, through trade restrictions. Moreover, as far as international liquidity was concerned, as the chief creditor there appeared a danger of an excessive creation of international credit or reserves, over which the United States would have limited control and in relation to which she would bear the burden.

The upshot was the Bretton Woods Charter, which bears some of the hallmarks of compromise, although the United States had most of its own way. While flexible exchange rates were ruled out, the Articles of Agreement of the International Monetary Fund established currency parities. The dollar provided the anchor for the new system in that the United States agreed to buy and sell gold at the fixed price of $35 a fine ounce. The United States was not expected to deal in foreign exchange markets, but other countries would buy and sell dollars with their own currencies to keep their parities within the agreed limits with the dollar. However, provision was made for the alteration of the parities unilaterally up to 10 per cent, but any change in excess of that required the approval of the Fund. Only if the balance of payments of the country was deemed to be in 'fundamental disequilibrium' would such assent be given. This represented the compromise between the fixed and flexible exchange rate regimes.

As far as the liquidity problem was concerned, quotas were established with the Fund, backed by each country subscribing 75 per cent of their quota in domestic currency and 25 per cent in gold. At the insistence of the United States, these quotas were kept relatively small. There was to be an automatic right of access to the Fund of 25 per cent of the initial quota - the so-called gold tranche - but thereafter Fund approval had to be obtained and certain conditions observed, up to a maximum of 200 per cent of the quota.

The Articles of Agreement also provided for currency convertibility after a transitional period, at least with respect to current account transactions on a non-discriminatory basis. That is to say, individual countries would be required to redeem, if requested, outstanding balances of their currency either in gold or in a denominated currency. Direct trade restrictions on imports from any member country were prohibited except in the special case where a member's currency was deemed to have become 'scarce' in the Fund. However, while convertibility was to become the case as far as current account transactions were concerned, exchange

controls were to be permitted, and indeed encouraged with
regard to the capital account, largely because of the belief
that disorderly capital movements had been a cause of undesirable exchange rate instability in the pre-war period.

The establishment of the Fund, the International Bank for
Reconstruction and Development (the World Bank) and the General Agreement on Tariffs and Trade provided the framework
of the international trade and monetary system for the
peacetime years. With hindsight it is easy to be critical
but, as many commentators observed, it represented the first
concerted attempt for the world to take control of the international system. The subsequent attempts to reform it
have proved in large part more difficult to achieve than the
original conception was to establish.

However it became rapidly obvious, as indeed Keynes had
feared, that the new system would not be capable of dealing
with the post-war difficulties that beset countries, not
only in war-torn Europe, but elsewhere in the world. A dash
for convertibility by Britain in 1947 ended in disaster. The
capacity of the other industrial countries to achieve rapid
trade liberalisation, on which the United States had set its
heart, was fraught with difficulties, and set against a
background of political instability in France and Italy. The
foreign exchange reserves of both European countries and
Japan were rapidly depleted as they sought to finance their
rising deficits with the United States on current account.
In the event, the United States took command of the situation and launched the European Recovery Programme (the Marshall Plan) to make grants and loans available to the European economies over a four-year period.

In return for the Marshall plan, the European economies
were expected to commit themselves to a joint self-help programme, an early fruit of which was the establishment of the
Organisation for European Economic Cooperation (OEEC). In
addition to the Plan, however, the European countries were
encouraged to liberalise trade amongst themselves while
maintaining restrictions on imports from the dollar area. On
the financial side, a European Payments Union was established to facilitate the liberalisation of European trade and
payments on a multilateral basis, while the countries concerned conserved their scarce holdings of gold and dollar
reserves. Additionally in 1949 the United States supported
the devaluation of sterling by 30 per cent and the ensuing
concomitant readjustment of exchange parities with other
countries. Recipients of dollars under the recovery programme were also permitted and encouraged to retain a certain portion of the funds provided to rebuild their reserves, and to pursue policies designed to yield balance of

payments surpluses on current account with the same end.

All this was predicated partly on the immediate and direct need of the European countries and, in another sphere, that of Japan for aid in promoting recovery. It was also based on the view of the United States, widely held in Europe, that the international economic world would be dominated for many years to come by a shortage of dollars. Even as late as the mid-fifties, works of substance relating to the persistence of the dollar problem were being written as far as the eye could see. In fact, as far as Europe was concerned, the direct aid obtained through the Marshall Plan was not replaced when the four-year period of the Plan came to an end. This loss was partly offset by a substantial flow of dollars emanating from the United States' military aid in the first six years of the fifties.

Meanwhile, the economic recovery of Europe in general was dramatic. Industrial production in the OEEC countries between 1952 and 1960 grew by 60 per cent. With the notable exception of the United Kingdom, productivity increases outstripped those in the United States by a substantial margin. The growing strength of the outside world permitted it to ride two — by historical standards — relatively mild American recessions, in 1953/4 and 1957/8, with scarcely an interruption in economic progress. At the other end of the world Japan, having benefited from American aid, encouragement to pursue trade discrimination and the direct favourable impact of the Korean War, doubled its share of world exports during the 1950s. By the end of the decade, Japan also was poised to exploit the opportunities of expanding trade that the sixties were about to bring.

Thus, by the end of the fifties, the post-war recovery outside the United States was well and truly complete. Despite this fact, progress toward liberalising trade with the dollar area was not as fast as one might have expected, and it was not until 1959 that the post-war provisional arrangements were completely abandoned. Meanwhile the overall United States balance of payments continued in deficit, although with a substantial surplus on trading account. The reserves of the European and other countries grew during the fifties, with the result that by 1959 the aim of convertibility — at least as far as current account transactions was concerned — was at last reached. The dollar had become the principal reserve currency, and the system of fixed parities following the bout of devaluations in 1949 was substantially in place. After a slow start, the Fund had begun to operate in the style that had been expected of it, including making substantial loans to the United Kingdom and France in 1957 and 1958 as both the closure of the Suez

Canal and the Algerian war made an impact on payments positions. On the surface, it might have appeared that all was
well. However, at the peak of achievement, cracks in the
system began to appear, although it was another twelve years
before it finally split asunder.

THE MIDDLE YEARS : 1959-71

With the advent of the sixties, the international monetary
system came under increasing pressure. The underlying forces
that pointed to the need for change were rooted in the fundamental shift in the balance of economic power already seen
in the fifties, which continued in the period under review.
The fifties had reflected the economic dominance of the United States *vis-à-vis* the rest of the world, a position that
had subsequently been eroded. The United States had become
the world's banker and, apart from such increases in the
supply of gold that took place, the major creator of international reserves. Insofar as the underlying trade position
of the United States remained strong, and the dollar shortage persisted, the overall deficit on the American balance
of payments appeared both desirable and acceptable. However,
as time went on, the position on trade deteriorated as the
competitive position of the rest of the world improved. In
addition, the net outflow from the American balance of payments as a whole no longer materially reflected the giving
of aid both for military and for economic purposes, but was
substantially the result of a major outflow of private capital.

From an historical point of view, the first sign of unease
within the system was the flurry in the London gold market
in October 1960. The price in that market had normally been
directly related to the official price of $35 a fine ounce
around which, as we have seen, the initial currency parities
had been set after the war. The buying and selling of gold
by the United States Treasury had maintained this relationship between the so-called private and official markets for
gold. In October 1960 the market price broke free and reached a level of $40 an ounce, reflecting the operations of
certain central European banks which now found themselves
with excess dollars which they wished to convert through the
open market rather than exercising official conversion
rights with the United States.

Apart from the fact that these banks believed their holdings of dollars to be excessive, the episode also reflected
the increasingly unfavourable attitude of the United States
towards official conversion of dollars into gold. The United

States authorities themselves were beginning to be nervous
about the American balance of payments and this increased as
the sixties wore on. In the event, the cracks were papered
over by the formation of the so-called gold pool, which was
a joint arrangement between the United States and seven
other countries to buy and sell gold in the market with the
aim of stabilising the free market price at the official
rate of $35.

While this episode was successfully managed, it reflected
a fundamental weakness in the Bretton Woods arrangements
which dominated the sixties, namely that it failed to provide any explicit mechanism through which international reserves could grow in line with world trade and output. The
quota system established with the Fund had done nothing to
deal with the long-term liquidity problem that we identified
earlier. During the fifties, there had been something of a
problem insofar as there had been a perceived shortage of
dollars. However, the outflow of dollars had been sufficient
not only to deal with the problem of imbalance between the
United States and the rest of the world, but also to enable
the rest of the world to build up acceptable reserves. The
basic problem of the sixties was the validity of this mechanism of supplying reserves and the dependence of the value
of those reserves on the activity of the United States.

The recognition of this problem is widely and correctly
ascribed to Robert Triffin. The 'Triffin dilemma' was posed
as follows. The world was dependent on the United States'
overall deficit for the supply of reserves. However, if this
process were to continue, the reserve liabilities of the
United States would rise relative to its reserve assets. The
credibility of the dollar as a reserve asset ultimately depended on the commitment of the United States to the gold
exchange standard under which dollars might be converted
into gold at the official market price. But, as the dollar
liabilities grew concomitantly with a weakening in the underlying American balance of payments, there were fears that
the value of their dollar holdings in relation to gold might
change.

The other horn of the dilemma lay in the fact that, if the
reserve centre sought to try and strengthen its own reserve
position, for example by deflationary action designed to improve the underlying balance of payments, there would be a
double consequence of a deflationary impact on the world at
large and a cutting off of the source of reserve growth. As
a consequence of this Triffin proposed a scheme, in principle not unlike that-proposed by Keynes at Bretton Woods, for
the creation of a new reserve asset on an international
basis under the aegis of the International Monetary Fund.

While the Triffin proposal was not accepted, the basic argument was echoed elsewhere, notably in France, which had emerged as the major critic of the gold exchange standard as it was practised.

The particular position of the United States and, to a lesser extent, the United Kingdom as creators of reserve currencies focussed attention on the asymmetry that existed between the countries that had predominantly surpluses on their overall balance of payments, and those that had deficits. The general problem was the establishment of some kind of global equilibrium in the balance of payments positions of individual countries at an acceptable level of output and employment, i.e. the solution of the adjustment problem that we have already defined. Insofar as the deficits of the deficit countries resulted in the acceptability of the net currency outflows as international reserves without redemption either in gold or some other currency, there was — it was said — no pressure on the deficit countries to put their houses in order.

The consequences of this, it was argued, were two-fold. Firstly, the deficit countries were accused of exporting inflation since the absorption of foreign currency without redress imposed problems of maintaining internal monetary control, and the subsequent lack of monetary control made the control of inflation difficult. Secondly, the reserve status of the currency in effect gave its owner a licence to print international money. Since much of the currency created passed overseas in the form of overseas investment, a graphic description of what was going on was that money was being printed to take over other people's industry.

The debate that sharpened during the sixties produced two answers to these accusations. Firstly, it was argued that the burden of adjustment should be shared between the surplus and the deficit countries, and no attempt had been made by the surplus countries to make their contribution. Secondly, it was argued that part of the problem of the outflow of capital from the United States stemmed from the fact that the surplus countries had not opened their own capital markets sufficiently to outside borrowers.

The last major problem of the sixties also stemmed from the initial weakness of the Bretton Woods agreement, in particular from the compromise reached on the balance between fixed and floating exchange rates. The original agreement laid the foundation for exchange rate changes to take place in discrete jumps, with a subsequent *de facto* assumption that such changes would not take place in other than exceptional circumstances. This provided the basis for extreme and successful speculation against the value of cur-

rencies and sharp and destabilising movements of short-term
capital. Since exchange rate changes were looked on as taking place *in extremis*, their direction became obvious, and
the problem of assessing the upside or downside risk of a
particular currency became simplified. Advance warnings of
possible changes made it possible to take up substantial un-
covered positions *vis-à-vis* the future movement of a particular currency with virtually no risk. Speculators were in
effect given a one-way bet, a fact which gave rise to problems both in relation to the pound sterling and to the German mark. Governments were faced with the difficulty of
either adjusting the parity at the first sign of pressure,
which was inconsistent with the spirit of the Articles of
the Fund, or sitting the storm out in the hope that events
would subsequently make the problem go away. The result was
a desperate and sometimes frenetic commitment to maintaining
currency parities, with the implication that an ultimate adjustment of the exchange rate represented something of a de-
feat for the government concerned and for the system as a
whole.

These interrelated problems weave through the international economic history of the middle years. They begin with an
increased concern in Washington with the overall United
States balance of payments, which coincided with the elec-
tion of President Kennedy in 1960. From being the beneficent
provider of resources for post-war recovery, the United
States moved into a position of defence of the existing system. Paradoxically, the Administration recognised the position of the United States as the banker of the world, yet
drew the conclusion that, in the future, the position of the
balance of payments should be an important factor dictating
the general conduct of economic affairs.

The formation of the gold pool already referred to was the
first of a number of expedients adopted by the United States
to preserve the *status quo* or, as some commentators put it,
to avoid any decision on the value of the dollar in terms of
gold. To sustain the dollar, the Administration indicated
its own willingness to borrow from the Fund should that be
deemed necessary. In conjunction with this, a new agreement
(General Arrangements to Borrow) was negotiated to enlarge
the potential resources of the Fund, at the discretion of
ten major countries, should the United States seek to exercise its drawing rights in the Fund and thus exceed the
Fund's existing resources of usable currencies. A variety of
measures were adopted to strengthen the overall balance of
payments. A network of 'swap' arrangements or reciprocal
credit facilities were negotiated by the Federal Reserve
Bank of New York. An interest equalisation tax was intro-

duced to discourage the purchase of overseas securities by
United States residents. Special United States Treasury
securities were issued, denominated in foreign currency to
avoid the exchange risk (the so-called Roosa bonds after the
American Treasury Under-Secretary who invented them). Other
minor measures were taken, both to strengthen the balance of
payments and to discourage the investment of American capital abroad.

Such measures contributed to shoring up the system and
dealt with the short-term pressures as they arose. But, in
themselves, they did not - and indeed were not designed to -
tackle any of the major deficiencies in the system outlined
above. Moreover, it can be argued that in alleviating the
short-term problems by the various means employed, the overall system was being progressively weakened. With hindsight,
it might be said that the very pursuit of such measures de-
liberately taken to maintain the status quo only made its
weakness more apparent. Moreover, they served to emphasise
that while in the fifties the asymmetry that had arisen between the United States and the rest of the world had largely emerged voluntarily in response to the needs of the time,
the system was now being sustained by the United States as a
deliberate act of policy. In the light of the increased economic strength of the other industrial countries, what appeared to be a unilateral decision by the United States to
maintain its position as the world's banker was unacceptable
without discussion and without conditions, although it was
not always clear what those conditions were.

Notwithstanding these developments, the issue of reform of
the international monetary system was on the international
agenda as the sixties unfolded. In 1962 Britain's own
Chancellor of the Exchequer, Reginald Maudling, had proposed
the development of a new reserve asset into which dollars
could be converted. The issue of liquidity was discussed in
a Fund study in 1964 and by the deputies of what was known
as the Group of Ten countries. At the Fund's meeting in
1964, the issue of reform became more alive and the align-
ment of the respective parties clearer. The French were in
favour of re-emphasising the importance of gold and the
creation of a new reserve asset linked to it. On balance,
the Americans were lukewarm toward the creation of any new
asset.

The intricate details of the subsequent negotiations are
beyond the scope of this book. Suffice it to say that, after
protracted meetings and debates, it was agreed in March 1968
that a new supplement to existing reserve assets in the Fund
should be created as Special Drawing Rights. SDRs were not
to be backed by currencies since it was their general

acceptability that ensured their success or failure. Nor
were they to be related to gold as the French had hoped. Nor
again was their distribution to be related to the deficit
position of individual countries, but distributed across the
board to the members of the Fund according to quota. In July
1969 it was agreed that $9.3 billion of SDRs (one SDR=$1)
would be distributed over a three-year period, beginning in
1970.

But the fat was effectively in the fire. While debates on
the future of international liquidity continued, the central
problem of adjustment had already reared its ugly head. The
devaluation of the pound sterling in 1967 pulled the first
brick out of the fixed exchange rate wall. Fear that a similar fate could befall the dollar, despite the difficulties
inherent in such a development, set the gold market alight.
A weakening American balance of payments under pressure from
the war in Vietnam, coupled with the uncertainty as to the
fate of the system, put heavy pressure on the American gold
reserves. A solution was cobbled up, resulting in a two-tier
price system in the gold market, one for private and the
other for official monetary transactions. Uproar in France
in 1968 added to the difficulties of maintaining parity between the franc and the mark. In 1969 pressure on the mark
followed by the guilder resulted in an upward float and re-
pegging of both currencies. The franc was devalued, and the
stage was set for the last gasp of the system as it was. By
1970-71, the American balance of payments was again in deep
deficit. American banks were busy repaying the debts that
they had incurred during the late sixties by borrowing
through their branches abroad. The fall became an avalanche
and, in August 1971, President Nixon formally suspended the
convertibility of the dollar into gold. It was the end of
an era.


FROM SMITHSONIAN ONWARDS

The American reaction to the crisis was sharp and decisive.
Along with the decision to suspend convertibility of the
dollar into gold went a 10 per cent surcharge on imports and
the disallowance of capital investment overseas for tax purposes. Despite the protests from elsewhere, the United
States took a hard line, and there followed four months of
American intransigence built around the personality of the
then United States Secretary of the Treasury, John Connally.
Only by the end of 1971 had matters calmed down sufficiently
to complete the task of negotiating a new set of exchange
rates in the Smithsonian Institute in Washington.

The Smithsonian agreement was based on a new technique of multi-currency realignment. In practice there is no real answer to the question of how much the dollar was devalued, or other currencies appreciated. The French had been insisting for some time that the dollar should be devalued, and this seemed to assume a symbolic importance out of proportion to the reality of the problem. The upshot was a series of net appreciations of the other major currencies against the dollar, although not to the extent that the Americans had hoped. The devaluation element was reflected in a rise in the official dollar price of gold from $35 to $38 an ounce. The 10 per cent surcharge was suspended forthwith. Henceforth the band of fluctuation around the par values of currencies was raised from 1 to $2\frac{1}{2}$ per cent. In grand style, President Nixon hailed the agreement as 'the most significant monetary agreement in the history of the world' which finally set the world on a thoroughgoing dollar standard. However its durability bore no relation to the glowing terms in which the President had greeted its conclusion.

The tension throughout had reflected the continental European countries' belief in a system of fixed parities against a growing feeling in the United States in favour of more flexibility. A move to greater flexibility, even if only visible through the wider bands of possible fluctuation, cut across the incipient plans of the European Economic Community for exchange rate fixity and eventual monetary union. In particular, the so-called Werner Plan for European monetary union was still on the table. The European response to this apparent step backward was to create what became known as the snake inside the tunnel. The effect of the Smithsonian agreement on fluctuating bands was to permit a maximum fluctuation of 9 per cent between two European currencies, if one fell from the top of the band to the bottom, while another rose vice versa. The snake provided for more limited movement so that, when the weaker currency fell to a discount of $2\frac{1}{4}$ per cent on its parity based on a given currency, the strongest currency should be used to purchase the weakest. The snake came into being in March 1972. It comprised the Six and, in addition, the United Kingdom, Denmark and Eire.

As in the case of the devaluation of 1967, it was the United Kingdom that took a significant step that had repercussions throughout the system, by floating the pound. Britain's current account had moved into deficit at a time when the government was concerned to expand the economy and reduce unemployment. The fear was that the expansion would be cut off by the deteriorating payments position, as had happened several times before. In practice, given the massive

increase in the supply of money that was under way in the
United Kingdom, there was really little choice. As in 1967,
the final outcome was the response to an excessively lax
fiscal and monetary policy which was incompatible with a
stable value of the currency. In floating sterling, the United Kingdom withdrew both from the snake and from the tunnel. Moreover, the decision to float sterling also meant the
end of the sterling area, since only about a dozen of the
sixty-five countries that hitherto pegged their exchange
rates to sterling continued to do so.

For the rest of 1972, the world outside remained calm.
However, in the first quarter of 1973, the foreign exchange
markets of the world began to take fright again. The gold
price in the free market rose sharply, and a further flight
from the dollar was in progress. By March, the brief reign
of the dollar standard was over. Germany revalued 3 per cent
against her snake partners, and the members of the snake
agreed a joint float. The practice of countries varied,
either floating freely against the dollar or, in some cases,
sticking with it. The general practice of pegging against
the dollar was at an end.

The reasons for the collapse of the Smithsonian agreement
were several. Despite the effective devaluation of the dollar in 1971, Germany and Japan had continued to take in vast
amounts in dollar reserves. The adjustment process simply
did not seem to be working although, ironically, the
strength of the United States trade recovery became apparent
in the autumn of 1973. Moreover, the events of 1971 had palpably reduced the long-term confidence in the dollar required by the system as a standard against which to peg. The
feeling was that what had already happened could happen
again and, in an international game of pass-the-parcel, no
one wanted to be left excessively exposed to further dollar
devaluation should the case arise. In addition, there had
been a long-standing argument about the need for more or
less active participation in foreign exchange markets to
maintain the parities. The European complaint was of American inactivity, leaving the burden of correction to fall
elsewhere. In part, this no doubt reflected a growing attitude in the United States towards letting the market look
after itself. One way of interpreting events is to argue
that the United States was in effect preparing to float.

The question of an overall reform of the monetary system
had been mooted by the British Chancellor of the Exchequer,
Anthony Barber, at the Fund meeting in 1971. The American
response was not encouraging. However, the tide turned and,
in July 1972, the Governors of the Fund established a Committee of Twenty, under the chairmanship of Jeremy Morse, to

undertake an overall re-examination of the workings of the system. The Committee embarked on a new 'Grand Design' for the international monetary system. The results of this lengthy enquiry appeared in June 1974. By then it had been blown far off course from its original terms of reference, firstly by the financial crisis of 1973, followed by general floating, and secondly by the dramatic consequences of the rise in the price of oil later in the year. Against this background, it was hardly propitious to advance any new scheme based on a return to fixed parities, given the fact that floating was already taking place, and given the differential impact of the oil crisis across countries.

Despite the passage of events, there remained a number of basic reasons why agreement was bound to be difficult. The disposition toward floating on the part of the United States has already been mentioned. While there were many who saw, and wished for, the period of floating after March 1973 to be temporary, there were many officials, politicians and academics in America who wished the perceived experiment to persist and who, after recent experience, had developed a hands-off rather than a hands-on posture in the international field. Secondly, even those in America who were favourably disposed toward a return to fixed parities in some form, were not prepared to envisage such a development without assurance, possibly in the form of sanctions which would ensure that adjustment burdens would be equally shared between the surplus and deficit countries. At the back of the discussion there was, on the part of the Europeans, an unacceptable tacit assumption that their surpluses would persist, a position that is perhaps understandable given the history of the previous decade. Thirdly, in the process of establishing some new reserve asset, or widening the role of SDRs to the point that the dollar became simply one currency among many, there was no apparent solution to the problem of how to deal with the large amount of dollars already in reserve portfolios, the so-called overhang problem. It was unacceptable that the United States should redeem its dollars by running a trade surplus on the back of an undervalued dollar, and it was not easy to agree that the dollars would be redeemed in SDRs, thus transferring former American liabilities to the other member countries.

But, technical questions aside, there was a further overriding issue bearing on the question of international liquidity and currency reform, and that was the rate of inflation. Bretton Woods and much of its aftermath, including the discussions that took place during the sixties, focussed attention on the implications of the international monetary system for the behaviour of output and employment. As exem-

plified by the quotation from Oppenheimer and Hirsch at the
outset of this chapter, the post-war period continued to reflect a major shift in thought and emphasis from the financial consequences of international money to its influence on
management of the real economy. The failure of the system
owing to lack of adjustment or, more immediately, to a lack
of liquidity, was perceived almost solely in terms of depression and unemployment. Even the French concern with the
role of gold as a stabilising factor in the growth of world
money owed more to political considerations relating to the
balance of power between the United States and the rest of
the world, than to a direct concern that the failure of the
international monetary system might be seen not immediately
in depression but in runaway inflation with depression as a
consequence.

With the rapid rise in commodity prices in 1972 and 1973,
and the rise in the price of oil, opinion grew that the major concern could be too much rather than too little liquidity. Against this background, some influential views saw
no need, and indeed positive disadvantage, in promoting the
wider use of Special Drawing Rights. Thus the work of the
Committee of Twenty was accompanied by a preoccupation with
more immediate issues, and by an emerging lack of interest
in additional international credit. Both these stemmed in
part from the same sources, namely the increasing concern
with inflation and the new problems resulting from the price
of oil.

Indeed, the rise in the price of oil - while highlighting
the difficult issue of inflation - had a direct effect in
alleviating concern over the excessive supply of dollars.
The general rise in the dollar value of imports, both on
account of commodity price increases and the rise in the
price of oil, reduced the import cover that dollar holdings
represented. In addition, there was the important fact that
oil imports were paid for with dollars, and this created a
new demand for the currency. Of course, in other respects,
both then and subsequently the rise in the oil price posed
serious problems for the dollar and for the United States
economy. But in the shorter run some pressure was taken off
the excess supply of dollar liquidity and this, too, contributed to a lack of interest in the creation of additional
reserve facilities. Inflation discouraged the issue of SDRs
*on top of* existing liquidity. The greater need for dollars
discouraged the issue of SDRs *in substitution for* existing
liquidity.

The oil problem itself presented a major challenge to the
existing monetary system, one for which the decision to
float currencies had little or no relevance. It was impossi-

ble for the non-oil countries to deal with the problem by
devaluing against the oil producers, insofar as the latter
were quite incapable of balance of payments adjustment by
offsetting the oil revenues through higher imports. Short of
cutting off the supply of oil, there was no alternative for
the oil producers other than to lend their surpluses abroad
and, to this extent, the deficits of the rest of the world
on oil account were automatically financed. Of course, that
was not the end of the story since the distribution of oil-
country deposits obviously failed to match the needs of individual countries as they arose. Official facilities created through the Fund and the World Bank made some contribution to dealing with individual needs but, in many cases,
the would-be borrowers were not prepared to incur the restrictions that might be placed on them if they sought official finance. In the event, the greater part of the provision of facilities, insofar as they can be identified, was
undertaken through the operations of the private banking
system. Large dollar deposits were made, particularly with
Euro-banks, and then lent to individual countries.

On the first round of oil price increases, the operation
must be reckoned a major success. It was not, however, without its difficulties, since there was a limit to the debts
of this kind that banks wished to hold in their portfolios
and, in addition, such an expansion of lending created pressure on the capital base of the banking system. On top of
this, the presence of the mass of petro-dollars created
potential instability insofar as, remaining liquid, they
might be rapidly transferred from one financial centre to
another, with consequent effects on interest and exchange
rates. In some cases, such as the United Kingdom and Italy,
recourse had to be made to the Fund on a large scale. But
this did not reflect the impact of the rise in the price
alone. The difficulties that both countries suffered were
rooted in the fiscal and monetary policies that they followed in response to the oil price rise.

For the various reasons outlined above, the pressure for
the 'Grand Design' that had led to the establishment of the
Committee of Twenty in 1972 melted away. The climax to the
subsequent period of extended negotiation came in January
1976 at a meeting of the Interim Committee of the Fund in
Jamaica. Agreement to amend the Articles of the Fund in
order to formally permit floating had already been achieved.
Action had also been agreed on in 1975 to deal with the
contentious question of gold, another chapter in the long-
drawn-out story of the American wish to 'demonetise' gold
and dispense with its role in international financial
transactions, and the French desire to sustain it in some
way. A compromise was reached. One sixth of the Fund's hold-

ings of gold was to be sold for the benefit of developing countries, and a further sixth was restored to Fund members. There would be no official action to peg the price of gold for at least a two-year period, and the stock of gold in the hands of the ten major countries and the Fund was not to be increased. The agreement in Jamaica tidied up the details and, far from establishing a new 'Grand Design', effectively legalised the realities of floating exchange rates and the role of gold that had come to exist after the collapse of the dollar standard in 1973. The Bretton Woods system was officially buried.

These developments did not of course dispose of the underlying and recurrent economic problems to which they were a reaction. Almost immediately in 1976 sterling was plunged into crisis and, in November of that year, the Fund had to be called upon. As has already been noted, the crisis was not directly related to any further short-comings of the international monetary system as such, but to the excessively expansionary monetary policies pursued by the United Kingdom in an attempt to spend its way out of the deflationary consequences of the rise in the oil price, sterling suffering the same fate that befell the Swedish krona for the same reasons. The subsequent strengthening of sterling was attributable initially to a reversal of previous policies and to a sharp deceleration of domestic monetary growth through 1977, and subsequently to the shift brought about by the development of North Sea oil. Subsequently, the problem of sterling seemed to have become a different one, in the face of the further leap in oil prices at the end of 1978. Concern was now expressed at the 'overvaluation' of sterling when considered in terms of the trade account bolstered by a large capital inflow on the back of the oil reserves.

As the seventies drew to a close, the central focus was again on the persistence of the imbalance between the strong surplus countries, Germany and Japan, and the deficit countries, particularly the United States. Relatively rapid growth in the United States, combined with further increases in the price of oil, created a new dollar problem and fears about the lack of capacity of the monetary system to bring about the necessary adjustments. In some quarters, this produced a call for an examination of 'planned trade'. In the European Economic Community, the perceived instability of exchange rates led to the proposals for a new European Monetary System. These issues and the current state of affairs are taken up in the discussion that follows.

## EXCHANGE RATE SYSTEMS AND ADJUSTMENT

As we have seen in our survey of events, a large part of the time up to 1970 was spent discussing the international monetary system in terms of the problems of reserve creation and international liquidity. A much smaller portion of the time was devoted to discussion of the adjustment problem, and particularly the exchange rate regime. In the sixties in particular, attitudes toward exchange rate fixity became ossified in defence of the dollar and the gold exchange standard as it operated. The advent of more general floating in 1973 was imposed on grave uncertainty as to how the system might operate. There was a sense of venturing into uncharted waters in which dangerous reefs might lurk, any one of which might plunge the system into further instability and chaos.

The reaction in some quarters to managed floating in its earlier years was one of marked relief in that none of the supposed reefs were in fact struck. At the outset there was no collapse in the development of world trade and investment, attributable to the change in the international monetary system as such. The world survived the sharp recession of 1975 which was largely due to the deflationary impact of the rise in the price of oil and, in 1976, world output bounced back sharply. The rate of inflation fell everywhere from the post-oil-crisis peaks, and the storm appeared to have been weathered. However, as time has gone on, opinion has become less favourable. The further problem of the dollar, the apparent persistence of imbalance between the deficit and surplus countries and - by historical standards relatively sharp movements of currencies in international markets, created a hankering after greater exchange rate fixity and backward-looking glances were tinged with regret. The European Economic Community returned to its original theme of currency stability between the trading partners, manifesting itself in the proposals for the European Monetary System, which came into being in January 1979. Moreover, as we shall see later, while by the mid-seventies there was some self-congratulation that the crisis of 1973 had not been followed by extensive controls on trade and beggar-thy-neighbour policies of the thirties, in fact over the period since 1974 there has been a persistent growth in the proportion of managed trade as the protectionist tide has encroached on the sands of free trade. A balanced view would suggest that the period of managed floating has not proved the disaster that some feared, but has proved disappointing to those who placed great hope and expectation upon it.

In discussing alternative exchange rate regimes, it is important to recall that fixity as against flexibility is a matter of degree. Even in purely theoretical terms, a country cannot in general unilaterally choose to have a fixed exchange rate irrespective of the domestic financial and trade policies that it pursues. If it chooses to peg its currency against another then, on the assumption that it is operating in a free market, such a policy of pegging will prescribe limits of behaviour that its domestic policies must observe. In the long run all exchange rates are variable. The more pertinent issue is not between fixity and floating, but between stability and instability of exchange rate behaviour. If for one reason or another a preference is indicated for stable rates, the question of how this might best be achieved arises. It does not follow logically from this that the best way of achieving exchange rate stability is by some form of institutionalisation such as the system that emerged in the post-war period, or on a regional basis such as the European Monetary System.

Moreover, in between the polar aims of complete stability and free floating, there is a wide spectrum of possibilities which imply more or less flexibility in exchange rate behaviour. As explained in Chapter 4, under a free floating exchange rate system, in theory, two important conclusions follow. The first is that the liquidity problem disappears. There is no need for official reserves since the overall balance of payments is maintained in constant equilibrium as the exchange rate reflects the interaction of the total demand and supply of foreign exchange. The second is that the individual economy gains control over its domestic money supply and effective choice over its own inflation rate. In practice, neither of these things is likely to occur completely. Indeed, it has been argued that, since the move to more general floating after 1973, there has in practice been more rather than less intervention on official account in foreign exchange markets than previously. The need for reserves has not apparently diminished since much of Bretton Woods has been swept away. Free floating has by no means been observed. Moreover while in practice more flexible exchange rates have done something to insulate the domestic economic policies of individual countries from the world outside, that insulation has been far from complete.

We should also bear in mind the important distinction between changes in nominal and real exchange rates. Correspondingly we should recall the distinction clearly drawn by Keynes and set out in Chapter 4, namely that exchange rates may be altering as the result of monetary changes relative to the outside world, or because of fundamental changes in

productivity and efficiency that occur in the real economy.
Insofar as relative real efficiency remains constant, it was
pointed out in Chapter 4 that fluctuations in the nominal
exchange rate brought about by monetary changes will, in the
long run, have no effect on the balance of payments. The
consequence of such change will be borne entirely by the
general price level. However, it is wrong to conclude from
this that, since it cannot affect the balance of payments
adjustment process, exchange rate flexibility is at best use-
less and at worst undesirable, since it will only encourage
inflation. While it may be true that in the long run nominal
exchange rate changes with no change on the real supply side
will be fully reflected in prices, what evidence there is
suggests that, even on this assumption, the period of adjustment is in years rather than in months. Consequently,
nominal exchange rate changes can alter the real exchange
rate over a time scale that may be regarded as relevant to
economic policy-making. It may from time to time in the
short run prove to be better to permit exchange rates to
absorb both real and monetary shocks to which individual
economies are exposed while, in the long run, flexibility
should exist to cope with longer-run trends that reflect
fundamental shifts in real price competitiveness.

The argument that floating or more flexible exchange
rates are inherently inflationary is clearly at the back of
the minds of many who advocate a return to some institutionalised form of fixity. In retrospect, there is something
of a paradox here. It is arguable that the gold exchange
standard, as practised in the fifties and early sixties when
accompanied by a conservative American monetary policy, was
a key factor in stabilising the overall rate of inflation
in the industrial countries over that period. At the same
time, it has been argued that the system was inherently
inflationary. Even before the dollar outflow associated with
the war in Vietnam, the United States was accused of using
the system to export inflation. On this view, the period of
persistently high inflation rates that began in 1969 was
attributed to the behaviour of the international monetary
system. The counter-argument advanced by certain American
commentators was that European monetary expansion and subsequent inflation were the result of domestic monetary policies, rather than the result of the dollar outflow. As a
practical matter, it is difficult to escape the conclusion
that the system as operated in the fifties and sixties, when
combined with American financial conservatism, was stabilising, and that the disturbances of the late sixties and
early seventies were conducive to a general weakening of
monetary discipline.

It has been argued that this assertion is inconsistent
with the evidence, if applied to the United Kingdom, on the
ground that Britain persistently inflated faster than her
trading partners, and frequently provoked foreign exchange
crises. However, this can partly be explained by the under-
valuation of the pound in 1949 and the stop/go precisely
reflected the imposition of discipline and deflationary
measures designed to protect the currency. The fact that, in
the end, the brink was crossed does not invalidate the importance of the influence in earlier years.

However, none of this points logically to the conclusion
that some form of fixity is inherently desirable. On the
assumption that fundamental changes on the supply side take
place relatively slowly, the most important cause of exchange rate fluctuations and variations in relative inflation rates is likely to be found in unstable and divergent
patterns of monetary growth between countries. Stability in
both inflation and exchange rates needs to be rooted in the
pursuit and maintenance of realistic monetary growth rates.
In principle at any rate, the pursuit of such policies by
individual countries does not require any major institutional change from the present system. Such a view has not
been shared by members of the EEC, and the creation of the
European Monetary System has been the result.

The EMS can be looked at from several different points of
view. In the shorter run it can be perceived as an attempt
to deal with the problem of unstable exchange rate regimes
reflecting in part arguments of the kind discussed above
with regard to monetary discipline. Secondly, it can be seen
in politico-economic terms as picking up the thread of
thought manifest in the Werner Plan of 1970. The scheme itself required member countries to keep their currencies
within a narrow band around fixed rates. A new European Currency Unit (ECU) was to be created, backed by deposits of
gold and dollar reserves from the individual members, in
terms of which the rates of exchange of national currencies
would be expressed. The original scheme also contained a
proposal to constitute a European Monetary Fund which would
control the supply of ECUs, and also their issue to deficit
countries in excess of their original reserve deposits.

It is important to grasp the essentially political character of the EMS which, at the same time, is both its vice and
its virtue, depending one one's stance in relation to the
Community. In essence, there is a strong analogy between
what is proposed for the EMS and for the International Monetary Fund itself. In this sense, the proposal stands as an
integral part of the movement toward European unity and it
is largely on this ground alone that much of the argument

concerning Britain's entry into the EMS has been advocated. The analogy with the decision for the United Kingdom to join the EEC is also very strong. In that case, much argument based on an economic calculus was put forward to justify entry, the substance of which was very hard to evaluate.

The case for joining the EMS is equally hard to make on purely economic grounds. As already pointed out, it is not at all clear that a general case for exchange rate fixity can be made, as opposed to the more general case for exchange rate and price stability, supported by sensible national policies with regard to monetary control. Moreover, in the light of the fundamentals of sound underlying monetary policies, the immediate outcome smacks of putting the cart before the horse. Convergent monetary policies could ultimately ensure exchange rate stability between the member countries. However, fixing rates at the outset, before the process of monetary adjustment has been achieved, puts patently unsatisfactory strains on the overall system. In some respects, it might have made more sense to have pegged European currencies explicitly against the mark, and to have developed the use of the mark as an additional reserve currency, a step that Germany was really not prepared to take. To move responsibility for European monetary stability away from the IMF to the EMS is hardly in the spirit of present international needs. In terms of economic theory, it is not always the case that half a loaf is better than no bread, and an international monetary system without the dollar resembles the performance of Hamlet without the Prince of Denmark. Against this background, any argument for the EMS must be rooted in its political implications.

In considering the overall balance of payments adjustment process and the role of alternative exchange rate systems, a key issue to be resolved concerns the nature of persistent imbalances. In particular, it is important to reach a conclusion as to whether such imbalances emerge from some underlying structural problem that is reflected in the supply side of the world economic system, or whether the problems largely stem from the way in which the financial system operates.

The theory of balance of payments adjustment in the context of the monetary approach to the balance of payments was discussed at length in Chapter 4. The general conclusion was that the balance of payments was essentially a monetary phenomenon and reflected imbalances in monetary behaviour between countries. In the absence of government intervention, in a floating exchange rate system, the coordination of monetary policies across countries should in principle enable balance of payments problems between countries to be resolved

while, at the same time, restraining overall world monetary
growth in line with productive capacity, so ensuring general world price, exchange rate and monetary stability. Such
a world would not imply a fixity of exchange rates, but
would permit exchange rate adjustments to long-term changes
in fundamental competitiveness.

In practice, there are major political obstacles to the
efficient working of such a system. The institutionalisation
of fixed parities represents one kind of attempt to ensure
an arm's length form of coordination although, for reasons
already advanced, it is not clear that this is necessarily
either the best or the most feasible route to go on a world
scale. However, at present, excessive intervention in
foreign exchange markets, combined with sterilisation and a
reluctance to allow inter-country currency flows to be reflected in changes in domestic money supplies, mean that the
system functions relatively inefficiently.

However there are those who believe that the problems are
inherently structural and stem from a basic imbalance of
economic power and competitiveness which is getting worse
over time. Such a diagnosis, coupled with a conclusion that
the world requires protectionism and managed trade, is discussed at length in the next section. Here we are concerned
with a particular form of the argument propounded by John
Forsyth.

Forsyth's analysis focusses *ab initio* on three issues. The
first is to note that, as described in Chapter 4, the post-
war discussion of the problem of balance of payments adjustment has until recently been concerned with the current account. The role of the capital account has been substantially neglected. In large part, and certainly in more
immediate manifestations of this neglect, the origin lies
in the fact that, while ostensibly discussing the problem
of balance of payments, the major preoccupation has in fact
been with the consequences of a particular shape to the
balance of payments from the point of view of industrial
health. It is the real rather than the monetary consequences
of the behaviour of the current account that have been at
stake. To this extent, reference to the so-called problem of
the current account as a balance of payments problem can be
seriously misleading.

The second issue is that while most of the post-war period
has focussed, in the spirit of Bretton Woods and after, on
the liberalisation of trade, extensive restrictions have
been widely maintained on the movement of capital. There has
been a bias in favour of the free movement of goods and
against the free movement of capital. Finally, a mechanism
is postulated which supposes that under free market condi-

tions, the allocation of real investment between the domestic economy and the world outside will be determined by relative rates of profit.

The upshot of this is said to result in a bias in favour
of the surplus countries continuing to invest domestically,
and particularly to invest heavily in the trade sector. The
argument suggests that profit rates in the traded goods sector have been maintained by a combination of direct controls
and exchange rate policies, which have discouraged or prevented the offsetting of surpluses on current trading account by outflows of private capital. The analysis is
applied in particular to the historical behaviour of Germany, Japan and Switzerland. Under a fixed exchange rate
system, which characterised much of the post-war period,
some tendency will exist to equalise rates of inflation, as
explained in Chapter 4. However that will not in itself
serve to equalise rates of return on investment, in the absence of free movement of capital.

In practice, it is argued that official behaviour and
subsequent exchange rate intervention by the authorities
have meant two things. The first is that surpluses on current
account have largely been financed by official capital
exports, often of a short-term nature, while at the same
time official intervention in foreign exchange markets has
prevented the appreciation of the exchange rates of the
surplus countries, to a point that reduced domestic profitability of investment and so encouraged outflows of private
capital. The lack of access to the domestic capital markets
of the surplus countries is thus deemed to play an important role in the creation of asymmetry between the surplus
and the deficit countries. As a general idea this is not
new. As we saw earlier in this chapter, the lack of access
to the capital markets of the surplus countries was an issue strongly raised by the United States in the sixties in
the context of the same problem of the asymmetry of adjustment.

The second is that the long-term consequence of this apparent protection of the rate of return in the traded goods
sector of the surplus countries is said to be excessive investment in the traded goods sector. Subsequent pressures
arise in political terms, not to protect the balance of payments as such, but to protect the export industries which
contribute so much, both on average and at the margin, to
national welfare in terms of output and employment. Moreover, it is argued, the longer this situation continues the
greater the tendency of the surplus countries to get locked
in on their traded goods base.

The Forsyth thesis can be seen as a particular case of the

general unwillingness of surplus countries to permit capital
flows to play a role in altering both the competitive position of imports and exports and to permit changes in the
overall structure of the surplus countries as between traded
and non-traded goods. As argued earlier, official financing
has insulated export and import behaviour from the money
flows that arise as a consequence of the balance of payments
overall disequilibrium. The problem is generally the same as
could arise under the old gold standard in that, under the
gold standard, a deficit of country A with country B would
be corrected by changes in their relative rates of monetary
growth which, other things being equal, would occur as the
deficit country lost and the surplus country gained money.
Insofar as these changes were not permitted to work their
way through to consequent changes in prices and interest
rates, or in different regimes to exchange rates, the equilibrium mechanism would fail to function. In the event that
restrictions on capital movements in foreign exchange markets prevent adjustment, either directly through regulation
or indirectly through intervention, attention is then focussed on protection and on the restriction of movements of
goods to offset the restrictions on capital account.

Thus we may see that, in general, the argument between
fixed or flexible exchange rates cannot be conducted in a
vacuum, ignoring the implications of whatever regime is in
force for capital movements. On this analysis the alternative would seem to point to a freeing of real and financial
capital movements, permitting them to influence the overall
behaviour of domestic economies, or to some form of 'managed
trade', to which we now turn. In practice, matters are currently complicated in the real world in which we live by
the impact of developments in world oil markets which are
impinging on both the deficit and the surplus countries.

MANAGED TRADE

As already recorded, the history of the post-war period up
to 1973 was substantially one of trade liberalisation. In
the adjustment period of the fifties, discrimination against
imports from the dollar area by both Japan and the European
countries was permitted and encouraged by the United States,
a period which ended in 1961 as far as trade restrictions
were concerned. Since the onset of floating in 1973, and in
the face of the subsequent recession, there is clear evidence that discrimination has increased, not only of a tariff but also of a non-tariff kind. The proportion of world
trade subject to tariffs and direct controls of one kind or

another has grown, partly because of the rise in the share
of world trade attributable to the developing countries who
have historically made more use of controls as part of the
process of development. But currently something over a fifth
of trade in manufactured goods is controlled or managed to
some degree, and controls imposed by the developed countries
have largely come into effect in the years since 1974.

Though much lower than for the developing countries, the
proportion of trade managed by the developed countries has
risen substantially. The European Economic Community
applies a wide variety of measures against non-EEC members.
Japan has used a variety of trade controls, although it is
commonly supposed that other features of the Japanese economy, such as the distribution system, constitute *de facto* important barriers to expanding trade.

The growth of protection, particularly with regard to
manufactured goods, stems in part from the depression of
1975 and subsequent problems arising from the energy price
increase and, in a period of uncertainty, a shift to the
criteria of stability and preservation in the face of a
sharp overall decline in the rate of economic growth of the
industrial countries. It has been estimated by Deborah Page
that the share of managed world trade in manufactures rose
from 14 per cent to 23 per cent in 1979 and the share of
managed exports in the OECD countries from 4 per cent to
15 per cent. In the case of non-manufactures such as food
and other commodities, where protection has been most common, the share of managed trade of the OECD countries rose
from 36 per cent in 1974 to 42 per cent in 1979.

While the apparent trend toward protectionism is a cause
for concern for many, a general argument in favour of the
need for protectionism and in favour of a move to 'managed
trade' has been advanced by the Cambridge Economic Policy
Group. The particular implications of their argument for the
management of the United Kingdom economy are considered in
subsequent chapters. Here we are concerned purely with the
contribution of such ideas to the development of the international and monetary trading system.

The starting point of the Cambridge argument lies in the
observation of sustained imbalances in rates of economic
growth and balance of payments behaviour on current account.
Simplifying the argument, we can think of the world as being
divided into two groups of countries, the 'weak' and the
'strong', or more specifically those that are constrained by
their balance of payments and those that are not. The strong
are so competitive and accumulate such large reserve
balances that they can 'choose' their levels of output and
employment. Those that are constrained by their balance of

payments are forced to restrict the growth of monetary demand below what is required to generate full employment,
particularly in the face of what is perceived to be 'real
wage resistance'. The rigidity of real wages also precludes
the use of devaluation to correct matters between the weak
and the strong.

Given the presumption of the persistence of past trends in
export behaviour, and in the relationship between the out-
puts of the weak countries and their imports, extrapolation
of history into the eighties suggests to the Cambridge Group
that the situation will become critical, particularly for
the United Kingdom. The imbalance in competitiveness and the
need to achieve equilibrium in the balance of payments will
mean that the weak countries will have to grow below their
underlying rate of productive potential, and the consequence
will be a persistent growth in both spare capacity and unemployment. Given past history, this imbalance, it is argued,
will not be corrected by movements of capital, labour and
technology nor, as we have seen, by devaluation.

The conclusion that follows is that the weak countries
should therefore discriminate on trade account against the
strong. If protection is only adopted by the weak or constrained economies then, in the absence of retaliation,
there is no presumption that total world output will fall or
that trade would be reduced. On the contrary, starting from
a position where the balance of payments is in equilibrium
for the weak against the strong, the argument is that this
will permit the monetary expansion of demand, increasing
output and employment in the constrained countries but, at
the same time, maintaining the volume of imports at its
existing level. Protection would simply be used to prevent
the additional growth of imports that otherwise would have
been sucked in by the expansion in monetary demand.

However, returning to one of the themes of the last chapter, it is inherently misleading to pose the problem in terms
of a constraint being exercised by the balance of payments,
or necessarily from the way in which the international monetary and trading system functions. As we have seen, this
confusion arises in part from the persistent tendency to
focus only on the current account of the balance of payments, excluding the role of the capital account and of monetary changes in achieving overall balance of payments equilibrium. This is not to say that the state of the current account, the implications for exports and growth of output are
not relevant – they certainly are. But the focus on the current account reveals the fact that the essential problem of
the so-called weak countries is an industrial one rooted in
the general character of the supply conditions in those

countries.

The key problem is not the balance of payments as such, but a lack of competitiveness that prevents the weak countries from securing and maintaining a sufficient share of world output to maintain what is perceived as a desirable level of unemployment and an acceptable rate of economic growth. It is misleading to represent this as a balance of payments problem for two reasons.

Firstly, it suggests that the real problems facing these countries are in some sense external problems that can be dealt with by some form of insulation. Attention is diverted away from the real points of concern which, as we saw in the last chapter, are related to direct labour productivity and product quality. Simply removing the so-called constraint will not in itself have much - if any - effect on either of these variables. To be fair to the proponents of the arguments for managed trade, the proposals for protection are generally part of a wider scheme for change including elements such as increased direct investment by government in industry, and perhaps increased labour participation. The logical extension of the protectionist argument in this case, which implicitly rests on the assumption of international market failure, is to a belief in market failure generally, and therefore arguments such as have been applied in certain developing economies for close economic planning and direction in general. Protectionism is the thin end of a very large wedge once it is accepted that, as far as the longer term is concerned, it will not in itself directly affect overall efficiency.

Secondly, it persists with the argument that the weak countries are constrained by lack of monetary demand which, even at face value, is a curious argument in view of one of the oft-cited characteristics of the weak countries, namely an inherent tendency to greater inflation. Leaving on one side the question of additional intervention to increase competitiveness, the possible impact of increased monetary demand behind trade restrictions has two dimensions. The first is the once-and-for-all effect of increasing the utilisation of existing resources of both capital and labour up to what might be described as 'full employment'. There is an inherent presumption that, given the level of real wages and the current state of competitiveness, more output can be profitably produced and sold on a permanent basis if only the monetary demand were there. While in the case of some industries at some points of time this may be true, there is little case for supposing that it is true in any significant sense across the board. Moreover, there is no guarantee that, in general, additional monetary demand will be spent on the problem industries which are import-competing. Additional demand may be spent on the tertiary sector and on traded goods, or diverted in an attempt to make increased purchases from the exporting industries for domestic consumption. In the short run, the proposed strategy of general protection for manufactured goods may not succeed in permanently raising output and reducing unemployment. One may also add the fact that a substantial proportion of manufacturing imports into the weak countries are intermediate and not finished goods, with the possible consequence that successful exporters may have to switch from cheaper to more expensive sourcing so in turn restricting their own competitiveness in world markets.

The second dimension is that of the longer run. Accepting, for the sake of argument, that an expansion of internal demand behind barriers does succeed in eliminating excess capacity, we must clearly distinguish between a possible once-and-for-all effect of this kind in reaching some quasi short-period equilibrium, and the longer-term issues posed by the continuation of divergences in the underlying rates of growth of the weak and the strong countries. The protectionist argument does not explain how demand in the weak countries can be allowed to grow faster than in the strong, or at least as fast, either closing the gap in living standards or at worst preventing it from widening.

Much has been made by the protectionists of the rather dubious argument that the slower growth of demand in the weak countries has prevented them from exploiting economies of scale. If this is the case, it would appear on the surface that, after an initial leap to a new short period equilibrium, the continued divergence of growth rates will simply cause the problem to reappear. Moreover, the protectionist argument carries the implication that free trade cannot improve economic performance through the mechanism of replacing uncompetitive domestic industries by imports, so releasing scarce resources to be employed by the efficient. Insofar as there is a need for changes in structure rather than preservation, the argument points not to protection but to the need for policies to assist in the process of change. Finally, as Forsyth has pointed out, if protectionism is combined with continued controls on the behaviour of the capital account, the net effect may simply be to divert the surpluses of the strong into the faster-growing markets of the third world.

While the Cambridge Economic Policy Group plays down the issue of retaliation, it must not be forgotten that here we are discussing problems of the world trading and monetary system, which stem in large measure from the difficulties of reconciling an economically interdependent system with the aspirations of nation states. We have seen the kind of problems that have arisen in the attempts to manage international money. To shift these problems to the management of trade is largely simply to put them in another place. The key issue remains that of establishing the right kind of international monetary and trading rules based on international cooperation. To pretend that the problems can be solved by unilateral action within the boundaries of nation states is a dangerous illusion that should not be encouraged.

# 7 Macroeconomic Policy

Previous chapters have focused on those aspects of economic behaviour which help to explain the functioning of the economy that is relevant to macroeconomic policy-making. The nature of economic policy-making considered in this chapter is macroeconomic in character although, in practice, the distinction between macro- and microeconomics becomes blurred. We distinguish between *stabilisation policy* which concerns the use of fiscal and monetary policies in the determination of output, prices, the balance of payments and associated economic variables, and *industrial policies*. The latter deal with the structure of the economy and have particular significance for the rate of economic growth in the long run. This chapter is concerned with stabilisation policy and the discussion of industrial policy will be taken up in Chapter 8. The application of industrial policies involves questions of social organisation which are conveniently discussed separately, and are important in determining the limits of government intervention in industrial affairs.

We attempt to clarify the nature of the relationship between fiscal and monetary policies and consider certain matters of definition. Secondly, we take up an issue of central importance for macroeconomic policy-making, so far neglected, namely how the public forms its expectations about future events, and the consequential limits that may be imposed on government action. To simplify, both monetary and fiscal policy and the role of expectations are initially discussed in terms of a closed economy. The complications of the balance of payments and foreign trade are taken up in the third section, which leads to some general conclusions about the limits of stabilisation policy.

## MONETARY AND FISCAL POLICY

The definition of fiscal policy seems relatively straight-
forward. It may be thought of as determining the level of
public expenditure and the complex structure of tax rates,
allowances and regulations. The difference between the current value of government spending and the collection of
taxes and other income represents the additional money that
government has to find, or what is defined as the public
sector deficit. If the government is in financial deficit,
it must issue financial assets either by selling its own
debt or by creating new money which passes into the hands of
private portfolio holders. However, knowing all this does
not tell us much about the nature of fiscal policy changes
and the government's *fiscal stance*. To assess policy people
often wish to know whether the government's fiscal stance is
'loose' or 'tight'. This requires a measure of comparison
between alternative fiscal policies which is not a simple
matter.

Monetary policy is defined in terms of the level or rate
of change of some monetary aggregate (the 'quantity' of
money) or some interest rate or structure of interest rates.
In analysing the effects of changes in fiscal policy on output and prices, the quantity of nominal money is often kept
fixed to isolate the fiscal policy effects, suggesting that
unchanged monetary policy should be measured in terms of the
monetary aggregate. In practice, much Keynesian thinking has
focussed on interest rates to judge whether monetary policy
is tight or relaxed, the money supply as such being regarded as of relatively little importance. This reflects in
part the Keynesian belief that interest rates represent the
main channel through which monetary changes affect the economy, and in part the fact that the monetary authorities moni-
tor the behaviour of interest rates rather than the supply
of money.

There are reasons for believing that a focus on the behaviour of the stock of money is important. The first is that
changes in the stock of money can have significant direct
effects on the economy. As we saw in Chapter 3, the crude
Keynesian analysis neglects the effects of changes in the
money stock on wealth, private sector spending, and wages
and prices. Secondly, in practice, changes in the real stock
of money are a good guide to the actual stance of fiscal
policy. Consequently, we define the monetary stance in terms
of the real stock of money. Monetary policy is easy when the
growth of the real money supply is faster than the underlying growth of output, i.e. when the growth of the nominal

money supply is faster than the underlying growth in output
plus the rate of inflation, and vice versa.

In traditional Keynesian economics, the budget deficit or
surplus assumes a special importance. It is believed that
its size should be related to the overall state of the economy and, in particular, to the state of output and employment. Consequently, if changes in the fiscal stance are reflected in the budget deficit, one wishes to know whether
the changes are neutral, contractionary or expansionary. To
measure a change in fiscal stance by comparing the budget
deficit between two points of time will not do because,
while the budget deficit affects the economy, the economy
also affects the budget deficit. A fall in output brought
about by some external shock increases the budget deficit
since tax receipts fall and social security payments rise.
A substantial budget deficit may simply represent a depressed economy rather than the authorities' intentions.
This explains the popularity of the full employment budget
deficit as being the most appropriate measure of the government's fiscal stance.

This is calculated by choosing a level for 'full' employment and estimating the budget deficit at the consequent
level of output, for a given tax structure and set of government spending plans. A large budget *deficit* observed at
a depressed level of output could be consistent with a budget *surplus* calculated as if the economy were at full employment. In Keynesian terms, such a situation would be
deemed to reflect a very tight fiscal stance, preventing the
economy from reaching full employment.

Unfortunately the complications do not end there. The
effect of a given change in the budget deficit on the economy
depends on its composition. An increase of £100m in public
spending will not have the same effect as a reduction of
£100m in taxes collected, since part of the latter will be
saved and not spent. Correcting for this leads to the idea
of the weighted full employment deficit. Moreover, discretionary changes in tax rates may have perverse effects when
comparing their consequences at a relatively low level of
output with the consequences at full employment. A shift of
taxation from personal income to profits could reduce tax
yield at the lower level of output while profits are relatively depressed, and increase it at full employment when
profits are relatively buoyant. In this case the full employment deficit, weighted or unweighted, loses much of its
interest. Finally we have to face up to the fact that, even
at full employment, there remains the problem of fiscal drag
because, with a progressive tax structure and growing nominal income, there is a persistent tendency for the economy

to be paying an increasing proportion of its income in tax if allowances and tax rates are left unchanged. It can be argued that once one recognises the practical relationship between fiscal and monetary policy, some of these concerns disappear. The need for a unique measure of the fiscal stance stems from a wish to isolate and measure the effects of fiscal policy alone. The theoretical issue at stake is whether fiscal policy has permanent effects of any magnitude on output and employment if the supply of nominal money is kept constant. In the closed economy the question is whether an expansion in public spending, financed by the issue of government debt, will permanently increase output and employment. According to the strict monetarist argument presented in Chapter 3, the answer is 'no' because the issue of debt will raise interest rates and eventually 'crowd out' an amount of private spending equal to the additional public spending.

It has been argued by Alan Budd and Terry Burns that variations in the change in the money supply in the United Kingdom have been dominated by changes in the budget deficit in the medium term. The change in the money supply is identically equal to the government's borrowing requirement plus additional net lending by the banks, less the sales of public sector debt to the public. But, it is claimed, total net lending comprising the last two items is related in a stable way to interest rates and output behaviour. This relationship does not necessarily hold in the very short run, but expresses itself in the longer term.

For any given set of interest rates and output level, monetary growth rates will be determined primarily by different levels of the borrowing requirement or budget deficit. This does not imply that there is any simple relationship between the borrowing requirement and the rate of monetary growth in the short term. The actual fiscal deficit requires adjustment for the rate of inflation and for deviations of the level of output from its full employment level or, more generally, from its trend rate of growth in order to allow for fiscal drag and for the effects of output on the deficit rather than the effects of the deficit on output.

In the closed economy, the budget deficit must be equal to the overall financial surplus of the private sector. This is a matter of accounting because in financing its deficit, the government is issuing assets to the private sector by adding to its debt or by the creation of money, which must be taken up in the overall private sector surplus. Crude estimates suggest that over the period since 1964, a rise in the inflation rate of 1 per cent led to an increase in the private

sector surplus of about 0.25 per cent of the gross domestic
product, requiring an equal rise in the public sector deficit to finance the additional inflation. Similarly, it was
estimated that if output were 1 per cent below its trend,
additional net lending by the banks less sales of public
sector debt would fall by about 0.6 per cent of the value
of the gross domestic product, i.e. a given budget deficit
would generate a smaller increase in the money supply. Applying these estimates, the observed budget deficit can be
adjusted for inflation and output to obtain the equivalent
effect on demand if inflation were zero and output were on
its trend. As shown in Table 7.1, changes in the monetary
aggregates are closely related to the adjusted fiscal
stance, from which we conclude that changes in the monetary
aggregates are a relatively efficient measure of the overall monetary and fiscal stance, since the output and inflation effects are automatically contained in the monetary
measure.

This reflects an underlying symmetry in that deficit
spending tends to lead to the creation of money, while increases in the supply of money will tend to require deficit
spending. This symmetry and the argument presented leads to
two important conclusions. The first is that if the money
supply is chosen as a policy target, the stance of fiscal
policy must be consistent with it. They cannot in practice
be operated independently in the medium term. For this
reason academic debates about the 'pure' effects of fiscal
policy lose much of their *raison d'être*.

The second is that the interaction between monetary and
fiscal policy throws light on the debate between those who
argue that the budget deficit should be zero, and those who
argue that it should be adjusted to the needs of full employment. In the closed economy, the budget deficit is equal
to the financial surplus of the private sector. If that
equality represents portfolio equilibrium, the private sector must be prepared to absorb into its portfolio the precise amount and distribution of money and debt that the
authorities are issuing in order to finance their deficit.
A faster rate of growth of nominal income in the private
sector will tend to promote a higher demand for the financial liabilities issued by government in the form of bonds
and money. If the economy were stationary with zero inflation and zero output growth, maintenance of a stable ratio
of wealth to income would require the government deficit to
be zero. In a growing economy, however, it should not necessarily be zero.

The trick would be to determine the fiscal deficit as a
proportion of the value of the gross domestic product which

TABLE *7.1  Adjusted financial surplus and growth
of the real money stock*

|  | Adjusted financial surplus (% of GDP) | Growth of the real money stock (annual rate) |
|---|---|---|
| 1964 | −3.6 | 3.1 |
| 1965 | −2.5 | 1.7 |
| 1966 | −1.8 | 2.0 |
| 1967 | −2.8 | 3.1 |
| 1968 | −3.5 | 3.7 |
| 1969 | 0.7 | −1.5 |
| 1970 | 3.4 | 0 |
| 1971 | 2.6 | 2.4 |
| 1972 | −0.4 | 13.2 |
| 1973 | −3.4 | 15.5 |
| 1974 | −1.2 | −2.2 |
| 1975 | 0.5 | −12.9 |
| 1976 | −1.9 | −8.5 |
| 1977 | 0.3 | −4.6 |

SOURCE   A.P. Budd and T. Burns, 'The Relationship between
Fiscal and Monetary Policy in the LBS Model',
*Discussion Paper No 51* (Econometric Forecasting Unit,
London Business School, June 1978).

was consistent with satisfying the growth in asset demand, the underlying rate of growth of output and stable prices. In practice it is an easier matter to deduce the budget deficit from some desired rate of growth in the money stock than from direct attempts to measure the fiscal stance. This again emphasises the importance and significance of monetary policy measured in terms of changes in the money stock, rather than focussing solely on fiscal policy, which has been the British economic tradition.


EXPECTATIONS AND POLICY ADJUSTMENTS

We have argued that, in practice, monetary and fiscal policy are closely related in the medium term. If a particular monetary target is to be achieved in a closed economy, then fiscal policy must be consistent with that target. There is a case for believing that in practice the behaviour of the real money stock is a good guide to the fiscal stance. In what follows we therefore concentrate on the behaviour of monetary policy in affecting output and prices in the short and medium term, bearing in mind that changes in the nominal supply of money reflect underlying policy changes measured in fiscal terms.

One of the disagreements between the so-called Keynesians and the so-called monetarists was whether the ultimate effect of changes in the nominal supply of money was neutral with respect to real output and employment. The monetarist belief was that output and employment were determined by the interaction of supply and demand in the labour market. Consequently the natural rate of unemployment was fixed independently of the behaviour of the nominal supply of money in the long run. In the closed economy, the ultimate effects of changes in the nominal supply of money were reflected in changes in the price level.

It was suggested that the dispute between the monetarists and the fiscalists is less important in practice than might appear. By the same token, the question of whether monetary change is neutral in the longer run has also been debated on too abstract a level. We may construct models of the economy so that the neutrality of money follows as a consequence. The neutrality of changes in the quantity of nominal money depends on the conditions of supply. Whatever the underlying logic of the determinants of aggregate supply, it should be common ground that, at some point, an expansion of supply in response to increased monetary demand will not take place and the consequence of the monetary expansion will be entirely on prices.

The issues that divide the protagonists are both theoretical and empirical. However, the important issue is not one of strict logic as to whether fiscal and monetary policy changes are exactly neutral. At any given moment that is a matter of degree. Even in theory such changes are never likely to be exactly neutral. If taxes are cut, this alters the relationship between work and leisure, and so will in theory have some effect on the supply of labour and output. Strict neutrality cannot be proven. But this does not matter. The important question is an empirical one, whether monetary expansion will affect prices primarily in the longer run. The monetary approach places emphasis on the fact that output does not react automatically to changes in the level of aggregate monetary demand, but is also conditioned by the profitability of producing it.

Whereas the crude Keynesian story limits the supply of output in a physical sense through shortages and bottlenecks in both labour and capital, the monetarist approach suggests that there will be a limit to the supply of output generated by the behaviour of wages, prices and profitability. It evokes the possibility that, even under conditions of what appears to be spare capacity in terms of both capital and labour, economic considerations at the micro-level can severely limit the supply response. This means that in practice the power of the authorities to choose a given level of employment is limited, even though casual empiricism suggests that the level of unemployment is greater than is socially desirable.

Even if monetary changes are neutral in the longer run, the possibility and desirability of discretionary fiscal and monetary changes are not *ipso facto* ruled out. The response to a demand shock to the economy will not be immediate, and it will take some time before wages, prices and output adapt to it. It has been argued that, even if neutrality does hold in the long run, the stickiness of the economy's response may justify discretionary intervention to speed up the process of restoring employment to its equilibrium level. So it has been suggested by Professor Modigliani that:

In reality, the distinguishing feature of the monetarist school and the real issues of disagreement with non-monetarists is not monetarism, but rather the role that should probably be assigned to stabilisation policies. Non-monetarists accept what I regard to be the fundamental practical message of the General Theory; that a private enterprise economy using an intangible money *needs* to be stabilised, *can* be stabilised and therefore *should* be

stabilised by appropriate fiscal and monetary policies.
Monetarists, by contrast, take the view that there is no
serious need to stabilise the economy; that, even if there
was a need, it could not be done, for stabilisation policies would be more likely to decrease stability...

This definition of monetarism goes beyond the definition
that we have implicitly used in this book. Believing that
changes in the nominal supply of money have important consequences for the rate of inflation does not rule out discretionary fiscal and monetary policy.
    We have so far paid little or no attention to the problem
of expectations. It is clear that the behaviour of the economy and of markets over time are affected by the expectations of economic agents as to the future course of events.
In making economic forecasts for the economy some assumptions must be made about how individuals make their own
forecasts. Stock-market behaviour, the behaviour of interest
rates and exchange rates, the rate of investment and wage
bargaining are all affected by expectations.
    Economists and statisticians have made use of a wide va-
riety of formulae to represent the way in which expectations
are formed. One simple formula is to assume that the best
guess for tomorrow's value of an economic variable is today's value, which is defined as having static expectations.
A more common approach used in economic models is to suppose
that the expected future value of a variable can be represented by some weighted average of its past behaviour. In
this case, expectations are said to be adaptive. Forecasts
of the future value of a variable incorporate past errors
in making forecasts. The important point about this, and a
wide class of other formulations of the way in which expectations are formed, is that they are backward- rather than
forward-looking. An alternative view is that economic agents
do not form their expectations in this way, but instead
form them *rationally*.
    A general technical definition of rational expectations is
beyond the scope of this book. We limit the discussion to a
particular definition of rational expectations which has
been used in the macroeconomic debate on the feasibility of
discretionary stabilisation policies. Rational expectations
are said to be formed in any given situation by the expected or predicted values derived from the relevant economic model.
    To illustrate, suppose that the government, starting from
a position of employment equilibrium, decides to attempt to
create a higher employment level through monetary expansion.
Suppose also that it is predicted that the ultimate conse-

quence of the monetary expansion is to raise prices in the
longer run, leaving the level of real output and employment
unchanged. This is a result derived from the 'relevant' economic model which is assumed to be known both to economic
agents and to the government. In this case, the rational
expectation of the behaviour of output and inflation will
anticipate this result. In the extreme case of perfectly
rational expectations, since the longer-term outcome of
the monetary expansion is anticipated, there will be no
temporary change in output before returning to the original
equilibrium. The rational thing to do is simply to raise
prices and wages directly to their new equilibrium levels.
The private sector will thus frustrate the attempt by government to raise the level of output and employment by an-
ticipating the ultimate outcome. The result in this extreme
case is that not only is the effect of the monetary change
neutral in the long run, it is also neutral in the short
run. Money is said not only to be neutral, it is also *super-
neutral*. There are no effects on output, even in the short
term. Under these conditions it is not a question of whether
using discretionary monetary and fiscal policy to affect
output and employment is desirable, it becomes simply impossible.

It is easy to show that models of the economy which have
this property can be constructed, and they automatically
rule out any discretionary role for fiscal and monetary
policy. It is equally easy to show that the extreme result
of super-neutrality is not robust, and that generally plausible modifications to the model cause it to break down. By
and large, super-neutrality is an interesting *curiosum* which
is not consistent with the empirical evidence available.
From observation we conclude that, generally speaking, adjustments in the macroeconomy are not of such an instan-
taneous nature. Lagged responses of some considerable dura-
tion have been observed in the markets for capital, labour
and output.

Evidence shows that the rational expectations hypothesis
has made a fruitful contribution to our understanding of
market processes in stock markets, exchange markets and
speculative markets in general, but such markets have relatively rapid speeds of response. As it happens, the significance of the rational expectations hypothesis is not
vitiated in principle by the existence of lags in macroeconomic behaviour or by the non-existence of super-
neutrality. Rational expectations are themselves uncertain.
The hypothesis, it must be emphasised, does not say that
forecasts based on rational expectations will be correct,
but only that they will be unbiased and, on average, not

consistently wrong. There is a risk to be taken in acting on
a particular forecast and, to the extent that economic
agents are risk-averse, there will not be an immediate reaction to changes in expectations. A more cautious policy
may be followed, with the result that the adjustment is
spread out over time. In this case the argument against discretionary fiscal and monetary policy takes a more subtle
form.

The more general case against discretionary fiscal and
monetary policy, when expectations are formed rationally,
turns on the presumption that, if economic agents are acting
in their own best interests, it is not at all clear that
government has any superior knowledge or capability to act
on their behalf. The classic case for government intervention in the field of microeconomics rests on the identification of market failure. Markets may not work efficiently to
equalise private and social costs and benefits, in which
case there is scope for intervention by government to establish these equalities by the use of taxes and subsidies.
By parity of reasoning, macroeconomic intervention should be
subject to the same criterion. Market rigidities could prevent individual economic agents from acting in their own
best interest, i.e. they might be prevented for some institutional reason from responding to their own expectations, even if rationally formed. In addition, it is possible that government may have access to information that economic agents in the market place do not have and which could
be exploited for the general good. If such market failure is
not present, then with rational expectations and efficient
markets there is no case for intervention, irrespective of
the size of the disequilibrium that exists in terms of unemployment, and however long any inbuilt adjustment process in
the economy takes. If markets are efficient and expectations
are formed rationally, the actual time path taken by the
economy will be optimal and there is no reason to believe
that, by intervention, the government can improve on it. Before a case for intervention can be made, a source of market
inefficiency must be identified, and it must be shown why
the path being pursued by the economy is not optimal.

The hypothesis of rational expectations and the resulting
conclusions with regard to discretionary fiscal and monetary
policies have been attacked from a number of points of view.
Leaving on one side a number of technical details, the most
important issues concern the actual formation of expectations and the possible nature of market failure.

At the outset, rational expectations are defined as predictions from the relevant economic model, which should be
used to analyse the consequences of government economic

policy. This raises the obvious question of how agents in the market place know what this model is. In cases such as speculative markets where the hypothesis has proved extremely useful, the models used are often very limited, and all relevant information is easily available to participants in the market. It is however questionable how far economic agents can make structured sense of the economy as a whole and its workings, when apparently even economists cannot agree on what the relevant model is!

One could of course take the view that in practice economists, like governments, actually don't know any more than the man in the street. Remember that predictions do not have to be strictly correct, and one of the intuitive points in favour of rational expectations is 'Why should economic agents systematically get things wrong and governments systematically get things right?' There is little hard evidence that economic agents actually do form their expectations rationally, and it may be the case that governments do have an information advantage, although it does not follow directly from either of these propositions that discretionary intervention is justified. Moreover, there is a further problem of specifying how it is that economic agents learn the consequences of changes in government policy rules and converge to rational expectations about them. The literature on rational expectations has established that the behavioural responses of economic agents will vary with different policy rules, which is in itself an important insight with direct relevance for the construction of economic models and for forecasting. However, at present the learning process remains something of a mystery.

The second basis for criticism of rational expectations is the belief that markets for both labour and goods do not correspond to the free and perfect markets on which conventional monetarism depends. Under certain conditions, price and wage rigidity may offer scope for an expansionary monetary policy to have a permanent effect on output. To see this, suppose that money wages and prices are fixed, and output is below its economic optimum. In this case a rise in the supply of nominal money can permanently raise the real stock of money, and hence the level of real output and employment. The economic literature on the subject has therefore concerned itself with establishing that sufficient rigidities and imperfections exist to justify intervention with regard to output and employment - but at the same time seeking to justify such imperfections as either being themselves determined by institutional conditions, or as being in the best interests of the economic agents concerned.

It is difficult to conclude at this stage of the debate

that a case has been made out for non-discretionary fiscal
and monetary policy on the basis of the rational expectations hypothesis alone. Nevertheless, the hypothesis is a
challenging one which, apart from its other fruitful appli-
cations, has underlined the fact that conventional views
about stabilisation policy imply that people do not recognise their own self-interest and are less intelligent and
rational in the market place than those who pull the levers
of economic policy. Moreover, the proponents of rational
expectations have done us a service in emphasising the importance of a more rigorous justification of monetary intervention, which requires market failure to be identified and
exposed, rather than relying on *ad hoc* explanations of the
apparent rigidity of nominal wages and prices. Finally, it
is worth noting that while under certain conditions the
existence of rational expectations is a sufficient condition
for non-intervention and for the pursuit of non-feedback
policy rules, it is certainly not necessary, as we shall see
later in this chapter.


INTERNATIONAL CONSIDERATIONS

Before reaching any definitive conclusions with regard to
the feasibility or desirability of using discretionary fiscal and monetary policy to affect real output and employment, it is important to abandon the assumption of the
closed economy and to incorporate into our analysis the
balance of payments and the behaviour of exchange rates. We
discuss the effects of fiscal and monetary policy on the
assumption of free trade and free capital movements, drawing at length on the discussion of the open economy in
Chapter 4. It has been extensively argued in some quarters
that positive attempts should be made to impose trade restrictions, possibly in the form of a global tariff, in order to achieve consistency between the objective of a satisfactory balance of payments and full employment. Accordingly, we examine the arguments put forward for this view.
   It is important to re-emphasise the point made in both
Chapter 4 and Chapter 6 that, in economic terms, there is
no such thing as a fixed as opposed to a floating or flexible exchange rate regime. The authorities cannot unilaterally choose a given exchange rate independently of constraints imposed on the conduct of fiscal and monetary policy. The important constraint is that which is imposed on the
behaviour of the supply of money, at least in the medium
term. The authorities may set an exchange rate target, so
that what appears on the surface to be a fixed exchange rate

regime is in effect a commitment to pursue a monetary policy designed to keep the effective exchange rate stable. *De
facto* such an objective characterised the British economy
from the devaluation of 1949 to the mid-sixties, and was
finally abandoned in 1972. The principal concern of the
United Kingdom authorities, and those of most of the industrial countries, was to maintain parity with the dollar, and
the story of this period has been set out at length in Chapter 6. Our concern here is to recall from Chapter 4 the main
results that help us determine the nature and scope of fiscal and monetary policy when the stable exchange rate objective is in force.

As we have seen in previous chapters, the behaviour of the
nominal exchange rate is in part affected by the relative
behaviour of a country's money supply to money supply in the
world outside and in part by changes in relative real efficiency. For immediate purposes we will assume that the relative real efficiency of the country and the relative position of traded as against non-traded goods remains constant.

Under these circumstances, the objective of a stable exchange rate also makes the overall balance of payments itself a policy objective. The conduct of economic policy must
be such as to ensure that the rate of growth of monetary demand is consistent with balance of payments equilibrium,
i.e. a state of the balance of payments that is consistent
with the stable exchange rate objective. In this case, as
explained in Chapter 4, the key control variable becomes the
rate of domestic credit expansion.

While in this case both the nominal exchange rate and the
balance of payments become interrelated objectives of economic policy, the rate of inflation of traded goods in world
markets cannot. The average rate of inflation in the prices
of traded goods will be determined in world markets and will
be affected by the interaction of world demand and world
supply. By the same token, the average rate of world inflation will also be affected by the growth of the world money
supply relative to the growth of world output. This will not
necessarily be the only factor in the short run, since there
may be supply shocks to the world economy induced for example by the rise in the price of oil or by harvest failures.
Nevertheless, world monetary growth has been of major importance in determining the behaviour of world commodity and
raw material prices and, through them, the general rate of
inflation of industrial traded goods.

Given the world rate of inflation, the behaviour of an individual country's rate of inflation in traded goods prices
will be closely related to the behaviour of its exchange
rate. Given a stable exchange rate policy, this in effect

amounts to accepting the world rate of inflation for traded goods. Insofar as the traded goods sector in manufactures is the pace-setter for wage settlements, and given a transmission mechanism based on comparability, the average world rate of inflation will be a central factor in determining the overall domestic rate of inflation.

This is not to say that the domestic rates of inflation between countries will be the same since there will be differences both in the proportions of goods traded and in the efficiencies of the non-traded goods sector. The important point is that, under the conditions stated, in the absence of direct attempts to influence domestic inflation through incomes policies and price controls, the authorities cannot materially influence the rate of inflation. Monetary policy can be directed toward the exchange rate and the balance of payments, but it cannot be used primarily in an attempt to determine the general rate of inflation.

In the long run, expansionary monetary policy cannot be used unilaterally to determine the level of output and employment. Starting from a position of equilibrium in the level of output and employment, the unemployment rate may be above what appears to be socially desirable. Assuming that conditions in the world outside remain the same, an attempt to expand monetary demand to increase employment will result in a deterioration in the balance of payments which, if not corrected, will cause the exchange rate to fall, so violating the original policy objective. As a consequence, not only will the exchange rate fall but also the rate of inflation will be increased as the world rate of inflation is transmitted into the economy at the lower exchange rate. The effect of this will be to reduce the real stock of money, thus driving the economy back toward its original position. For a time, of course, the increased output and employment that results initially from the monetary expansion may be sustained by using reserves to prop up the exchange rate, or by borrowing from abroad. But these are only short-term measures and, in the end, the deleterious consequences of the monetary expansion have to be faced.

Thus we conclude that, under a stable exchange rate policy in equilibrium, the authorities cannot control the rate of inflation or unilaterally determine the level of output and employment by the management of monetary demand. Nor, for that matter, can they exercise much control in the long run over the level of interest rates. With freely-operating world financial markets and a stable exchange rate, the behaviour of domestic interest rates will be primarily determined by world rates. In addition a fiscal policy that is consistent with the monetary policy required to stabilise

the exchange rate is needed. The budget deficit and its
method of finance must be consistent with the world level
of interest rates, so restricting the behaviour of bond-
financing by the authorities, while the new money created
must not be excessive in relation to the balance of payments
and exchange rate objective.

The situation described is broadly that which persisted
during the fifties and sixties when the pound sterling's
parity with the dollar was an important objective of economic policy. The periods of so-called stop/go that occurred
simply reflect the working-out of the mechanism that we have
described. From time to time, attempts were made to stimulate output and employment by expansionary fiscal and monetary policies which had to be reversed when it appeared that
the parity was coming under pressure, except in the period
1964-7 when matters went too far and the pound was devalued.

These historical episodes led to two main conclusions that
had, and in some quarter still have, wide support. The
first, as we have seen in Chapter 5, is the erroneous view
that the growth of output and employment in the United Kingdom is in a meaningful sense balance-of-payments constrained. The second, which accompanied the devaluation of 1967
and the floating of the pound in 1972, was that control over
the level of output and employment might be secured by abandoning the stable exchange rate objective. After 1972 the
pound was left to float to take care of the balance of payments, while fiscal and monetary policy were again directed
toward expanding monetary demand in order to stimulate more
output and jobs. Admittedly the possibility of a successful
incomes policy played a part in the story, and this will be
taken up in the next section.

Once the exchange rate was floating, it and the overall
balance of payments ceased to be an object of policy in its
own right. The behaviour of the exchange rate was now sub-
servient to the policies pursued by the authorities in relation to other objectives. However, the key freedom given to
the authorities as a result of floating was not a new power
over the determination of output and employment, but a
responsibility for the rate of inflation. The floating exchange rate became a channel through which the excessive
creation of money in the interests of output and employment
was transmitted in a rapid escalation of the inflation rate
greater than average world levels, in a process in which the
power of organised labour was reactive rather than proact-
ive. The proper response to the new 'freedom' from the exchange rate objective was not to set monetary and fiscal
policy in line with one's desire for output and employment,
but to set it in line with one's desired rate of inflation.

Failure to do so turned out to be an egregious error which
was recognised by the then Labour Prime Minister of Britain,
Mr Callaghan, in a speech to the Labour Party Conference in
September 1976.

> We used to think that you could just spend your way out of
> a recession and increase employment by cutting taxes and
> boosting government spending. I tell you in all candour
> that that option no longer exists and that, insofar as it
> ever did exist, it worked by injecting inflation into the
> economy. And each time that has happened, the average
> level of unemployment has risen. Higher inflation followed
> by higher unemployment. That is the history of the last
> twenty years.

It is widely recognised that, for differing reasons, demand management or stabilisation policy is not enough to enable control to be exercised by the authorities over the
level of output and employment, although the case has by no
means been given up by some economists on both sides of the
Atlantic. In the United Kingdom, however, the two main,
although not mutually exclusive, lines of approach to reha-
bilitation are firstly to espouse the adoption of a permanent incomes policy, and secondly to impose overall controls on the level of imports. Here we confine ourselves to
the effects of restraints on trade.

The question of whether the balance of payments constitute
a constraint on growth, and the extent to which balance of
payments performance is a cause rather than a symptom of
economic behaviour across countries, has already been discussed at length in Chapter 5. The main conclusions for the
purposes of assessing the role of stabilisation policy are
implicit in that discussion. The most important conclusion
is that apparent difficulties with the current account of
the balance of payments are another feature of the inelas-
ticity and uncompetitiveness of supply, rather than reveal-
ing in any meaningful sense a lack of monetary demand that
can be made good by the fiscal and monetary authorities.
Insofar as this is the case, it follows immediately that the
case for the imposition of import controls, either in the
form of a tariff or in the form of quotas, must be justified
primarily not in making it possible to expand demand as such
without undesirable side effects, but in altering the fundamental conditions of supply.

This exposes the weakness of the analysis of those who have
advocated import controls as part of the process of increasing the level of employment by expanding monetary demand. The
approach, as set out by the Cambridge Economic Policy Group

in the United Kingdom, contains no theory or explanation of
how the supply of goods and services in the economy is determined. The underlying rate of growth of productivity and
productive potential of the economy is taken as given. Unless monetary demand grows at this arbitrary rate, unemployment will rise. Attempts to increase the rate of growth of
monetary demand fail as spending leaks out into imports. The
imports must therefore be restricted so that the increased
monetary demand is spent on domestic goods, increasing domestic output and employment. Since there is no economic explanation of supply, it is not possible to know whether or
why additional supply corresponding to the additional monetary demand will be forthcoming.

Even if it were possible, there is no clear analysis of
the second-round effects of the consequences of a combination of import controls and expanded monetary demand for the
rates of inflation, beyond the expressed belief that protection would enable more resources to be distributed to wage
earners, resulting in a reduction of wage claims. There is
no credible evidence for such a belief. In recent times, the
record rise in real disposable income between 1977 and 1979
did not serve to ameliorate wage demands. The incomes policy
of the government of the day actually collapsed, while standards of living were getting better at a rapid rate. Moreover, in view of the Cambridge belief that, following the
imposition of import controls, profits should not rise substantially, it is clear that the main beneficiaries of the
policy in the short run are not intended to be profit-
squeezed firms but organised labour. The notion that the imposition of protection would in itself reduce trade union
militancy is difficult to swallow, although one should be
clear that import controls are only part of a wider strategy
which envisages a great degree of worker control allied to a
high degree of centralisation of investment in the hands of
the government.

As far as discretionary monetary and fiscal policy is concerned, however, the imposition of controls is not likely to
permit monetary expansion without the familiar problem of
further inflation. Part of the inflationary consequence is
avoided in the Cambridge analysis by the curious assumption
that producers of import substitutes will price their products according to some cost-plus formula, as in the case of
a number of non-traded goods. Only exporters are assumed to
price competitively against the competition. Why those who
are competing with imported products and are experiencing
low profitability would not take the opportunity to raise
their prices to the new effective world levels, after adjusting for a tariff, is not made clear. It follows from

this, and from what has already been said in Chapter 5, that
there are a number of serious gaps in the protectionist case
that need to be made good before a case for stabilisation
policy behind tariff walls can be established.

All this is of course purely at an analytical level and
ignores the political considerations that relate to retaliation. Retaliation, it has been argued, is not a serious issue since it can be shown that the intention is not to reduce imports but to make the current volume of imports consistent with full employment. To object to the unilateral
imposition of protection would thus appear to be irrational.

However, this is to ignore two points. The first is that,
on a number of calculations, the imposition of tariffs would
not simply be temporary or even once-and-for-all, but their
level might have to increase over time if the protectionist
strategy were adopted. The second is that international
codes of conduct can at best be described as fragile. Let he
who is without sin cast the first stone. Unilateral protectionism hardly seems a good way to start building more co-
operative international relationships in the eighties. The
wise men who lived through the difficult period of the thirties and then advocated free trade were not so stupid.

## THE LIMITATIONS OF DISCRETIONARY STABILISATION POLICY

As we have seen earlier in this chapter, under certain conditions the existence of rational expectations is sufficient to cast doubt on the case for widespread discretionary
intervention in fiscal and monetary policy. The debate between those who espouse rational expectations and their
critics has focussed on the question of whether the authorities should follow some simple rule such as a constant rate
of growth in nominal money, or whether it should operate according to feedback rules based on optimising the behaviour
of the rate of growth of nominal money in response to observed information. An example of a simple feedback rule
would be to raise the growth of the money supply if the unemployment rate rose above a certain upper level, and lower
it if it fell below a lower level.

At the extremes in the discussion we find, on the one
hand, those who believe that rational expectations are all-
pervasive and quite generally destructive to discretionary
intervention. On the other hand there are others who believe
that output and employment can be legitimate objectives for
the conduct of discretionary monetary policy, and that government is capable of successfully fine-tuning the economy
in pursuit of such objectives. The general position adopted

in the discussion that follows is somewhat more pragmatic
with respect to both these positions. Rational expectations
keep us alive to the danger of excessive reliance on government and unjustified beliefs in government's knowledge and
capability. Limitations in government knowledge and the relevance of medium-term responses of the economy to policy
changes suggest the need for caution and a longer time perspective in dealing with the economy than has been enshrined
in the conventional economic wisdom in the United Kingdom
for nearly forty years.

In a non-trivial sense the conduct of fiscal and monetary
policy is always relevant to the behaviour of output and
employment which are affected by changes in the unanticipated rate of inflation. This should hardly be a matter of
dispute. Even on conventional monetarist grounds, inappropriate fiscal and monetary policies can be damaging to both
output and jobs. Repeated attempts to push the economy beyond the limits of its economic potential through monetary
and fiscal expansion will eventually cause output to be lost
and unemployment to spend some time above the equilibrium
rate as the resulting inflation is brought under control.
Thus, it may be necessary for there to be a change in policy
in order to correct previously made, or inherited, errors
which will in the longer run have beneficial effects both
for the growth of output and for the rate of unemployment.

This of course says nothing more than that monetary stability and therefore price stability is an important pre-
condition for steady growth and the efficient operation of
markets. It leaves unresolved the question of whether fiscal
and monetary policy, in combination with other measures such
as incomes policy and protection, can enable the government
to eliminate all unemployment that cannot be agreed to be
voluntary or structural in nature.

The key analytical issue relates, as we have seen throughout this book, to the way in which supply responds to an increase in monetary demand. Leaving rational expectations on
one side, conventional monetarism isolates the real economy
from monetary and fiscal effects in the longer run by determining the level of output through the clearing of the labour market. This gives rise to the notion of an equilibrium
level of output and employment when the demand for and supply of labour are equal. Added to this is the proposition
that, given some degree of stability in the outside world
and aggregate monetary growth in line with the underlying
rate of real growth in the economy, the inflation rate will
be relatively stable. Finally, the assumption is made that,
once the equilibrium level of employment has been achieved,
it will be relatively stable and self-correcting in response

to demand shocks. The main danger to stability is not seen
to derive from unanticipated shifts in the behaviour of the
components of final demand, such as fixed investment, consumers' expenditure or stock behaviour, but from the behaviour of governments in administering policy shocks, thus
inducing unanticipated inflation or unnecessary depression.
Fluctuations in the economy are interpreted as depending
substantially on unanticipated changes in the supply of
money which, in principle, is under the control of the authorities.

Two main criticisms are made of the conventional monetarist story of the labour market. The first is that, even
supposing that the labour market overall exists so that in
the long run, the supply and demand for labour will eliminate the effects of demand shocks on the level of output and
employment, the long term is in fact very long indeed. By
the same token it is argued that, while the neutrality of
money in the sense in which we have defined it may also hold
in the long run, that is also sufficiently far into the
future to be irrelevant from the point of view of policy-
making. Powerful institutional and frictional forces are
seen as preventing rapid adjustment in the market, with the
result that the authorities may intervene and speed up the
process, in the case of recession by injecting extra purchasing power into the economy.

If expectations are formed rationally, it is likely that
adjustments may be more rapid than is conventionally thought
and, in any case, with rational expectations the case for
intervention is not related to the time period of adjustment
since, by definition, the time path being pursued by the
economy back to full employment will be optimal. Thus rational expectations must be rejected by those who see a role
for discretionary stabilisation policy based on the length
of the adjustment period.

The evidence on this point is not easy to interpret. Insofar as one attempts to test the proposition that the labour
market exists and functions, statistical evidence for the
United Kingdom suggests that, by political standards, the
lags in adjustment are long, i.e. they extend well beyond
the life of a single Parliament, a fact that is not without
significance in the world of political economy. However,
whether because of the existence of rational expectations
or for other reasons, attempts at fiscal and monetary
expansion may be largely offset by inflation before the
labour market adjustment process is speeded up. Evidence
relating to the United Kingdom economy in recent years is
consistent with the view that monetary and fiscal expansion
passes more rapidly into price and nominal wage increases

than the conventional wisdom has supposed, and certainly
rapidly enough to be of major significance in the formation
of policy in the medium term.

The second set of criticisms of the conventional monetarist's view of the labour market tend to imply that there
is something peculiar about the labour market as opposed to
other types of economic market or, as in the case of some
British economists, the whole concept of a labour market is
ignored or rejected. The level of real wages is left suspended by its own bootstraps or passes into the hands of
organised labour. However, the absence of an adjusting labour market in the conventional monetarist sense does not
rule out the possibility of severe limitations on the capacity of the authorities to determine the level of output and
employment at what might be regarded as socially desirable
levels. The important question here is whether, and at what
point, the level of real wages and the profitability of
production imposes a limit on the supply response to increased monetary demand.

To take an extreme case, suppose that the level of real
wages is set by the institutional power of trades unions.
If the profitable demand for labour by firms, and their
ability to produce profitably, is affected by the real wage,
the willingness to supply output in response to an increase
in monetary demand will be limited at some point. The assumption is that, for a given level of monetary demand, output will be produced at minimum cost subject to the ruling
level of real wages. If firms behave in this way, i.e. they
produce according to demand, it is possible that the level
of monetary demand might be below what they are prepared to
produce at that real wage level. But there will be a limit
on the extent to which demand can be expanded in the closed
economy without severe inflation since, at some point, firms
will be producing their most profitable level of output.
At higher levels of real wages, fewer firms will find it
profitable to produce, and the marginal firms will go out
of business. Thus over time a limit will be set to the
capacity of expanding monetary demand to promote output and
jobs which, other things being equal, will vary with the
level of real wages.

This at least corresponds with the commonsense notion that
the profitability of production is an important element in
determining output and employment. It is also possible that
a further expansion of monetary demand will not produce
further output and jobs, even if involuntary unemployment in
the Keynesian sense remains. Involuntary unemployment implies that there are those unemployed who are willing to
work at the ruling wage rate or below, but who cannot get

work because of a lack of monetary demand. The point is
that, even if such people exist, the power and practices of
organised labour will prevent them from offering their labour at a lower real wage.

The upshot for stabilisation policy aimed at output and
employment, either in the case just discussed or in the
story as told by the conventional monetarist, is not very
different. The behaviour of the profitability of production
will affect the level of employment and limit the ability
of stabilisation policy to go beyond a certain point, call
it the natural rate of employment or call it what you will.
It is only in the extreme and unrealistic case where no
economic considerations enter into the determination of output that the matter is otherwise. In both cases there might
be scope for discretionary monetary and fiscal policy below
the equilibrium level of output if one was sure where the
level was. In practice, the evidence from the conduct of
British fiscal and monetary policy since the war clearly
demonstrates a persistent tendency to overestimate the
supply capacity of the economy in the short term in response to changes in the level of monetary demand engineered
by the authorities. This in itself should suggest severe
caution on the part of the authorities, even if the effect
of rational expectations were to be fully discounted.

Even supposing that the economy were in one of these
senses below equilibrium, how it got there is not a trivial
matter. The nature of the shocks that affect the economy is
important. In the typical Keynesian story, the economy is
regarded as inherently unstable and subject to substantial
unanticipated shifts in monetary demand, stemming originally
from a strong belief in the volatility of fixed investment
responding to the unstable moods and expectations of entre-
preneurs. In fact, the evidence up to the early seventies
for the industrial countries at large does not suggest that
capitalist economies have been typically unstable and unable
to cope with such shifts in demand as have taken place. Nor
is there evidence that this was brought about by a sudden
worldwide conversion to the pursuit of stabilisation policies in the Keynesian manner. The major problems and disturbances which have characterised the world industrial
economies since the late sixties are more plausibly traced
to the breakdown of monetary stability as described in the
last chapter, associated with the decline in the dollar and
a natural slowing down in the growth rate of the industrial
countries, upon which was imposed a severe supply shock
emanating from the rise in the price of energy in 1973. The
major rise in world commodity prices in 1972 was, without
doubt, a response to an excessive pressure of world demand

produced by monetary expansion aimed, in the main, at the
reduction of unemployment.

Even in the absence of the rise in the price of energy,
the attempt would have failed. Moreover, even if it were
agreed that there is a role for discretionary intervention
of a fiscal and monetary nature in the presence of demand
shocks, in the case of supply shocks such as the rise in
the external price of energy there is no miracle cure. The
maintenance of price stability in the face of a once-and-
for-all deterioration in the terms of trade can only be
achieved after a painful period of above-equilibrium unemployment and inflation, unless it is possible to offset it
by direct intervention in the setting of prices and wages.
But in this event the purpose of the prices and incomes
policy should be made clear. It is not simply to try and
control the rate of inflation; its central purpose would be
to ensure that the real wage level falls by an appropriate
amount to maintain employment equilibrium. No wonder organised labour has been so resistant to the application of
incomes policies.

The belief in the need for discretionary stabilisation
policies has been dominated by the experience of the thirties, and a particular interpretation of that experience.
The conventional Keynesian explanation applied to the
United Kingdom economy was that experience demonstrated the
inherent instability of the capitalist economy which
operated in such a way as to generate chronic recession.

The alternative explanation for the United Kingdom economy
is twofold; firstly, that the depression of the twenties
was the result of excessively tight monetary policies and
excessively high real rates of interest. Depression was not
produced by an unstable economy but by inappropriate policy
shocks. As we have seen, while we have concentrated on the
possible ill effects of excessive monetary expansion aimed
at artificially stimulating output and employment, equal
damage can be done by pursuing an excessively tight fiscal
and monetary stance in relation to the underlying potential
rate of growth of output. Thus it can be argued that the
monetary stance of the twenties, aimed at supporting the
high rate of exchange to which the economy had returned in
1925, was an important part of the depression story.

The second explanation of the United Kingdom's problems
derived from the general world situation which it was hardly
in a position to offset. The collapse in the United States
itself constituted a dramatic monetary failure arising from
the restrictive monetary policy of the Federal Reserve.
Thus the experiences of the twenties and thirties, together
with those of the first twenty-five years after the Second

World War, do not offer a case in favour of extensive discretionary fiscal and monetary policy but do support the
idea of the importance of stable monetary growth related to
the underlying supply potential of the economy.

While it is widely agreed that stabilisation policy is
not enough to ensure full employment, there is a school of
thought which believes that the efficacy of stabilisation
policy would be increased with a policy of direct, presuma-
bly statutory, intervention in the fixing of nominal prices
and wages. Even conventional monetarists might agree that a
case for such intervention might be made if matters have
got out of hand as a result of previous errors leading to
excessive monetary expansion and inflation. In such a case,
a freeze on prices and income might be desirable as part of
the process of breaking the spiral of inflationary expectations on the one hand, and attempting to reduce the amount
of unemployment in the adjustment period on the other. Such
a policy would be temporary in nature and in no way intended
as a substitute for the ultimate objective of establishing
control over the rate of monetary growth. This is a far cry
from the view held in many quarters that a permanent prices
and incomes policy of some kind is necessary in order to
ensure that fiscal and monetary policies can be directed
toward the determination of output and employment.

The notion of a permanent incomes policy has been criticised on a number of different grounds. One is that such
policies are not feasible in the long run. They will be accepted only in extreme circumstances, and eventually collapse, with the result that nominal incomes and prices tend
to move back toward levels that they would otherwise have
achieved in a free market situation. Certainly the history
of prices and incomes policies in the United Kingdom is in
accord with this view. However, the protagonists of permanent incomes policies often argue that they must not be
seen in isolation from other inducements to maintain any
permanent effect such as power-sharing in both industry and
government by trade unions, and major voices in the formation of economic policy. It is clear however that a substantial part of the price of such policies is the distortion of differentials, not only within skill grades but
also in practice often between the public and the private
sector and, in general, the distortion of markets in the
allocation of resources. In practice, a permanent incomes
policy would be the thin edge of a very large wedge which
would demand a high degree of centralisation in the allocation of economic resources.

The major analytical confusion with regard to a permanent
as opposed to a temporary policy, introduced for reasons

already discussed, is a failure to distinguish between whether the policy is primarily directed toward the control of inflation or whether it is part of the process of ensuring a higher level of employment.

Taking the closed economy case, suppose that the level of output and employment are the most profitable, given the existing level of real wages. In this case, given that physical constraints are not binding, a permanently higher level of output and employment can only be sustained by ensuring that the growth path of real wages is permanently lower than it would otherwise have been. If the incomes policy means that nominal incomes cannot offset the inflation resulting from monetary expansion, increased employment is purchased at the cost of the standard of living of those already at work. In effect the incomes policy results in an inflation tax on the employed which subsidises increased employment through increased profits. An effective incomes policy of this kind, leaving on one side the disadvantages that have already been referred to, restores a choice between a higher level of employment and a higher price level, as against lower employment and lower prices. The basic trade-off is between unemployment and real wages and, as we have already noted, it is for this reason that organised labour is instinctively opposed to pay policies. If a prices policy is introduced along with pay policy so that there is no effect on real income per head, and particularly on real wage costs, then there is no trade-off and no possibility for a monetary expansion to permanently raise output and employment levels, beyond what the market is prepared to produce at the ruling real wage rate.

The notion that in principle - however difficult in practice to achieve - organised labour would hand over the determination of the real wage to the authorities on a permanent basis is implausible. As far as the inflation rate is concerned, given proper monetary control on the one hand and firm control over public pay settlements on the other, economy-wide statutory intervention in the setting of nominal wages and prices in the long run is at best unnecessary and at worst distorting to the efficient working of the economy.

The central conclusion emerging from this discussion is that there is no general presumption that, within the limits of physical capacity, the authorities can choose the level of output and employment by the use of fiscal and monetary means. This is *not* to say that government policies in general will have no effect on levels of employment and the growth of output of the economy, a point that will be taken up in Chapter 8. It simply states that the results that can

be achieved from fiscal and monetary control without serious
side effects for the economy at large are limited. The
notion that the government can spend its way to full employment through monetary and fiscal expansion is not in
general valid.

If the economy is in substantial unemployment disequilibrium as a result of previous mistaken policies, such as
perhaps in the twenties, there may be a case for a shift in
the stance of monetary policy aimed at improving output and
employment. It is not obvious that disequilibria occurring
on such a scale, as the result of unanticipated shifts in
monetary demand, cannot be coped with by market adjustment
within a stable fiscal and monetary framework. However,
even in such cases governments are wise to proceed with
caution, given the evidence of history on the one hand and
the difficulty of determining the supply potential of the
economy on the other. The perceived existence of unemployment in itself does not, and should not, constitute a sig-
nal for expansionary monetary and fiscal policies, although
it may suggest the need for other types of policy to be
considered.

Since in general it has been argued that monetary and
fiscal policy should not be directed toward output and employment, that leaves the question of how the fiscal and
monetary stance should be set. It is possible for government
to choose another target for its monetary and fiscal policies that it may seem to have some capacity to influence.
The chief candidates are the rate of inflation or the nominal exchange rate. It should be clear that in the absence of
other interventionist policies, and with the operation of
free goods and foreign exchange markets, it cannot seek to
determine both. Clearly the rate of inflation and the nominal exchange rate are interrelated, as we have already
seen, and a policy directed at one will have clear implications for the other.

As we have already argued, the implicit policy of the
fifties and early sixties in the United Kingdom was directed toward maintaining parity with the dollar. Given the
low rate of inflation in the United States and the moderate
rate of inflation in traded goods prices in the world in
general, such an exchange rate policy was accompanied by a
relatively low rate of inflation in the domestic economy.
In such circumstances, the choice between an inflation target and a nominal exchange rate target did not raise any
real problem of choice, given that it was thought desirable
to keep the inflation rate as low as possible. However,
under other circumstances, the choice can become a real one
Suppose that output is growing at 3 per cent, the supply of

money at 3 per cent and the rate of inflation at 3 per cent. Suppose also that world inflation is 3 per cent and the nominal exchange rate is stable. If a major monetary expansion occurs in the world outside, followed for the sake of argument by a doubling in the world rate of inflation, then, other things being equal, the authorities must be prepared to accept a sharp increase in the domestic rate of inflation and an increase in the rate of domestic monetary growth, or permit the exchange rate to rise, thus offsetting the effect on domestic inflation.

The opposite problem can arise as in the case of the United Kingdom in 1980, where a high rate of inflation was accompanied by an exchange rate which, for reasons largely associated with oil, reached a level at which the price competitiveness of British industry had been reduced substantially, resulting in calls for an exchange rate policy to bring the nominal rate down. However, to direct fiscal and monetary policy toward lowering the exchange rate as such seriously weakens the counter-inflation policy. The most sensible approach would seem to be to aim to set the growth of the money supply in line with the desired rate of growth of total monetary demand, allowing the nominal exchange rate to reflect changes in relative efficiency and to offset nominal shifts in the inflation rate of the world outside.

While we have discussed the inflation rate as an alternative target for monetary and fiscal policy, it is important to emphasise that this cannot be achieved with great precision. One must avoid the danger of falling into the trap of believing that either the exchange rate or the price level can be fine-tuned in the short run, an error associated with previous beliefs about the ability of governments to fine-tune the level of output and employment. The behaviour of prices in the short run will be subject to shocks both of a domestic nature and from the world outside which are not of a specific monetary nature. Chasing the price level on a month-to-month basis is inconsistent both with our short-term forecasting ability and with the nature of the relationships between fiscal and monetary policy, and the behaviour of total monetary demand. Such relationships hold over a period of years rather than months.

This argues for the desirability of a medium-term financial strategy which directs the growth of the money supply and the formulation of a consistent fiscal policy. The main aim is to create a stable financial environment within which the economy can develop, subject to other policies that the authorities may pursue in order to encourage a faster rate of economic growth. Such a plan requires the

setting of the desired rate of monetary growth, together
with broad plans for public spending and taxation. In some
quarters it is argued that such a plan is, or should be,
completely independent of any view as to the future behaviour of real output. This seems excessively severe since,
subject to the cautions scattered through this chapter, an
upward shift in supply potential for whatever reason might
justify the encouragement of a faster growth in the money
supply, or be seen to permit a higher rate of increase in
real public spending. If this is seen as the re-emergence of
discretionary monetary and fiscal policy through the back
door, so be it. Even if rational expectations are believed
to hold, it is unlikely in practice that governments will
commit themselves completely to an automatic monetary rule
which sets the money supply to grow at a constant rate per
annum, irrespective of all events. Moreover, it might be
added that sustaining such a target in a literal sense would
in itself require precise forecasting and fine-tuning, on
which we have already cast doubt.

# 8 Economic Management in the Mixed Economy

The argument just presented constitutes a case for 'practical monetarism'. This rests on three main propositions. Firstly, in the medium term, there is a stable although not precise relationship between the growth of the supply of money and the growth of nominal expenditure although this relationship may vary from year to year because of the lags in behaviour in the economic system. Secondly, in the medium term, monetary changes mainly influence nominal rather than real magnitudes, and the period of adjustment is relevant to current policy making. Thirdly, while in the medium term the behaviour of the money supply is relevant to the behaviour of the inflation rate, in the short run prices may change for other reasons. The practical monetarist does not seek to replace one spurious target, the level of employment, by another, namely the price level. Fine-tuning the price level is not the name of the game. The general thesis is that a stable and relatively low rate of growth of the money supply is a *necessary* condition for the control of inflation, and for ensuring steady growth in real output and a stable level of employment.

The case for practical monetarism is not rooted in *a priori* theory. It is derived from the historical record of the United Kingdom over the post-war period. It does not imply that discretionary monetary and fiscal policy is *impossible* (as in the case of some versions of the rational expectations story) or *always* undesirable. However, the supporters of active discretionary policies have spent less time on positively justifying their approach than on seeking to discredit the position taken up by their opponents. They have sought to show that discretionary intervention *may* result in an increase in social welfare under certain assumptions about market clearing and the formation of expectations.

None of this promotes confidence in the power of governments to exert a major and permanent effect on the deter-

mination of output and employment through fiscal and monetary expansion, whether accompanied by incomes policies,
protection or both. The ultimate test must be empirical, in
particular whether the aggregate supply of output is sensi-
tive in response to monetary and fiscal changes.

In the United Kingdom economy since the war, a 'high'
elasticity of supply in an economic as opposed to a physical sense has been taken for granted. It has been presumed
that demand will always create its own supply up to 'full'
employment. It has been accepted that there may be unfortunate side effects on the inflation rate and the balance of
payments, the details of which have varied with the exchange
rate regime that has been in force. In this framework, inflation and the balance of payments have been interpreted as
constraints on fiscal and monetary policies. However, both
inflation and balance of payments behaviour over the period
are themselves reflections of supply constraints in an economic sense. This has been widely misunderstood and has
promoted the repeated calls for incomes policies and latterly for general protection.

The practical monetarist has grave practical reservations
about what might be achieved with incomes policies and about
the costs of the benefit attainable. If the rate of inflation is the central policy objective, temporary control of
prices and wages might reduce the rate of increase of nomina
*per capita* income in line with a tightening of monetary
discipline, accelerating the process of adjustment and
minimising the loss of output and employment during the adjustment period. A good reason for this is that if individual groups reduce their claims, others may not, so those
that do lose out. There must, it is said, be some mechanism
that coordinates the reduction of income claims and ensures
that individual groups do not suffer. Taken literally this
is impossible and, indeed, all the evidence on the behaviour
of incomes policies since the war shows that individual
groups suffer and this is one of the short-term costs that
such policies incur, with the subsequent restoration of differentials and comparabilities when the policies break down.
However, in extreme circumstances it may be worth a try,
taking into account not only these costs but also the
distortions to the labour market which such policies have
created. In reaching agreement, organised labour may seek to
impose conditions that are not acceptable to the rest of
the community. Whatever the costs and benefits of establishing a temporary policy, it must be clear that such
policies are no substitutes for the actual reduction in the
rate of monetary growth that is required in the medium term.
Incomes policies do not change the remedy. If they have

virtue it is in reducing the pain.

As we saw in Chapter 7, this is far from the belief that such policies enable the authorities to regain control over levels of output and employment through fiscal and monetary means. It is not sufficient to exercise permanent control over nominal wage settlements; government would need to have the power to control real wages. No one has yet adduced any theoretical explanation or empirical evidence as to how this might be achieved in an economy in which any significant semblance of freedom in labour and product markets remains. Traditional economic thinking denied the power of determining real wages even to organised labour. Short of determining all money incomes and prices by central statutory directive, it is not possible to envisage state control of real wages and the distribution of the national product other than in a society in which the power of organised labour has become subordinated to the power of the state.

This highlights a central issue of this book, views about which are useful in classifying economic positions. The question is whether the economy exhibits widespread market failure. In practice, responses to this question are strung out along a spectrum. We can distinguish four views. The first is that economic markets are objectionable in principle because those who deal in them do so for personal gain or profit rather than social interest, and because such markets are a part of a capitalist system that needs replacing. The second is that, without prejudice to the merits of free markets compared to socialism, the former have failed to deliver what the country desires and market failure is widespread. The third view acknowledges the importance of market behaviour in the allocation of resources, but tempers this with a belief in some market failure that requires regulation and government intervention. Finally, there is the view that free markets constitute the best of all possible worlds and, if left to themselves, they will provide the best economic environment consistent with the maximum of individual freedom.

Each of these representations is a caricature but they span much of the disagreement that exists with regard to market behaviour. Moreover, such a spectrum does not neatly divide the holders of each view into left and right. Traditional Toryism was not rooted in a belief in market efficiency. As compared with the Liberal Party of the nineteenth century, and in its later activities, the Conservative Party was the party of protection and intervention of both a direct and paternalistic nature. It was not traditionally the party of free markets.

Practical monetarism does entail some belief in both the
importance and efficiency of market behaviour. It rejects
the view that market failure in the economy is all-
pervasive. Practical monetarism in itself has nothing to
say on whether the market system as such is inherently desirable or undesirable. Its predictions and judgements are
conditional on the way in which the economy actually
functions assuming that it remains a mixed economy in
which the private sector plays a major role.

The economic thinking of Keynes, as interpreted by his
followers, represented a challenge to market efficiency
as far as the behaviour of aggregate output and employment
were concerned. Keynes did not challenge market efficiency
at the microeconomic level. Nominal magnitudes such as
wage rates, interest rates and prices were perceived as
sticky, so offering scope for permanent changes in real demand brought about by nominal fiscal and monetary changes.
In practice, disequilibria in economic markets were believed to result in adjustments in quantities supplied and
demanded rather than in changes in nominal prices. The
evidence of the seventies, however, suggests quite the
reverse. Changes in nominal wages, prices, interest rates
and exchange rates have responded rapidly to changes in the
rate of monetary growth, not only in the United Kingdom but
also in the world at large.

Practical monetarism (no more nor less than Keynesianism)
has nothing to say about the nature of the underlying rate
of growth of output as we saw in Chapter 5. In Chapter 7 we
were principally concerned with the limits and legitimate
objectives of discretionary fiscal and monetary policy. We
drew a somewhat arbitrary distinction between stabilisation
policies and industrial policies. The reason for this was
not derived from any profound belief that they can be dis-
tinctly separated. The purpose of drawing such a distinction was to focus on the dangerous and facile assumption
that manipulating the overall level of monetary demand is
the key to advancing the rate of output, employment and
economic growth.

The central theme has been the distinction between the
behaviour of monetary demand and aggregate supply, and the
belief that important policy errors have been made and mis-
conceptions established by a failure to emphasise this
distinction. This has imposed a burden on conventional demand managment which it cannot bear. This is not to say
that government should not be concerned with either the
rate of economic growth or the level of unemployment, but
in realising both objectives, demand management has little
to contribute. Similarly, practical monetarism says nothing

about the overall proportion of the national output that
might be absorbed by the public as opposed to the private
sector, except to the extent that it has consequences for
monetary control and financial stability.

Practical monetarism by definition is therefore insufficient. In the remaining sections we pick up these issues.
We begin with the determination of public expenditure and
then discuss industrial policy, emphasising North Sea oil
and its effects on British industry. Recent problems of
the world economy are then reviewed as a background to the
future of the mixed economy.


GOVERNMENT EXPENDITURE

Attitudes toward public expenditure which include the use of
real resources and transfers within the community are determined by many considerations. If there were a consensus
about social and economic objectives, the resolution of disagreements about the share of resources going to the public
sector and the desirable extent of transfers would be
easier. It is important to distinguish between practical or
positive judgements about the consequences of public expenditure policy and value or normative judgements about
what is intrinsically desirable. Those in favour of extensive
state involvement in economic life on social grounds are
predisposed towards a higher share of public expenditure as
a proportion of national income.

Views about public expenditure are political insofar as
such views have implications for the organisation of society
and the way in which its business is conducted. Attempts to
de-politicise such views and to present objective assess-
ments will cut across the political and value judgements of
others. Practical monetarism leaves open a variety of questions with regard to the extent of state involvement, the
distribution of income and the micro-role of taxation and
subsidies in affecting economic behaviour and economic
structure. For a mixed economy, practical monetarism closes
down the options to the extent that it implies that economic
markets have an important role to play in the allocation of
economic resources. The existence of such markets limits
public intervention. The practical monetarist does not object to efficient free markets on moral or social grounds.

Arguments for and against a high share of public spending,
and control over national resources on principle, emanate
from both the left and the right of the political spectrum.
The provision of welfare by the state is not necessarily a
matter of principle but a matter of determining how much

needs to be provided, whether for sickness, pensions, unemployment benefit or simply misfortune. For the left, it becomes a matter of principle that certain kinds of service and benefit should be provided solely or largely through the state, and that the state should take a large share in the ownership of productive assets. Given such principles, the actual current performance of the economy and the present distribution of well being is irrelevant, except that it is believed that changes can always be made for the better. The political right believes that welfare programmes and the provision of public goods and services are deficient in principle, insofar as they reduce personal independence and responsibility, depreciate moral fibre and reduce the significance of the family unit. For both left and right, the arguments for and against public spending, other than on public goods such as defence or law and order, assume a moral character. From a more pragmatic point of view what may be said about the size of public spending and its consequences?

While favoured by some and deplored by others, an extension of public spending is generally accompanied by a growth of state interference and regulation. There is no logical necessity that this should be so. Increases in the provision of welfare might take place unaccompanied by any increases in regulation and intervention. In practice, however, public spending expands in line with the increased demand for the control and regulation of the economy, which increases the cost of society's overhead. The increase in this overhead, associated with increased intervention and regulation, takes place with the best of intentions. The control of land use, the protection of tenants, the extension of regional supports, the establishment of minimum wages and wage tribunals, the subsidisation of industrial investment, are all rooted in humanitarian instincts; the desire for conservation, the provision of minimum living standards, the protection of the exploited and the maintenance of jobs. However, such measures frequently produce the opposite of what was intended. Free market land prices rise, protecting the better-off rather than the community at large, the availability of rentable property at acceptable rents disappears, unprofitable employment is preserved, wage levels prevent the employment of young people, and money is poured into unprofitable and, from an international point of view, uncompetitive investment. With the best of intentions, the extension of the activity of the state, supported by major increases in public spending, undermines market efficiency without producing the expected micro-benefits of public expenditure. The record on this point is clear. The disap-

pearance of rentable property and excessive dependence on
private house ownership leads to demands for interference
in the private housing market, with additional subsidies to
encourage home ownership. Minimum wage levels have to be
supported by additional measures to deal with the resulting
unemployment. The failure of regional policies and investment subsidies leads to demands for state ownership and
protection.

As already emphasised, none of this is logically necessary. There are three issues as far as the determination of
public spending is concerned. The first is the level of resources that should be redistributed from one section of the
community to another through the mechanism of taxation and
subsidy. The second is the need to identify market failure
as the justification for state intervention, bearing in mind
that what appears as market failure may have already been
induced by prior government action. The third issue is the
consequence of a given *level* of public expenditure for the
operating of the economy.

Maintenance of a healthy mixed economy associated with
price stability and stable employment imposes constraints
on the size of the claims made by government on real resources and the scale of transfers made from one part of
the community to another. The order of magnitude of public
spending in absolute terms, or as a proportion of the national income, depends in a crude sense on what the community is prepared to pay for, and how this is paid for.

Since the war there has been a tendency in the United
Kingdom to see public expenditure as a free good and to mis-
interpret its consequences for employment. The problem
stems in part from a failure to distinguish between real and
nominal money, and in part from confusion as to the role of
government as agent or principal. Government is personalised
in its financial dealings. When it spends what appears to be
too much money, it is 'profligate', and when it spends what
appears as too little, it is characterised as being 'mean'.
However, government is more like agent than principal,
acting as an intermediary between the suppliers and
consumers of real resources. By contrast, in the United
States it has been more clearly recognised that governments
do not have money. They may raise money in taxation, they
may borrow it and they may create it. But the burden of
supplying the real resources that are directly used by
government or transferred to others falls on the productive
marketed sector of the community.

As the size of the public sector increases, so generally
does the average rate of taxation. Throughout the industrial
world, the rise in the average rate of taxation has been

accompanied by an extension of the tax burden from higher to
lower income earners as it becomes less possible to raise
significant tax revenues from higher incomes and from companies faced with shrinking profits.

The consequences of this are two-fold. The first is that
a conflict emerges between the demands for increases in real
take-home pay and the demand for extra state welfare. The
idea that extra benefits may be provided by the state without additional personal cost has been fostered by a number
of beliefs. The first is that there is always some person
or group of persons who can better bear the burden, and
that the rich can always be squeezed further until the pips
squeak. This ignores the fact that in the United Kingdom,
the bulk of those paying the taxes actually receive the
benefits. The scope for massive redistribution to finance
additional services and benefits is a myth. As a result,
demands for higher taxes on so-called higher incomes have
assumed more of a punitive and symbolic nature rather than
bearing any major relevance to the financing of greater
public expenditure.

The second has developed against a background of sustained
growth in output and real income since the war, although
slower in the United Kingdom than elsewhere, which led to
the view that real increases in public expenditure could be
obtained painlessly from the growth dividend. When coupled
with a budgetary system in which public sector spending was
set in real rather than nominal terms, this view played a
key role in the apportionment of the adjustment burden between the private and the public sector, following the rise
in the real price of oil in 1973, and the subsequent shift
in the terms of trade for the major industrial countries.
While the private sector contracted, the public sector grew.

Finally, the confusion between real and nominal money has
sustained the impression that government can always find
money if it wants to, and that a refusal to do so must inevitably be based on ideology or wilfulness. But, as pointed
out in Chapter 5, all public expenditure must be paid for
out of taxation. It is simply a matter - and a fundamental
one at that - of what form the taxation takes. If government
fails to secure sufficient taxation to finance its activities, it may impose implicit taxes on borrowers by pushing
up interest rates for the private sector, beyond what would
otherwise be the case, or by reducing the value of take-home
pay by the creation of new money and the stimulation of inflation.

Arguments that during the seventies the real fiscal deficit had not risen, and that the ratio of the national debt
to the national income had fallen, have been used in an

attempt to show that the financial burden of the public sector is illusory. These are beside the point. The first tells us only that the rate of inflation, stimulated by large deficits and monetary expansion, has induced a massive increase in the surplus of the personal sector, so enabling the deficits to be financed. The second is equally the consequence of inflation in imposing taxation on lenders as the government's own debt burden is the major beneficiary from inflation in benefiting the issuers as opposed to the holders of fixed interest debt.

The second issue is the contentious question of the reduction in incentives to work, as both average and marginal rates of taxation are increased, the consequences of which are difficult to quantify. The fact that the burden of taxation has increased has had clear effects in accentuating the gap between private aspirations for take-home pay and the expectations of what the state ought to provide. The fact that governments have sought to finance so much of their increases in public spending other than through taxation constitutes an implicit recognition of the limitations of further tax increases to finance public programmes. The creation of money has been undertaken by governments to fill the credibility gap as a consequence of the problem of reconciling private and public demands. The belief that there is something for nothing, buttressed by political promises of more without pain, has been a principal cause of financial instability and inflation.

The issue of what, and how much, should be supplied by the state to its various constituencies is quite distinct from the idea that an essential role of government spending is to provide employment. In recent years, the horse has been put very substantially before the cart. We must distinguish clearly between the role of government in managing the general level of monetary demand and the role of government in directing its expenditures in such a way as to directly stimulate employment. The issue is one of the direct role of government as an employer. Arguments have frequently been advanced that, in periods of unemployment, government should increase its own payroll, or that in periods of monetary adjustment it should not reduce it. For many people the expansion of public spending has triple advantages. It provides jobs, it increases the provision of benefits and services, and it extends the power and influence of the state.

The belief that expanding public sector employment through increases in employment constitutes a net benefit at little cost depends on the elasticity of supply. Those employed in the public non-market sector are supported by goods supplied by the marketed sector, and if the marketed sector is will-

ing to provide a surplus for use in this way, there is no
inherent problem. We can conceive of a notional market in
which payment is made for the non-market sector through
taxes and the goods and services foregone by the market sector. If the supply of marketed goods and services is limited, shifts in the balance between the public and private
sectors must entail shifts in the resources available for
private consumption and investment. Judgements of the size
of public enployment should be made not on the basis of
short-term considerations relating to jobs, but on longer-
term considerations relating to the demand for public services and benefits and the willingness of the marketed sector to pay. Post-Keynesian orthodoxy has diverted attention
away from the needs of the *consumers* of public sector output to the needs of the *suppliers*. Insofar as public sector
output is not implicitly demanded by the community at large,
the expansion of public sector employment amounts to a form
of income redistribution unjustified by the social value
of the output.

There is plenty of scope for disagreement among practical
monetarists about the desirable size of public expenditure
and its allocation. They *will* agree that in the long run
there is no such thing as a free lunch. A rising share of
public expenditure must be traded off against a falling
share of real take-home pay and private sector profits,
whether brought about by increased nominal taxes, excessive
interest rates or inflation. For the community at large
there is never something for nothing. They will also agree
that, if there are not to be undesirable side effects, there
must be an overall consistency between public expenditure
plans in nominal terms, taxation policy and the desired
rate of monetary growth. In the mixed economy, the behaviour
of private sector markets for labour, for goods and for
financial assets limits the size and share of resources used
by or redistributed by government. For the practical monetarist rather than the moralist, the nature of these limitations becomes an empirical question.


INDUSTRY AND INDUSTRIAL POLICY

Views for and against government intervention in industry
are often based on principle rather than pragmatic assessment. The government must have an industrial policy. It has
the responsibility for determining the legal framework within which companies operate and for determining the rules of
competition. As a major purchaser from the private sector
and as a major investor in economic infrastructure it

influences economic activity. It is concerned with the protection of the consumer, with certain types of research and
with training, where the social benefits exceed those accru-
ing to any single corporate enterprise. Direct government
intervention in industrial affairs should reflect judgements
as to the existence of market failure and the balance of
private and social benefits. Unfortunately, as an operating
principle this leaves much to be desired, since the calcula-
tion of such costs and benefits is in itself a matter of
subjective judgement. Rather than attempting to refine our
criteria with regard to the nature and extent of government
intervention, we focus on a number of issues around which
debates on industrial policy have taken place during the
last twenty years: industrial investment, employee participation, aid to industry and protection. The special problems
arising from the existence of North Sea oil are dealt with
separately in the following section.

It has been widely argued that the cause of a relatively
slow rate of growth has been a lack of industrial investment. This has led to demands for the nationalisation of
major companies to ensure that investment is carried out, or
for the establishment of separate state-controlled investment facilities. Such views seem to be based on two possible
kinds of market failure. One is that capital markets have
failed to act as efficient channels for investment funds,
and the second that profitable opportunities for investment
have not been exploited.

As argued in Chapter 5, evidence to the Wilson Committee
and the Report itself demonstrates that there is no proof
that a low rate of investment since the war has been the
result of a lack of financial resources. In any event it is
misleading to regard the low rate of investment as a cause
rather than a symptom of disappointing economic performance.
Investment is a necessary condition for economic growth and
increasing standards of living, but unless it is sufficiently profitable it is not enough. There is clear evidence that
the principal reason for the low rate of investment has been
the low prospective rate of return. In the case of the
seventies, the trend decline in the rate of return on capital has been accentuated by the high rate of inflation, the
rise in the real cost of energy, and high interest rates
resulting from the need to finance the large government borrowing requirements of the decade.

While the financial instability of the seventies made the
situation very much worse, the long-term fall in the rate
of return is another reflection of underlying competitive
failure. This poses the critical question of whether the
rate of return is low because investment has been low, or

vice versa. The former is related to the beguiling notion
that investment always generates its own profits, and is a
disguised version of the doctrine that demand always generates its own supply. But all we know about competitive behaviour in export markets and the importance of non-price
competition suggests that, while there may be justified criticism of industrial behaviour, the failure has been principally in business areas such as product quality, market-
ing and after-sales service. To describe this as resulting
from a failure to invest is to point the finger in the wrong
direction, and to ignore the important microeconomic factors
that underly the rate of return. The issue is not simply one
of the provision of resources; it invokes the wider question
of managerial control.

If the lack of funds argument is rejected, the case for
state control of investment, through some central fund and/
or nationalisation, must rest on the identification of
managerial failure to recognise and create profitable investment opportunities. We return to the question of whether
the free market has in some sense failed. Notice in this
context that market failure is not synonymous with disap-
pointment. The fact that performance has fallen below aspir-
ation is not in itself direct evidence of market failure. To
demonstrate market failure, it would be necessary to show
that industry predictions of market opportunities have been
systematically wrong, and that it is in the power of the
state to organise matters to perform systematically better.
The state would be a better profit-maximiser than the free
market.

The idea of increased state control of investment has been
linked with an extension of employee participation and employee control. This builds on two ideas. The first is that
poor industrial relations and low direct labour productivity
result from the alienation of the employee, which contri-
butes to the low rate of return on investment. With extended
employee participation, the alienation would disappear, so
making it easier to reduce restrictive practices and improve productivity. Secondly, it has been argued that the
increased power of employees in affecting the decisions of
their firms would improve the quality of decision-making
at the managerial level.

The importance of employee participation has been widely
accepted as a matter in its own right and as an important
part of the process of establishing orderly industrial relations. This goes without question. However, present developments in the British system do not aim at the enfranchisement of the employee, but the enfranchisement of the union.
Unions are primarily producer-protectors and in particular

the protectors of their own members. It is unlikely that such developments would favour an increased focus on competitiveness, which puts the consumer first. Moreover, much of the debate over employee participation has failed to distinguish between the importance of increased democracy in determining accountability, and democracy as an organising principle for managerial decision-making. There is little evidence that more democratic forms of decision-making as such result in increased efficiency. The expectations of those who believe that employee control would lead to a major improvement in the quality of managerial decision-making are liable to be disappointed. The importance of the accountability of management to its work-force is another matter.

Government must accept two major responsibilities. The first is to ensure a stable financial environment in which investment can take place, through monetary and fiscal policies designed to stabilise interest rates and prices. Major unanticipated shifts in interest rates and the inflation rate make rational calculations difficult and invoke unnecessary uncertainty. Secondly, government already has a major role as a direct investor in the infrastructure and support systems from which industry benefits. It is reasonable and necessary for government to take into account the plans and aspirations of private industry. Unfortunately, in the past the government's capital budget in times of crisis has invariably been cut in favour of the maintenance of public consumption, and has imposed a burden which falls directly on private industry. The balance between government investment and government consumption is an important concern which requires government to take an overall view of the industrial development of the economy.

In some cases, the demand for a state investment fund has been made on the ground that subsidised finance is required for industrial support. Alternatively there have been arguments in favour of two-tier interest rate structures. In general terms, there is no economic case for either of these ideas which deal with the symptoms rather than the real problems of industry. As already argued, the problem of high interest rates follows from inappropriate monetary and fiscal policies leading to rapid inflation.

Unfortunately there are rarely good economic arguments for schemes of this kind or for subsidising industry generally. In the main, arguments for industrial support are political and social. Most countries support their agricultural sector and give regional subsidies. Industries are supported for national and autarkic reasons. Subsidies are given to those who compete with subsidised competition. Payments are made

to preserve jobs. In the long run such policies preserve and
encourage inefficiency, however plausible the arguments for
imposing them seem to be at the time. The result is a mare's
nest of supports and support systems which often have the
opposite effect to that intended. Agricultural surpluses
mount. Regional policies preserve industries without change.
Payments made to preserve jobs are eaten away with even
higher wages which there is no cause to resist.

At the same time it must be recognised that, even if markets are relatively efficient in the longer term, there may
be a legitimate case for temporary support and aid to industry as its structure changes, provided that one can ensure
that change takes place. Problems of structural unemployment
are real and socially destructive. While, as we have argued
throughout, there is no case for the general direction of
monetary and fiscal policy toward output and employment objectives, this does not invalidate concern with structural
unemployment, which cannot be removed by general increases
in monetary demand. Declining industries pose particular
problems. While it may be believed that market failure is
not such a widespread phenomenon as to justify extensive
government support for industry and state aid, the market
will still require assistance from time to time in order to
minimise the costs of adjustment. A complete so-called
'hands-off' policy is as unrealistic as the view that superior wisdom always lies with the government.

By the same token, in certain situations a case can be
made for the use of temporary selective import controls although, as we have argued, there is no case for general protection. The problem in practice is that temporary measures
tend to become permanent and are built into the structure
of the system rather than being part of a programme leading
to either renewed strength or to the phasing-out of a particular activity. There is no evidence that general protection will do anything other than preserve inefficiency,
strengthen the hands of producers, both employers' and employees', against the consumer, and worsen the climate of
international economic relations.

It is a legitimate activity of government, through its
industrial and social policies, to strengthen the operation
of market forces and to assist in resource mobilisation and
the re-allocation of resources where problems of adjustment
are identified. This requires pragmatism and judgement in
the case of particular problems as they arise, rather than
any slavish adherence to a particular dogma. The ultimate
objective must be to try and ensure that industry stands on
its own feet. However, in achieving that objective, it must
be borne in mind that the dependence of industry on support

must be related to longer-term adjustment. The establishment of the fitness of the long-distance runner cannot be ensured simply by a programme of breathless sprints.


NORTH SEA OIL AND INDUSTRY

The economic effects of North Sea oil have been much misunderstood. Many have believed that the benefits of North Sea oil can support the regeneration of British industry and provide special capital resources to be channelled into improvements of domestic efficiency and productivity.

Such beliefs are part of a mirage, engendered by a failure to distinguish between nominal money and real resources, and a reappearance of the familiar and incorrect argument that the state of the current account of the balance of payments has, in the past, exercised a constraint on British economic growth. The existence of North Sea oil is seen as permitting a relaxation of this constraint, so providing opportunities for a faster rate of increase in demand. At the opposite end of the spectrum, the argument has been advanced that the existence of North Sea oil makes it inevitable that, to enjoy its benefits, there must be a structural shift away from manufacturing and into service industries. As we shall see, this is not in fact *inevitable*, although it is *possible* that some shift would be required.

In order to separate the various arguments, it is helpful to start with the assumption that the economy is fully employed, and discovers oil, all of which has been imported previously. There will of course be some direct effects on the economy in terms of employment, but these are clearly small, the principal effect of finding oil being to generate large financial flows which accrue in tax revenue to the state and in profits to the oil companies.

From the point of view of the economy as a whole, it is not too far-fetched to liken the discovery of oil to the discovery of gold. The major immediate effect is that the increase in nominal income reflects the saving of foreign exchange that was previously required to finance the oil import bill. But, since by assumption the economy is running at full employment, the only way in which the real income benefit of the value of the oil can be enjoyed is through overseas expenditure. The savings of foreign exchange, assuming that export revenue remains unchanged in the first instance, cannot be converted into sterling and spent at home since the economy is at full employment. However, if all the import savings are spent on additional non-oil imports or on the acquisition of overseas assets, balance of

payments equilibrium can be maintained at the existing level
of domestic output of traded goods. Real income and the
standard of living rise. There is no squeeze on the traded
output sector, of which manufactures are the largest part,
and no need for any permanent increase in the real exchange
rate. However, to the extent that the North Sea oil benefit
is not fully offset either by capital exports or by an increase in non-oil imports, the exchange rate will rise permanently, and a contraction in the traded sector must therefore occur, which will fall substantially on manufacturing.

The reason for this is that the existence of North Sea oil
is equivalent to a windfall increase in the supply of traded
goods. To put the matter another way, the supply of traded
goods is now greater relative to the demand for them, than
as compared with what was previously required to bring the
balance of payments into equilibrium at the former level of
import demand. Consequently, unless the demand for traded
goods rises sufficiently to offset the additional supply,
the real exchange rate will rise as part of the process of
restoring balance. Even if the North Sea oil effect on the
balance of payments is not fully offset by non-oil imports
and capital exports, the rise in the real exchange rate required to restore equilibrium need not necessarily result
in a contraction in the domestic production of tradeable
goods, although in practice such an effect is likely. This
depends on the extent to which the supply of tradeable goods
released from the balance of payments is absorbed domestically; that is to say whether the volume of traded goods and
services can be sold at home rather than abroad. In practice, this is generally unlikely to be the case, so a permanent upward shift in the exchange rate will almost certainly have some effect on the size of the tradeable goods
sector. Insofar as the burden falls most heavily on manufacturing industry as the major component of the traded sector, de-industrialisation would occur.

Notice that this stands on its head the traditional argument surrounding de-industrialisation, at least over the
life of the oil benefit. It arises not from a lack of competitiveness, leading to concern as to how the import bill
is to be met, but from a sudden increased capacity to pay,
that makes the old level of output of the traded sector
unnecessary. Notice also that, where this occurs, the rise
in the exchange rate is not in itself the cause of the problem, it is merely the mechanism through which adjustment
is brought about. In the case of an incomplete adjustment
through imports and capital outflows and a permanent upward
shift in the exchange rate, employment can only be maintained by shifting resources away from the traded sector to